HEGEL AND THE CHALLENGE OF SPINOZA

Hegel and the Challenge of Spinoza explores the powerful continuing influence of Spinoza's metaphysical thinking in late eighteenth- and early nineteenth-century German philosophy. George di Giovanni examines the ways in which Hegel's own metaphysics sought to meet the challenges posed by Spinoza's monism, not by disproving monism, but by rendering it moot. In this, di Giovanni argues, Hegel was much closer in spirit to Kant and Fichte than to Schelling. This book will be of interest to students and researchers interested in post-Kantian Idealism, Romanticism, and metaphysics.

GEORGE DI GIOVANNI is Professor of Philosophy Emeritus at McGill University. He is author of *Freedom and Religion in Kant and His Immediate Successors* (Cambridge University Press, 2005), editor of many essay collections, including *Karl Leonhard Reinhold and the Enlightenment* (2010), and editor and translator of numerous texts by Kant, Hegel, and Jacobi.

T0382139

HEGEL AND THE CHALLENGE OF SPINOZA

A Study in German Idealism, 1801–1831

GEORGE DI GIOVANNI

McGill University, Montreal

CAMBRIDGE
UNIVERSITY PRESS

Shaftesbury Road, Cambridge CB2 8EA, United Kingdom

One Liberty Plaza, 20th Floor, New York, NY 10006, USA

477 Williamstown Road, Port Melbourne, VIC 3207, Australia

314–321, 3rd Floor, Plot 3, Splendor Forum, Jasola District Centre, New Delhi – 110025, India

103 Penang Road, #05–06/07, Visioncrest Commercial, Singapore 238467

Cambridge University Press is part of Cambridge University Press & Assessment,
a department of the University of Cambridge.

We share the University's mission to contribute to society through the pursuit of
education, learning and research at the highest international levels of excellence.

www.cambridge.org
Information on this title: www.cambridge.org/9781108820400

DOI: 10.1017/9781108906999

First published 2021
First paperback edition 2023

A catalogue record for this publication is available from the British Library

ISBN   978-1-108-84224-2   Hardback
ISBN   978-1-108-82040-0   Paperback

For Felix and Oliver
who brought so much joy.

Contents

Preface

In an earlier study, *Freedom and Religion in Kant and His Immediate Successors: The Vocation of Humankind, 1774–1800* (2005), I documented the discussion regarding the nature of humankind that preoccupied the German intelligentsia in the second half of the eighteenth century. Jacobi intervened in the discussion bringing Spinoza to the scene, with results that affected the reception of Kant's Critique of Reason. In the present study I pursue the same theme but in the completely different conceptual and social context of early Romanticism. Humankind's vocation assumes rather the form of God's vocation. I explore this change with reference to the three canonical post-Kantians, Fichte, Schelling, and Hegel, with Jacobi occasionally interloping, all in their post-1800 phase, taking the date of Hegel's death (1831) as my occasionally moving end post. How to save subjectivity in the face of Spinoza's monism was still the challenge. I argue that Hegel met this challenge not by disproving monism, which was also the assumption behind classical metaphysics, but by simply rendering it moot. In this, Hegel was much closer in spirit to Kant and Fichte than to Schelling. I should also mention that I portray Spinoza exclusively through the eyes of the Idealists. I beg the Spinoza specialists for indulgence.

I owe many debts of gratitude for the production of this book. I should first mention Anna Ezekiel, Hadi Fakhoury, and Matthew Nini. Anna finely edited my typescript. Hadi assisted me with the footnotes and with issues of formatting. Matthew did the Index. James Devin, of Toronto, a sometime assistant of H. S. Harris, was an invaluable source of information. Working with all of them was a pleasure and, for me, a learning experience.

I am also indebted to my graduate students at McGill, both in the Department of Philosophy and in the School of Religious Studies – notably, Jeanne Allard, Jason Blakeburn, Joseph Carew, Hadi Fakhoury, Paolo Livieri, and Matthew Nini. Their interest in my work and their feedback in seminars and personal conversations have been a source of

motivation and instruction. Above all, however, my gratitude goes to
Garth Green, the director of the School of Religious Studies and a close
colleague. Without our long conversations at different stages of the book's
production, his constructive criticisms, and his constant encouragement,
this book might never have seen the light of day.

Of a different nature is the gratitude I owe to Sheila, my wife, and my
extended family. I thank them for their patience and their care. This book
is dedicated to my grandchildren.

Parts of Chapters 3 and 5 were previously included, respectively, in "The
Transcendental Spinozism of Fichte's 1804 *Wissenschaftslehre*," *The Bloomsbury
Handbook of Fichte*, ed. Marina Bykova (New York: The Bloomsbury
Academic, 2020) 197–215; and "¿Como de necessaría es la fenomenología
para la lógica de Hegel?," *La Lógica de Hegel*, ed. Edgar Maraguat. Collecíon
de filosofia (Valencia: Pre-Textos, 2017) 19–35. I thank the publishers for their
kind permission to reproduce them.

Abbreviations

German Works

Editions of collected works are cited by series number in Roman numerals, volume number, pagination, and, when possible and appropriate, line number.

AA= *Kants gesammelte Schriften*, edited by Königliche Preußische Akademie der Wissenschaften. Berlin: Reimer/de Gruyter, 1900–.

DWA= *Friedrich Wilhelm Joseph von Schelling: Werke 13 = Nachlaßband, Die Weltalter. Fragmente. In den Urfassungen von 1811 und 1813*, ed. Manfred Schröter. Munich: Beck, 1946.

GA= *J. G. Fichte – Gesamtausgabe der bayerischen Akademie der Wissenschaften*, ed. R. Lauth and H. Gliwitzky. Stuttgart-Bad Cannstatt: Frommann-Holzboog, 1962–2005.

GW= *Georg Wilhelm Friedrich Hegel: Gesammelte Werke*, ed. Rheinisch-Westphalischen Akademie der Wissenschaften. Hamburg: Meiner, 1968–.

KrV= *Kant: Kritik der reinen Vernunft*. English edition: *Critique of Pure Reason*, trans. Norman Kemp Smith. 2nd ed. New York: Palgrave Macmillan.

SSW= *F.W.J. Schelling: Sämmtliche Werke*. 14 vols, ed. Karl Friedrich August Schelling. Stuttgart: Cotta, 1856–1861.

W= *Johann Gottlieb Fichtes Sämmtliche Werke*. 11 vols, ed. I. H. Fichte. Berlin: Veit, 1845–1846.

English Works

EHF= *Philosophical Investigations into the Essence of Human Freedom*, trans. Jeff Love and Johannes Schmidt. Albany: State University of New York Press, 2006.

xi

EPW= *Fichte: Early Philosophical Writings*, ed. and trans. Daniel Breazeale.
　　　Ithaca, NY: Cornell University Press, 1988.
GPP= *The Grounding of the Positive Philosophy: The Berlin Lectures*, trans.
　　　Bruce Matthews. Albany: State University of New York Press,
　　　2007.
HCI= *Schelling: Historical-Critical Introduction to the Philosophy of
　　　Mythology*, trans. Mason Richey and Markus Zisselsberger. Albany:
　　　State University of New York Press, 2007.
HMP= *Schelling: On the History of Modern Philosophy*, trans. Andre Bowie.
　　　Cambridge: Cambridge University Press, 1994.
Logic= *Georg Wilhelm Friedrich Hegel: The Science of Logic*, trans. George
　　　di Giovanni. Cambridge: Cambridge University Press, 2010.
MPW= *Friedrich Heinrich Jacobi: The Main Philosophical Writings and the
　　　Novel Allwill*, ed. and trans. George di Giovanni. Montreal and
　　　Kingston: McGill-Queen's University Press, 1994.
PhRe= *Philosophy and Religion*, trans. Klaus Ottmann. Putnam, CT:
　　　Spring Publications, 2010.
PR= *J.G. Fichte and F.W.J. Schelling: The Philosophical Rupture Between
　　　Fichte and Schelling: Selected Texts and Correspondence (1800–1802)*,
　　　ed. and trans. Michael G. Vater and David W. Wood. Albany: State
　　　University of New York Press, 2012.
PS= *Hegel's Phenomenology of Spirit*, trans. A. V. Miller. Oxford: Oxford
　　　University Press, 1977.
SK= *J.G. Fichte: The Science of Knowing: J.G. Fichte's 1804 Lectures on the
　　　Wissenschaftslehre*, trans. Walter E. Wright. Albany: State University
　　　of New York Press, 2005.
SSW= *F.W.J. Schelling: Sämmtliche Werke*. 14 vols, ed. Karl Friedrich
　　　August Schelling. Stuttgart: Cotta.
WA= *F.W.J. Schelling: Ages of the World*, trans. Judith Norman. In Schelling
　　　and Slavoj Žižek, *The Abyss of Freedom/Ages of the World*, pp. 105–182.
　　　Ann Arbor: University of Michigan Press, 1997.

CHAPTER I

Introduction: The Spinoza Connection, or the Discovery of "Feeling"

"Every cause is a living, self-manifesting, freely acting power [. . .], and every effect is an *act*.
  And without the living experience of such a power in us, of which we are continuously conscious, [. . .] we should not have the slightest idea of cause and effect."

Jacobi[1]

"Hume himself grants [. . .] that we only derive the representation of power from the feeling of *our own power*, and specifically from the feeling of its use *in overcoming obstacles*."

Jacobi[2]

"Things in themselves can be recognized only *subjectively*, i.e., insofar as they affect our feeling."

Fichte[3]

1.1 Prelude: Jacobi and Spinoza

The reception of Kant's critical philosophy, generally referred to in his own day as the Critique of Reason, was for the intelligentsia of the late German Enlightenment the dominant issue in the final two decades of the eighteenth century. But, just like the Critique itself, its reception did not take place in a cultural vacuum. Both Critique and reception fit within a broader discussion on the nature of the human vocation to which all the luminaries of the day contributed, Kant included.[4] The discussion was initiated in 1774 by J. J. Spalding, a rationalist theologian with pietistic leanings, with the publication of a tract by the title of, precisely, *Die*

---

[1] MPW 291.   [2] MPW 292.
[3] *Über den Begriff der Wissenschaftslehre*, GA I.2:109. English trans. Fichte (1988), 95.
[4] For a detailed account of the historical context, see George di Giovanni (2005).

I

Bestimmung des Menschen (The Vocation of Humankind). Spalding repub-
lished the tract several times during the rest of the century, each time in
a revised form that reflected the discussion's current status. In the original
edition, however, he had already raised the three questions – What can
I know? What must I believe? What can I hope for? – to which Kant gave
his critical answers. Moreover, an event occurred in 1785 that, according to
Goethe's testimony, served as the spark for a truly societal explosion.[5] As
things turned out, it also steered the reception of the Critique into a course
Kant himself would not have expected.

I am referring to the Jacobi/Mendelssohn dispute over the meaning of
Spinoza and the implication that this meaning had for philosophy –
Enlightenment philosophy in particular but, by implication, also philosophy as such. The story of the dispute has been told many times and
from different points of view.[6] Seldom noted, however, is that the dispute
had its antecedents in a spat between Jacobi[7] and the poets of the *Sturm
und Drang* of which Goethe was the prominent exponent. Jacobi himself,
at least in earlier years, had fancied himself a poet but in the sentimental
style typical of the culture of feelings that the Enlightenment had
spawned alongside its rationalism. The *Sturm und Drang* movement
had sprung precisely in reaction to this culture, and Goethe had merci-
lessly ridiculed Jacobi's sentimentalism on more than one occasion.[8]
Nonetheless, Goethe and Jacobi moved in the same narrowly elite social
circles. The two met in person in 1774 and, as it happened, struck up
a lively and emotionally laden friendship (only intermittent, as things
turned out), in the course of which, apparently on the occasion of a trip
undertaken in company, Goethe presented Jacobi with the poem later
known as the *Prometheus*.

This is the poem that, in 1780, Jacobi gave to Lessing to peruse during
a stay at the latter's household in Wolfenbüttel, just one year before
Lessing's death. The poem occasioned a long conversation extending

---

[5] "[*Prometheus*, the poem at the origin of the event] became important in German literature because it occasioned Lessing to take a stand against Jacobi on important issues of thought and sentiment. It served as the spark for an explosion that uncovered, and forced to the level of spoken word, the most secret relationships of worthy men–relationships of which they themselves were not conscious yet lay dormant in an otherwise very enlightened society. The rapture was so violent that on its occasion, because of intervening contingencies, we lost one of our worthiest men, Mendelssohn." Goethe (1985), 681.

[6] For an account sympathetic to Moses Mendelssohn, see Altmann (1973), pp. 591–759.

[7] Friedrich Heinrich Jacobi (1743–1819), known to his friends as *Old Fritz*.

[8] That of his brother Georg as well. See *Das Unglück der Jacobis* (1772. *The Jacobis' Misfortune*); *Götter, Helden, und Wieland* (1773. *Gods, Heroes and Wieland*).

over a number of days between Jacobi and his host regarding Spinoza and the Spinozist leanings of all philosophy. Other visitors to Lessing's household joined in. The poem was also included in the tract that Jacobi published in 1785[9] in which he related the 1780 conversation, allegedly verbatim, and also made public the letters he had in the meantime exchanged with Moses Mendelssohn on the occasion of Lessing's death.[10] The issue in the exchange was Lessing's Spinozism, which Jacobi alleged but Mendelssohn denied, at least as interpreted by Jacobi. Quite understandably, the issue expanded into a discussion on how to understand Spinoza himself. This tract by Jacobi was the cause of the social stir that Goethe later remembered. In retrospect, the stir was not surprising. On the one hand, according to common opinion at the time, Spinoza was a pantheist: in effect, therefore, a God-denier. On the other hand, the *Aufklärer*, despite their uncompromising rationalism, were not as keen as the *philosophes*, their French counterparts, on jettisoning their traditional Christian faith wholesale. They wanted to retain at least its presumed rational core. In their way, they still championed the cause of religion. Lessing was looked upon as having been, together with his friend Mendelssohn, the artificer as well as exemplar of the enlightened mind. To accuse him of Spinozism, as commonly understood, was tantamount to accusing the Enlightenment itself of bad conscience. It was atheist *contre soi*. At the heart of the upheaval that Jacobi's tract caused was a crisis of identity on the part of the Enlightenment.

This was in 1785. In 1780, however, at Lessing's house, Mendelssohn was not on the scene at all. The issue of Spinoza arose in immediate connection with Goethe's poem, presumably – since in his report Jacobi did not comment on the poem at any length – because of the view the poem expressed of the human vocation. There stood Goethe's *Mensch*: defiant before the gods on whose whims his life nonetheless depended; fated to suffering and death yet asserting his existence with joyful exuberance, fully aware of its ephemerality.[11] This was only a poetic vision,

---

[9] Jacobi (1785). An English translation is given in MPW 173–251: *Concerning the Doctrine of Spinoza in Letters to Herr Moses Mendelssohn.*

[10] The circumstances of the exchange are very complicated but need not concern us here. See my introduction to MPW, especially 3–67.

[11] This was the poem's final strophe:

> Here sit I, shaping Men
> In my likeness:
> A race that is to be as I am,
> To suffer and weep,
> To relish and delight in things,

reflective of the *Sturm und Drang*. Yet the shift to philosophical discourse was all too easy, for, in Jacobi's view, philosophy, because of its reliance on empty abstractions, which it assumed for the sake of explanation, had to be inherently Spinozist, that is, pantheist, consequently also atheist. The discourse preempted the possibility of any personal relation between the human individual and God. It thus fostered precisely the existential attitude that Goethe's *Prometheus* expressed and that Jacobi found intolerable. Whereas for the Enlightenment philosophers (Kant included, in his critical way) the issue of the human vocation was one of determining humankind's place in an objectively well-ordered universe, one based on universal laws, Jacobi was, instead, preoccupied with what it would mean subjectively for the human individual to occupy that place. And since he personally found the implication existentially insufferable, he rejected the philosophers' universe as simply a figment of abstractive reason.

Jacobi eventually extended his charge of Spinozism to Kant's new type of idealism. Kant's own immediate disciples, under pressure from the charge, took their task to be to demonstrate that it was possible to adhere to Spinoza's monism in principle, while adding to it the personalist dimension that Jacobi found missing. This is the circumstance that gave the Kant reception its unexpected course. One striking result, and also a telling illustration of the kind of uncomfortable paradoxes one courted in the effort at reconciling Spinoza and Kantian idealism, was Fichte's tract of 1800, also entitled *Die Bestimmung des Menschen* (The Vocation of Humankind). Although Fichte, like Spalding, still saw the universe as a well-ordered totality governed by universal laws, unlike Spalding he no longer took the order as simply presupposed. He saw it as a moral achievement, the product of an act of the human will executed in faith. There was a paradox in this. Despite Fichte's language of subjective commitment and action, in his system the singular individual, the one who alone was of importance to Jacobi, was a vanishing quantity in this process of creating a moral world no less than in Spinoza's substance. Spinoza ended up having the last word.

Fichte's tract was also a striking witness to the truly revolutionary transformation that Enlightenment culture had undergone since Spalding's early reflections. At an intellectual level, Kant himself had contributed to the change. So had Jacobi, and, albeit at much distance,

And to pay you no regard—
Like me! (trans. Jeremy Walker, cited in MPW 186).

there was an affinity between Kant's critical project and Jacobi's existential worries.[12] It consisted in the fact that both, in opposition to traditional dogmatism, had insisted that the truth of experience be sought from the standpoint of one immersed in it, without transcending its limits. As Jacobi said addressing Mendelssohn, "we cannot experience anything without [. . .] *experience.*"[13] Jacobi objected to Kant because in his view he had not been true to his own agenda but, while starting out from the standpoint of a subject bound to experience, had in fact reintroduced in his system all the abstractions of the metaphysicians through the subject's subjective back door.[14] In other words, as of 1800, the truth of experience, or, since the content of experience is phenomenal, the nature of what truly appears in appearance, was still the burning issue, just as it had originally been for Kant. However, the conceptual context in which it was raised had changed, and it is precisely the ways that this issue worked itself out in this new context after 1800 that we want to explore it in the study that follows. The general theme is that, although Fichte and Schelling distanced themselves from Spinoza, repeatedly by name and in their systems according to method, they nonetheless accepted his monism, and this made a difference to the post-Kant realism they both defended after 1800. It was Hegel who made this monism moot by undermining its conceptual foundations, thereby also finally exorcizing Spinoza's spirit, the same that Jacobi was given to invoke even with religious fervor[15] against what he took to be the *Aufklärer*'s lack of illumination about themselves. The context was indeed different. In one respect at least, however, there was continuity between the late Enlightenment and the new Romanticism and that was in the still commanding interest in religion. This interest will shape the theme in crucial ways and will finally bring it to conclusion.

One can only speculate regarding the form that critical idealism would have taken if its reception had been left in the hands of Kant's more scholastic first reviewers, the likes of Christian Garve or Hermann

---

[12] Jacobi felt much affinity with the pre-critical Kant, for he saw him as placing existence ahead of essence. He was surprised when, in the debate of 1785, he found Kant siding with Mendelssohn. Kant's siding with the latter was not altogether unambiguous but not his rejection of Jacobi. See Kant (1996), p. 15. For Jacobi's early attitude towards Kant, see the dialogue *David Hume* in MPW 281, 284–285.

[13] MPW 237 (translation slightly modified).

[14] Appendix to the *David Hume* (1787), in MPW 331–338.

[15] As Jacobi exclaimed in a letter to Fichte: "May you be blest for me, you great, yea you holy *Benedictus!*" (MPW 520). In Jacobi's eyes, Spinoza had had the courage to bring his rationalism to its logical conclusions.

Andreas Pistorius, or of Carl Leonhard Reinhold, Sigismund Beck, and Solomon Maimon. Very likely, at their hands Kant would have assumed a more Hume-like face.[16] But in fact Jacobi hijacked the reception. Post-Kantian idealism was thus born under the sign of Spinoza. And there was something about Kant's Critique of Reason that fated it, so to speak, to this development.

1.2   The Critique of Reason and Classical Metaphysics

The Critique, while a rejection of classical metaphysics, remained at the same time bound to it. This not only made it vulnerable to misunderstandings; it generated a formalism that made it internally vulnerable to skeptical attacks. At its most innovative core, the Critique was a further elaboration of the well-known Socratic aporia regarding the acquisition of knowledge.[17] To wit: It seems that it is impossible ever to learn anything new, for to know that something is *truly* the case, one must recognize it as being such, and, for that, one needs prior knowledge. To the extent, however, that this prior knowledge does not exhaustively cover the object which is at the moment at issue, that is, to the extent that this object is new, its truth remains unfounded, problematic. Historically, this aporia set the stage for subsequent attempts at determining the source in experience of a pre-knowledge that would at once anticipate all that can possibly be known and save the possibility of genuine discovery. Kant's innovation – the centerpiece of his critical system – consisted in restricting this pre-knowledge to formal conditions of objectivity which, although universal in their own right, did not predetermine the content of any object. This last was a matter of actual experience: of discovery, in other words.

This was a brilliant strategy which, however, his contemporaries were not necessarily ready to appreciate, for it was based on the assumption that experience, contrary to the common view, is a complex process from its origin. It consists in the recognition of something as actually or at least possibly *there*, that is, *present* to a knowing subject; as such, experience is only achieved in a judgment (however spontaneous and self-unaware) that requires the satisfaction of two sets of conditions. The first is that the "something" at issue be recognizable for *what* it is: it has to be conceptualizable, in other words; as such, it can intelligently be looked for and

---

[16] Manfred Kuehn is a contemporary interpreter who makes the case for treating the historical Kant – not just Kant as the source of inspiration for current philosophical reflection – as a Humean. Kuehn (2001), pp. 259–265.

[17] Plato's *Meno* (80d–81a).

therefore also recognized if discovered. The knowledge of a "thing" thus requires that the thing be made part of an intelligible universe of conceptual intentions governed by categories of thought accessible in principle by simple reflection (or *a priori*, in Kant's terminology). As Kant said of his list of such categories, these are the determinations of the concept of an object in general[18] – in effect, what one *means* by, or is ready to recognize as, an object of knowledge. As for the second set of conditions, these have to do with the actual presence of the intended object. They are set by the limits imposed on this presence by the receptivity of the senses. The presence must occur, or the object be *given*, within the senses' spatiotemporal reach. Only within this reach can the object be intelligently, that is, conceptually, recognized as realized.

This was a simple, but at the same time conceptually elegant, depiction of what happens in experience. It deftly finessed the problems associated with both essentialism and empiricism. On the one hand, to know does not mean to grasp an essence, an intelligible *in-itself* for which one would require some sort of always mystifying intellectual intuition.[19] In experience, one only recognizes an intended presence as spatiotemporally attained or at least theoretically attainable. On the other hand, it avoids the problem, typical of any psychological empiricism, of explaining how allegedly disparate sensations can be meaningfully associated to yield together recognizable objects, without, however, thereby implicating them in an already ongoing process of experience, that is, without begging the *explanandum*. On Kant's scheme, sensations have *per se* no noetic value (they are "blind") unless they are spatiotemporally structured from the beginning; they consist in a *here/now* or a *there/then* event which is in principle already implicated in a play of intentions. Despite the psychological paradigms on which Kant relied to present his critical theory, the theory itself was not explanatory. It did not explain the psychological genesis of experience but only defined its form, and it was clear that this form is intentional from the start.

Very likely unwittingly,[20] Kant was in fact reviving the distinctive element of Aristotle's theory of knowledge, namely that knowledge is

---

[18] "But first I shall introduce a word of explanation in regard to the categories. They are concepts of an object in general, by means of which the intuition of an object is regarded as determined in respect of one of the logical functions of judgment." KrV B128; Kant (2007).

[19] For the fuzziness of intellectual intuition, see Hegel's preface to the *Phenomenology of Spirit*, especially PS §§ 16, 17; GW 9:17.12–18.17.

[20] Kant had a low opinion of Aristotle whom he criticized for having derived his categories haphazardly (*zufällig*) and whom he considered an empiricist of the Locke type. KrV A81/B107; A833/B86.

a form of life, the defining mark of rational existence. To partake in the
economy of this life – to be known, in other words – a thing must pass
a test of relevance, so to speak. Or again, it must satisfy norms of intelligibility as determined not by the thing to be known but by the form of that
life.[21] This was precisely Kant's claim. Together with the further claim that
a form of life that sets norms of intelligibility also establishes the conditions
for free action, it was also the insight that was to govern the whole of post-
Kantian idealism. Here is where the line of continuity between Kant and
his idealist successors lay. Nonetheless, despite this continuity of insight,
the post-Kantians all believed that they had to press the insight further than
their mentor had done. This was because Kant had in fact obfuscated his
own critical position. As we said, in presenting it, he had remained still
bound to pre-critical metaphysics.

   What was the obfuscation? Its source can be easily summed up in one
word: the "thing-in-itself." There is of course nothing particularly problematic about such a "thing," if taken as a conceptual fiction only intended
to express the ultimately sheer *givenness* of experienced objects or, in the
subjective language that Kant seemed to favor, the irreducibly passive
moment of all experience. Nor, for that matter, would it be particularly
problematic to say that this "thing," whatever it is, is known only to the
extent that it is *in fact known*, that is, only as given in particular experiential
situations. In the context of Kant's theory of knowledge, this would have
been a tautology indeed but not a pointless one. For it made clear that
whatever of that "thing" is yet to be known as the result of any given
experience must be sought in some other experience, without ever trespassing the limits of experience in general. The temptation to assume the
standpoint of one who stands outside experience and is thus capable of
presiding over its origin as a third uninvolved party must be resisted at all
costs. This is precisely what the metaphysics that Kant dubbed "dogmatic"
had done in the past. This kind of metaphysics explained the origin and
content of experience as if it had access to a source of knowledge other than
experience.

   But Kant famously also said that the "thing-in-itself" is not and
cannot be known *at all* – at least not by *us*, immersed as we are in

---

It was a belief widely held at the time that Aristotle was at the source of empiricism. The belief was
spread by Brucker (1742), vol. 1. Cf. Mollowitz (1935).

[21] For a parallel that Hegel would have appreciated, see PS §109; GW 9:69.23–31. What is edible *for* an
animal is determined by the latter's organic constitution. This requires discovering *what* a thing is in
itself. The norm of "edible" brings this "what" to light for the animal, precisely by rendering it
problematic.

experience.[22] This was a claim that his contemporaries found difficult to process. Lived experience is robustly realist, in the sense that it presumes that whatever is experienced also exists in some way or other independently of experience. The idea of the "thing-in-itself" is perfectly legitimate as a safeguard for this natural realism or the belief that the "thing" is known "in-itself," albeit within the limits of experience. Indeed, there is nowhere else where it could be known. The idea expresses the irreducible "in-itselfness" of the objects of experience even *as experienced*. But Kant was saying that this "in-itself" could not be grasped at all from within experience. He further claimed that it would, however, be known by a hypothetical someone who transcended experience and was thus capable of a kind of direct and exhaustive grasp of it only yielded by an intuition at once immediate yet intellectual. In other words, while denying such an intuition to *us*, subjects bound to experience, Kant nonetheless still assumed it *de facto* as the standard of *truly* (not just *experientially*) true knowledge. This is the sense in which Kant remained strangely bound to classical metaphysics. While distancing himself from it, at the same time he also framed his critical system within its assumptions. The capacity to step outside experience and to consider it in abstraction from it remained the default position so far as the nature of reality and the possibility of knowledge are concerned.

This had serious conceptual repercussions for the critical system. The most obvious is that experiential knowledge – the only one available to human beings – is reduced to a mere appearance of knowledge. It is subjective not only in the perfectly uncontroversial sense already mentioned, that for a thing to be present to a subject of experience it has to satisfy conditions of objective presence set by the latter, but in the much stronger and controversial sense that, in satisfying such conditions, the thing's phenomenal presence conceals the thing's truth. As Hegel later said: "This is like attributing right insight to someone, with the stipulation, however, that he is not fit to see what is true but only what is false. Absurd as this might be, no less absurd would be a cognition which is true but does not know its subject matter as it is in itself."[23]

---

[22] This is not how Kant need be interpreted, but the point is that he lent himself to this interpretation, and this made a difference to his reception, especially as mediated by an influential personality such as Jacobi. Consider, for instance, KrV A125 (Objects, "in the way in which they are represented, as extended beings, or as a series of alterations, have no existence outside our thought"), a text that Jacobi found especially contentious. MPW 334.

[23] Hegel, Logic, 26; GW 21:30.26–29.

There were two other serious consequences. The first is that Kant attributed to the postulated "thing-in-itself" the source of the passivity of the sense-affections, as if the "thing" were their cause. Quite apart from the confusion that this use of "causality" caused for Kant's first-generation interpreters,[24] the more serious implication is that sensations, because of their presumed origin outside the confines of intentional life, essentially resist conceptualization. Conceptualization remains for them no more than a form attached to them externally only by dint of theoretically dictated subjective requirements. However conceptually reworked they may be, sensations *per se* remain blind, an intractable surd of experience. To the extent, however, that they thus remain inherently unintelligible, there is no guarantee that the categorial constructions intended to bring them to objectification ever reach past the level of *imaginary*, not actual, presence. But according to Kant, sensations were the factor in experience that provide its existential traction. The assumption of the "thing-in-itself" undermined precisely this function attributed to them. This was the source of the new skepticism that Kant's critical work occasioned – the doubt whether, on Kant's own terms, there can ever be an effective connection between the conceptual reflection governed by the categories and the sense-content of experience.[25]

The other consequence relates to Kant's theory of freedom. On the one hand, the theory rested on the idealizing power of reason, that is, on the latter's capacity to generate norms autonomously. On the other hand, it also treated freedom as a kind of self-determining causality, such as is impossible on the side of the essentially heteronomous phenomenal nature but must rather be ideally projected on the side of the unknown "thing-in-itself."[26] On these terms, the problem was inevitably posed of how to relate

---

[24] Notably Jacobi and Schulze-Aenesidemus who capitalized on the ambiguity of "cause" according as it is used in schematized or in purely categorial sense. For Jacobi, see MPW 335–336. For G. E. Schulze, who wrote under the pseudonym Aenesidemus, the relevant text is in di Giovanni and Harris (2000), pp. 105–133.

[25] I am referring to Solomon Maimon's type of skepticism, not that of Schulze-Aenesidemus, which repeated Hume's skeptical doubts. For a somewhat more detailed treatment, refer to di Giovanni (2005), p. 98; also di Giovanni and Harris (2000), pp. 32–36.

[26] Pinkard alludes to this problem with reference to Hegel: "One crucial difference from Kant was Hegel's rejection of Kant's claim that if we were to be free, we had to be capable of exercising a kind of non-natural causality on ourselves, a 'transcendental causality' that stood outside the natural causal order of things and that could initiate chains of events without itself being the effect of any earlier causal chain. Hegel, by contrast, conceived of freedom not as the exercise of any form of causality at all but instead of having to do with the nature of the way in which we are capable of assuming a 'negative' stance towards our inclinations, desires, and impulses." Pinkard (2000), p. 473. This idea of "negative freedom" is, however, also present in Kant; indeed, it is the leading one.

the one concept of freedom to the other and both to the presumed heteronomous realm of natural causality.

These are the difficulties that interfered with the reception of Kant's critical system.[27] They played themselves out in a complex of contexts, both theoretical and moral, but they can nonetheless all be traced back to the point just made. Despite the critical stipulation that one should not define experience except from the standpoint of someone who is immersed *in it* and is bound *by it*, by assuming the allegedly unknowable "thing-in-itself" and by entertaining the idea of a possible intellectual intuition capable of grasping this "thing," Kant still framed his critical system on classical metaphysical assumptions, still making these assumptions the default position so far as the nature of reality and knowledge are concerned.[28] The consequent difficulties were especially insidious because Kant's position, while responsible for them, at the same time also provided the formula for keeping them at bay: "critical ignorance."[29] It allowed the results of a conceptual inconsistency internal to the transcendental system to be translated into cases of a non-knowledge endemic to the human situation. This was Kant's way of holding on to his original unimpeachable

---

[27] I have detailed this in di Giovanni (2005).

[28] Jacobi's claim that Kant was a Spinozist was quite general in character. Nonetheless, inasmuch as the reality *in itself* which can be thought (but not known) would have been for Kant the same as the reality assumed by dogmatic metaphysics, Jacobi could have made a case on textual grounds. Consider, for instance, the following texts, all from §76 of the *Critique of Judgment*, which Jacobi himself does not cite: "Now, however, all our distinction between the merely possible and the actual rests on the fact that the former signifies only the position of the representation of a thing with respect to our concept and, in general, our faculty for thinking, while the latter signifies the positing of the thing in itself (apart from the concept). Thus the distinction of possible from actual things is one which is merely subjectively valid for the human understanding." Kant (2000), p. 272; AA 5:402. "I cannot presuppose that in every [cognitive] being thinking and intuiting, hence the possibility and actuality of things, are two different conditions [. . .]. For an understanding to which this distinction did not apply, all objects that I cognize would **be** (exist), and the possibility of some that did not exist, i.e., their contingency if they did exist, as well as the necessity that is to be distinguished from that, would not enter into the representation of such a being at all." Kant (2000), p. 273; AA 5:402–403. "Now, however, although an intelligible world, in which everything would be actual merely because it is (as something good) possible, and even freedom, as its formal condition, is a transcendent concept for us, which is not serviceable for any constitutive principle for determining an object and its objective reality, still, [. . .] it can serve as a universal **regulative principle** [but] does not determine that constitution of freedom, as a form of causality, objectively." Kant (2000), pp. 273–274; AA 5:404. Spinoza would have agreed: modal categories are *only* subjective determinations.

[29] See Jacobi: "If Kantian philosophy were to distance itself even by a hairbreadth from the transcendental ignorance that transcendental idealism professes, it would not only lose every point of support at that very moment but be forced also to renounce what it alleges to be its main advantage completely – namely, that it sets reason at rest [in the sense that it provides no objective knowledge]. For this presumption has no other base than the *absolute and unqualified* ignorance that is claimed by transcendental idealism. But this ignorance would lose all of its power if even a single conjecture were to rise above it and win from it even the slightest advantage." MPW 338.

claim that thought without sensations are empty, and sensations without thought blind, despite the fact that he also framed the two terms of the required synthesis so as to make them mutually exclusive, thus rendering the synthesis merely formal. It was a way, in other words, of avoiding directly confronting the dissidence of the two terms by deftly retreating behind a veil of critical ignorance whenever the confrontation was otherwise unavoidable. When the post-Kant idealists came around and claimed the possibility, instead, of an *absolute* knowledge, or of knowledge of the "thing-in-itself," their claim must be understood in the first instance as a denial of this alleged "critical ignorance," not a simple retreat into pre-critical dogmatic metaphysics.[30] Their aim was to overcome the formalism of Kant's critical project.

1.3   Transcending Critical Ignorance

The difficulties affecting the critical system were reflected in the nature of the overarching unity that Kant sought to impose on the various parts of his system. His fundamental assumption was that reason is normative in nature, that is to say, that in its activities it generates its own norms of operation. And this it does in both the theoretical and the practical domains – in the one case, by determining in principle what counts as intelligible presence, that is, as "objective"; in the other, by determining what counts as effective action, the kind for which a subject can assume responsibility. The problem, as already indicated, was that, because of the passive moment of experience attributed to the unknown "thing-in-itself," there was no direct evidence, on the theoretical side that, despite the work of the understanding and the imagination, conceptual normativity was reflected immanently in actual sense experience. And on the practical side there was no evidence that, because of the assumed necessarily mechanistic character of natural events, moral intentions were ever immanently realized within their realm. Nature had to be perceived as mechanically organized, because, in the absence of any insight into its origin (such as could have been attained only by knowing the "thing-in-itself"), it was available for external observation only as held together externally in relations that were indeed necessary, but only *de facto*.

Kant confronted these problems by populating the ideal space made available by critical ignorance with such idealizing constructs as "moral

---

[30] The view that Hegel marks a return to pre-Kant metaphysics has been widely held. See Beiser (2005), p. 172; Horstmann (2008), pp. 58–78; Houlgate (2013), p. 12.

nature," "freedom" (understood as a kind of transcendent physical causality), God, the World. By virtue of these constructs one could have, if not objective, at least *subjective* warrant for believing that, in ways unbeknown to us, the otherwise intractable gaps in the texture of experience were in fact mended on the side of the "thing-in-itself." Albeit within critical restrictions, one could still hold on to Spalding's view of the universe. One could thus *think of*, though not *know*, nature as organically constituted, hence as internally attuned to moral intentions. One could also *think of* political institutions which, while treating human beings as mechanisms only responsive to external violence, would at the same time also promote their ideal status as subjects of rights and duties. Or again, one could *think of* the course of history as at once driven by the mechanism of nature, yet also indirectly and unwittingly playing into the hand of a putative universal reason. All this could be entertained without thereby incurring overt contradiction, for to think of something as x or y was not the same as knowing it as such. Moreover, at a most personal level of human experiences (the *hic et nunc* of human action), it was also possible to admit the reality of moral evil – to admit it indeed as an irreducible surd of experience, without needing to dissolve it into some greater good in the manner of classical theodicy. For the sake of confronting this evil existentially, one could equally bring into play such traditional religious beliefs as the effectiveness of divine saving grace, or the presence of an invisible yet universal church. But this was again despite the fact that, if Kant's conceptions of formal reason and phenomenal nature were taken *au pied de la lettre*, there was absolutely no objective room in his critical scheme for either evil or any accompanying soteriological history.[31]

Kant's was indeed a grand system that saved every aspect of human experience, bringing them together without sacrificing any. The problem, however, was that the union thus achieved was architectonic, in the sense that it was the product of external reflection. It was pieced together as if by one who had distanced himself from actual experience by means of abstraction; dissected it into its many components, and then, with the right formula at hand ("critical ignorance"), reassembled them, *ex post*

---

[31] As Kant admits, on the basis of either reason or nature (at least as understood by him), evil is not possible. Moral reason is incorruptible, and nature is innocent. See *Religion within the Boundaries of Mere Reason*, Kant (1996), pp. 81–82; AA 6:35. Nonetheless, that the human being is evil by moral nature is according to Kant an undisputed historical fact. Kant (1996), pp. 80–81; AA 6:33–34. Kant therefore proceeds in his philosophy of religion to *think of* the origin of evil coherently without thereby claiming to comprehend it speculatively. He reinterprets long accepted moral and religious tropes in this spirit.

facto. This would have been all right if Kant's interest had been simply one of conceptual art. It clearly was not, however, for the system included a critique of practical reason. Conditions of action, not just intelligibility, were at issue, and action is nothing if not engaged in the *here and now* of actual existence.[32] But can one act on the basis of what not only one does *not know* (as we all must do to some extent or other) but is *in principle* theoretically unknowable? To be sure, moral faith was Kant's reply. But what kind of faith is that? Is it the response to a truly universal human situation, or simply one rendered necessary by a philosopher's reflective account of that situation? In other words, is it philosophically manufactured, which is exactly Jacobi's contention? Perhaps there could be a *homo kantianus* who lived by that kind of faith; the question is whether such a *homo* could lay claim to universal status.

I am not implying that the post-Kant Idealists put their objections in the terms just stated or that they were all motivated by the same interests. Nonetheless, whatever their interests, and whatever the arguments in which such interests were invested, they all summed up their objection to Kant's system by claiming that his system was the product of formal reason – of a formalism that made it impossible for the system to connect with existence and therefore also made Kant's moral faith ineffective.

Was there a way of surpassing this formalism? It would have had to be a matter of further exploiting Kant's critical innovation by identifying within experience the structural component that would do the same systematic work for experience for which Kant had made recourse to the "thing-in-itself" and the consequent idealizing constructs; it would have had to make any need to transcend experience not only *de facto* impossible or only ideally possible but simply pointless. This presented indeed a formidable challenge. But it is remarkable how the post-Kant Idealists all tried to meet it by making the same two moves, equally fundamental and creative.

The first regards the required structural component and consisted in distinguishing within experience between a reflectively conscious level of intentional operations and these operations' still unconscious natural prehistory. The distinction corresponded to Kant's distinction between formal (conceptual) and material (sense-dependent) components of

---

[32] I suspect that Kant's aesthetic theory in the *Critique of Judgement* is very compelling because the aesthetic attitude is essentially theoretical in character. It requires *ex professo* a detached attitude with the respect to its object that sidelines any questions regarding speculative truth or, for that matter, moral appropriateness. But these are precisely the questions that are at issue in the other parts of the system and which expose the aesthetic attitude's abstractive character.

experience. But the difference, indeed the crucial difference, was that this still unconscious pre-history of reflective consciousness was still part of the latter, like an encumbrance affecting it from within and recognizable precisely by the limits it imposed on it. There could be no problem, therefore, of overcoming any gap between the two: their synthesis constituted experience in the first place. The problem, if any, was rather to explain why, and how, a gap might emerge between them.

In other words, the post-Kantians replaced Kant's distinction between "thing-in-itself" and phenomenal existence with one between "nature," as pre-conscious or immediate existence, and this same nature as reflectively retrieved in conscious existence; as objectified: as a *past* of consciousness reflectively recognized as such and thus made part of a *present* conscious existence. But where did the transition from the one level of existence to the other occur? Only there, if anywhere, would the problem of a gap seeming to emerge between the two levels might make itself felt.

Here the post-Kantians made their second move. Clearly the transition had to occur in an event that was at once immediate yet self-conscious and was the former precisely in being the latter.[33] This event was "feeling" – *Gefühl*, an immediate, yet already self-conscious experience that inchoately displayed in its *feel* the whole breadth of further experience. The unity of consciousness and self-consciousness which Kant indeed presumed to be the necessary condition of experience but, as his followers claimed, had failed to realize in the medium of representation, was now assumed as already exhibited in *Gefühl*.

To say that the post-Kantian Idealists discovered "feeling" is no doubt an exaggeration but not an inappropriate one. There definitely already was a language of feelings before them, in Germany notably in the culture of the *Herzensmensch* that made up one side of Jacobi's persona. Nonetheless, in the way the post-Kantians adopted and adapted "feeling," investing it with a meaning quite distinct from either "sentiment" (*Empfindung*) or "desire," distinguishing it, yet at the same time also connecting it, with "reason," the language acquired at their hands a new, conceptually significant dimension – all this, despite the widely differing theoretical

---

[33] This is how Kierkegaard defines "feeling" referring to Karl Rosenkranz's *Psychologie* (Rosenkranz was an eminent Hegel's disciple): "If a person now turns back and pursues his [Rosenkranz's] definition of 'feeing' as the spirit's *unmittelbare Einheit seiner Seelenhaftigkeit und seines Bewußtseins* [immediate unity of its sentience and its consciousness] (p. 242) and recalls that in his definition of *Seelenhaftigkeit* [sentience] account has been taken of the unity with the immediate determinations of nature, then by taking all this together he [Rosenkranz] has the conception of a concrete personality." Kierkegaard (1980), p. 148. Rosenkranz (1837), pp. 242, 320–322. *Seelenhaftigkeit* is best translated as "affect."

motivations for which they individually put it to work. There was much
fluidity in all this, especially in the case of Hegel, whose treatment of
"feeling" was often colored by his polemics against the Jena Romantics.[34]
Nonetheless, there was a normative concept of "feeling" at work against
which all complexities, even confusions, played themselves out. The norm
was first set by Fichte. As he said in 1794,

> The real controversy between criticism and dogmatism concerns *the connec-*
> *tion between our knowledge (Erkenntniss) and a thing-in-itself.* [. . .] Some
> future *Wissenschaftslehre* might well be able to settle this controversy by
> showing the following: that our knowledge is by no means connected
> directly through representation (*Vorstellung*) with things in themselves,
> but is connected with them only indirectly, through *feeling* (*Gefühl*); that
> in any case things are *represented* merely *as appearances* (*Erscheinungen*),
> whereas they are felt as things in themselves; that no representations at all
> would be possible without feeling; but that things in themselves can be
> recognized only *subjectively*, i.e., insofar as they affect our feeling.[35]

Feeling is at once subjective (i.e., immediately self-aware and therefore
transcending nature at origin) yet robustly realist (i.e., it never leaves its
natural pre-history behind). How this leads back to Jacobi and Spinoza will
emerge in what follows.

---

[34] It must be stressed that in idealist literature "feeling" does not carry a uniform technical meaning.
Especially in the case of Hegel, when used in polemical contexts, feeling is treated as an immediate
sensation of which even animals are capable. But this is not the term's meaning in other contexts, for
instance when at issue is the feeling of "devotion." There are places in Hegel, moreover, where
"feeling" does not occur when we would instead expect it, for example in the case of "prestige" or of
other attitudes defining such basic social phenomena as, for instance, "alienation." The presence of
feeling is absorbed in the description of the attitude in question. Nonetheless, as used by Fichte,
"feeling" provides the right conceptual guide. It connotes a definite basic existential attitude. For
Hegel's polemic against "feelings" and the Romantics, see especially Hegel's review of Solger's
Works, Hegel (1990); GW 16:77–129. Also Hegel's Foreword to Hinrichs' *Religion in its Inner*
Relation to Science ("the *beastlike ignorance of God* and the *sophistry of this ignorance* which put
personal feeling and subjective opining in the place of the doctrine of religious belief"), in Hegel
(1987), p. 267; GW 15:142.8–10). See also the Encyclopaedia (1830), GW 20:469–470, § 472.
[35] Fichte (1988), p. 95; GA I.2:109. See also, *Fundamental Principles of the Entire Science of Knowledge*
(1794): "It shows that the consciousness of finite creatures is utterly inexplicable, save on the
presumption of a force existing independently of them, and wholly opposed to them, on which
they are dependent in respect of their empirical existence. Nor does it assert anything beyond this
opposing force, which the finite being feels [*gefühlt wird*], merely, but does not apprehend." Fichte
(1970), p. 246; GA I.2:411. Regarding the relation of the human being to God in religion, which in
Hegel is paradigmatic of a subject's existential attitude in experience, Hegel says: "We have to
consider this relation according to its particular determinations. The first of this is feeling; and
certainty in general, or faith, is classed under it. The second determination is representation. The
third is thought, the form of thinking. We shall have to enquire more closely at this point to what
extent religion is a matter of feeling." Hegel (2006), p. 105. In the last sentence Hegel is preparing to
argue that true religious feeling has an objective content; it is not just *immediate*.

1.4   The Discovery of "Feeling"

Carl Leonhard Reinhold deserves mentioning because of his success at popularizing Kant's Critique of Reason by stressing the role moral faith played in it. Historically, his attempts at reforming Kant's theory of experience by providing for it a unifying positive principle, which it otherwise allegedly lacked, also proved to be a catalyst for the burgeoning new idealism. But in fact Reinhold never understood the true nature of Kant's moral faith, which he took as the basis for revalidating classical metaphysics, but subjectively. Nor did the desired principle he proposed, "representation" (*Vorstellung*), do more than wreck the finely articulated balance of Kant's own theory, exposing it to the worse kind of psychologism. Reinhold never saw formalism as the pressing problem of Kant's system; nor did he notice how this formalism, and the attempt at coping with it, gave Kant's concept of faith its defining character. At any rate, Reinhold famously changed his philosophical allegiances repeatedly. By 1800 he had already distanced himself from post-Kant idealism, eventually repudiating Kant's transcendental idealism altogether.[36]

For "feeling" as the factor that would address Kant's formalism head-on, one must rather turn to Fichte, specifically to the second paragraph he added to the second edition of his *Critique of All Revelation* (*Kritik aller Offenbarung*), the book that launched his authorship as philosopher.[37] This was in 1792, even before Fichte's Review of *Aenesidemus* in which, responding to Reinhold's "facts of consciousness," he first introduced his idea of a "fact-as-deed" (*Tathandlung*).[38] In the particular context of that 1792 paragraph, "feeling" means first and foremost "respect for the law." In the broader context of the *Wissenschaftslehre*,[39] however, the concept later assumed a much more generalized meaning. Feeling is for Fichte the "I" *in concreto*;[40] as such, it is the matrix of the more specialized functions of sensibility and reflection, the two fundamental dimensions of experience

---

[36] See di Giovanni (2005), pp. 272–284.

[37] *Attempt at a Critique of All Revelation*, first published in 1792, 2nd ed. 1793, GA I.1:15–162. English translation in Fichte (2009).

[38] Fichte (1988), p. 64. For the history of this term, see Franks (2005), p. 278. It was in fact older in use than *Tatsache*.

[39] The name Fichte gave to his philosophy which normally goes untranslated. "Doctrine of Science" would be a literal translation. I shall occasionally refer to it simply as Fichte's Science.

[40] This is the crucial text: "How is it possible for the I, in advance of all acting, to possess a cognition of the possible modes of action {in order to construct for itself the concept of a specific mode of acting}? These possibilities of action require that something positive and incapable of further analysis be present within the manifold-{something that simply is what it is, whose being must lie in something determinate} something by means of which the manifold itself first comes into being. {In short, we must assume} that there have to be certain basic or elementary qualities. A feeling is just

for which Kant had been unable to find a common internal ground.
However, despite these later developments, Fichte's original analysis
remained essentially unchanged. It was a masterly piece of phenomenological genetic reconstruction that sidelined anything that Reinhold, or, for
that matter, C. C. E. Schmid, his colleague and opponent at Jena, had
contributed.[41]

In Fichte's new paragraph, "feeling" is introduced in the context of
defining the concept of "free will." The problem is one of reconciling the
activity of reflection with the passivity of sensibility. It is a particularly
intractable problem because volition entails that one actively desire *something*. However, inasmuch as this "something" is external to the one
desiring it, it affects volition externally. The latter is passively related to
it. But volition would not be such if it were not a self-contained, spontaneous activity – as such, totally *reflective*. At root, therefore, this is the
problem: volition at once shuns, yet requires, passivity, where "passivity"
in the present context means "sensibility."[42] Although Fichte does not raise
the issue here, the possibility that any supposed experience of personal
freedom be only an illusion – the possibility, in other words, that freedom
be only an idea, and moral conscience, consequently, only a pathological
phenomenon – lies precisely in this juxtaposition of opposite
requirements.

The concept of *Trieb*, "impulse" or "drive," which Fichte develops in the
paragraph before broaching the problem of volition head-on, provides an
instance of a possible synthesis of activity and passivity, albeit limited to
nature-bound experiences.[43] The content of an impulse – what the impulse
is *for* – is determined by factors that are found in nature, and for which any
organism motivated by them is not itself responsible. Nonetheless, inasmuch as these factors have been appropriated by the organism in question
as part of its internal economy – and whether they are so appropriated

---

such an elementary quality; it is a determinate, limited state of the entire I, beyond which the
I cannot go. Feeling is the ultimate limit [of consciousness] and cannot be further analyzed and
assembled. [One cannot go beyond feeling. No action of the I can go beyond feeling, precisely
because the entire I is limited at this point: Its ideal and real activities, along with everything
contained in the I, are here constrained, and thereby the entire power of the I is originally limited.
That which is supposed to be originally limited or constrained cannot be further analyzed and then
assembled anew.] *A feeling simply is what it is and because it is.* What is given through feeling is the
condition for the possibility of all acting on the part of the I; feeling provides the I with its sphere of
action, though not with its object." Fichte (1992), p. 177 [italics added]; GA IV.3:377–378.
[41] The § 2 added to the second edition of *Kritik aller Offenbarung* was clearly written in view of the
debate on the nature of freedom going on at the time between Reinhold and Schmid. For details, see
di Giovanni (2005), pp. 118ff.
[42] Fichte (2009), pp. 9–10; GA I.1:135.   [43] Fichte (2009), pp. 10–11; GA I.1:136–137.

depends on the particular form of that organism's life – the externality of these factors is superseded (*aufgehoben*, Hegel would say). Here we have, therefore, the case of an otherwise passively received external influence being actively transformed into a spontaneous expression of an organism's internal form. *Trieb* in this context is the equivalent of Spinoza's *conatus*, and Fichte duly shows in the same § 2 how, when human life is the issue, a whole scale of ever more refined impulses can be generated through the intervention of the understanding. New forms of human behavior are thus created, without, however, the limits originally set by nature ever being transcended. Naturalism, or any form of comparative freedom, is based precisely on this fundamental concept of *Trieb*.[44]

The question is whether it is possible to transcend these limits of nature completely, totally abstracting from the original passivity of which they are the source. Here is where Fichte makes his creative move by introducing *Gefühl* (feeling), not to be confused with mere *Empfindung* (sentiment), or any subjective reaction directly dependent on just sensibility. Feelings definitively have nature as context.[45] They can be pleasant or unpleasant, joyous or painful. These are determinations that clearly require a corporeal presence, hence the passivity of sensibility. There is also no doubt that feelings are conscious events. One cannot feel without being consciously aware, albeit non-deliberately, of being in the clutch of a feeling. Yet there is something about feelings that renders them autonomous. Feelings are complex events. There is indeed the intimation of an "other" harboring in them: one always feels in context. Presumably, if this "other" were taken in abstraction from the particular feelings in which it is implicated, or considered from the standpoint of an observer external to the feelings, it would have determinations of its own. But feelings do not actively appropriate such determinations as happens in *Trieb*. On the contrary, they actively disconnect with them, generating determinations of their own, for they are first and foremost someone's *self*-feelings: they are reflective phenomena only *determinedly* manifested in a *feel for* the other. "Reflective" should be understood in this context in the sense of self-contained, that is, without implying a duality of reflected and reflecting. A feeling is a taking of a position regarding how one stands with respect to

---

[44] Fichte (2009), pp. 12–13; GA I.1: 138–139. "Comparative freedom" was the expression used in the literature of the time to signify precisely such a naturally conditioned type of freedom. It does not, however, occur in Fichte's present text.

[45] I am interpreting Fichte (2009), p. 15; GA I.1:141ff., deliberately diverging from Fichte's Kantian scholastic language to bring out in more accessible idiom the phenomenological insight at the basis of Fichte's analysis. See especially Fichte (2009), pp. 16–19; GA I.1:142.26–143.17; 144.28–145.17.

the "other" because of how one stands first and foremost with respect to oneself. At root, the feeling is thus a judgment of identity. In this it is inchoately rational from the beginning. This is Fichte's fundamental claim. In its basic structure feeling *is* already reason, for the judgment at issue is essentially about oneself, and, although made by way of determining the significance of the "other," it is the "oneself" that constitutes the norm of determination. The significance is for the "oneself." Whatever determination this "other" might presumably have *in itself* is entirely transformed into the new determination it assumes within the economy of the "oneself." When it comes to defining the latter (giving it a content, as it were), this has to be done in the medium of the "other." But the point is that this "other" has become the "oneself's other," the mere behavioral reflection of a *parti pris* regarding self-identity on the part of the one who feels.

This is clearly the case of the feeling of "respect for the law" which is Fichte's particular object of interest in the paragraph. Although not made explicit, it would also be the case for the feeling of "guilt," or of being constrained by the law, that Kant offered as subjective evidence of the effectiveness of the law.[46] To be bound by a law means to make oneself responsible for it; in effect, to stake one's identity on its normativity. Indeed, that one's identity would be an issue at all *is* the source of normativity – the *Faktum der Vernunft*, as Kant put it. It means to be rational, that is, to open up a new space (call it "moral")[47] within which the possibility of sensibility holding a position of its own is preempted *a priori*. It is as if, when answering to the law, the moral yet sense-affected individual were treading on holy ground, ever ready to yield to a higher presence, aware of the moral incapacity of his or her sensibility. This is what "respect" is about: "the cowing of sensibility," as Fichte put it. This is not to say that sensibility is therefore sidelined or left untouched by the presence of the law. On the contrary, it is first made significant, albeit negatively, by that very presence, no longer just a mere *given* but a given to be contended with in determining one's identity. Paradoxically as it might appear, in disconnecting with sensibility, feeling in fact appropriates it even more effectively than *Trieb* does in connecting with it positively.

[46] Kant (1956), chap. 3, "The Incentives of Pure Practical Reason." See especially pp. 81–85, 85; AA 5:78–82.

[47] The image of a "space of reason" is in Kant. In "What Does It Mean to Orient Oneself in Thinking?" (1786), Kant speaks of an "immeasurable space" which is a projection of reason's desire to know and to this extent is itself a creation of reason. Yet this space is obscure. Reason finds itself in it as in a "dark night" where it falls victim, as if naturally, to the illusion of being able to achieve knowledge of objects that transcend experience whereas these are in fact but projections of its theoretical needs. Kant (1996), pp. 10–11; AA 8:137.

Such was the shift in the paradigm of experience that was playing itself out in Fichte's paragraph. Kant's "I think" was at one with "I feel." In many ways Fichte was not straying from Kant. He was just making good on the latter's concept of "respect for the law"; also on his claim that at issue in all experience is the unity of self-consciousness attained in direct consciousness; on his claim, in other words, that identity is the determining issue. Radically new, however, was that the robust sense of realism that Kant wanted to save with the "thing-in-itself" was now being saved by the resistance (the *Anstoß*, as Fichte called it soon after) that was felt as coming from nature in one's assertion of self-identity – indeed, from a nature hitherto unconscious yet made consciously present and experientially significant precisely by the assertion.[48] In the new paradigm, experience was not a matter of traversing, by means of representations, a distance presumably separating a subject (the "I" of the "I think") and a given material object (nature). It was rather a matter of first creating such a distance and thereby generating the vital link between reflective subject and immediate nature (this last, however, already present *in* distance) that also made it possible, even necessary, depending on life-circumstances, to treat nature with a variety of attitudes, for instance, the detached attitude of the theoretical observer, the concern of the moralist, or any other attitude that found a place in Kant's system but remained only externally unified. Feeling was the experiential matrix that would hold the system together internally. This is what Fichte had in mind when, in the passage cited in Section 1.3, he said that "our [theoretical] knowledge is by no means connected directly through representation (*Vorstellung*) with things in themselves *but is connected with them* [viz., as thing of nature] *only indirectly, through feeling* (*Gefühl*)."[49]

This paradigm of experience made its way through all post-Kantian idealism – not, however, with identical motivations or equal results.

---

[48] The question that naturally comes to mind is how, and why, would this event ever occur in space/time. On this score, Robert Pippin puts it best: "Of course, it is possible and important that some day researchers will discover why animals with human brains can do these things and animals without human brains cannot, and some combination of astrophysics and evolutionary theory will be able to explain why humans have ended up with the brains they have. But these are not philosophical problems and they do not generate any philosophical problems. (The problems are: what is a compelling reason and why? Under what conditions are the reasons people give for what they do 'their own' reasons, reasons and policies they can genuinely 'identify with'?)." Pippin (2012), pp. 1–22. Not that Hegel would not be interested in the question. For this, see again Pippin, endnote 24.

[49] Stresses added.

Differences arose – serious ones at that, as should have been expected, for the paradigm itself invited them.

1.5   Nature As an Issue

Fichte always considered himself a disciple of Jacobi, even when the latter disavowed him in no uncertain terms. But Fichte could rightfully make a claim to the title, for already in 1787 Jacobi had suggested the feeling of power of which we are immediately aware in action as the source of the robust realism that pervades experience. He had also indicated how a whole theory of experience might be based on feeling.[50] Fichte was making good on Jacobi's insight that feeling is the matrix of all experience. On the other hand, Jacobi's was only the impromptu sketch of a theory only polemically advanced, as was usual with Jacobi, in this case against Kant. By contrast, Fichte's analysis of "feeling," besides standing at an altogether different level of conceptual sophistication, was presented as derived from Kant's own transcendental idealism. It shone light on precisely where that idealism, in the very idea of respect of the law, had already effectively saved, at least in principle, the robust realism of experience that the idea of the "thing-in-itself" otherwise only obfuscated. Prior to 1800, however, when Fichte translated his insight into a system of experience, namely the *Wissenschaftslehre*, itself the product of reflection, he easily exposed himself to Jacobi's criticism, even ridicule. He took as his starting point the thought of an "I = I" to which there immediately stood opposed a "not-I" (the moment of resistance in experience), and from this starting point he proceeded to derive *a priori* the rest of the system, including the phenomenon of feeling. Jacobi whimsically compared this science to a stocking deftly knitted out of a single thread to include in its texture all sorts of figures, a whole world of experience, which could nonetheless be reduced to nothing by just a pull on its single thread.[51]

---

[50] In 1787, in a fictitious dialogue published under the title of *David Hume*, Jacobi suggested a theory that made the robust sense of realism that pervades all experience depend on the feeling of power of which a subject engaged in experience is immediately and inevitably aware. The felt power would not be effectively such, as it indeed is, if it did not encounter real resistance. Jacobi indicated Hume as the source of the suggestion. And he went on to show how all the categories that Kant had supplied *a priori* can in fact be derived from this same feeling as further determinations of the irreducible sense of external reality that the feeling carries with it. Jacobi's was only the quick sketch of a theory, presented offhandedly and, as was usual for him, polemically – in this case against Kant. Nonetheless, even before Fichte, Jacobi had already brought feeling to the scene as a way of countering the formalism of critical idealism which he attributed to the latter's implicit Spinozism. MPW 290–297 (296, bottom, for the reference to Kant); for reason as a form of life, see MPW 301.

[51] MPW 509–510.

Let's leave aside whether Jacobi was being fair. After 1800 Fichte himself criticized this early starting point.[52] Nonetheless, the charge of crypto-Spinozism that, not unexpectedly, came along with Jacobi's criticism hit a note that at least sounded true, though not necessarily because of the religious issues that preoccupied Jacobi most. If, as we said in Section 1.4, feeling inchoately embodies a judgment of identity, a *parti pris* regarding how one stands with respect to oneself and reality in general, such a feeling must be certain of itself. It entails, in other words, a commitment, however unreflective, to what constitutes truth – a commitment which is historically conditioned, such as has been made from time immemorial. As Jacobi said in dispute with Mendelssohn, and Fichte repeated in his own way, "we are all born in the faith."[53] It is the task of the philosopher, as Fichte well knew, to bring this judgment to reflective awareness, exactly what he was doing in his *Wissenschaftslehre*. And it was clear that in this Fichte still assumed, as Jacobi rightly charged, the monism of the Enlightenment philosophical culture which for Jacobi amounted to crypto-Spinozism. That was the historical commitment that motivated him. And nowhere did this come more clearly in the open than in the controversy in which he became involved with Schelling in the early years of 1800 regarding the place of the idea of nature in a philosophical system. Schelling, who soon after became an avowed Spinozist, was at the time also coming to terms with Kant's widely alleged formalism. The ensuing controversy exposed the monism which Schelling and Fichte both spontaneously assumed, as well as the ambiguity that was inherent in it (indeed, is inherent in all monism) and came to a head precisely in their conception of nature.[54]

How this monism played itself out after 1800 in the systems of both Fichte and Schelling, and how Hegel finally rendered its ambiguity moot by simply transcending Spinoza, is the theme of the study that follows. Chapter 2 reviews the controversy between Fichte and Schelling. Very likely because of this controversy, both subsequently revised their earlier positions, each embracing a type of realism. Chapters 3 and 4 explore these positions, respectively. Chapter 5 brings Hegel on the scene. His break with

---

[52] See Chapter 3.

[53] MPW 230. Jacobi was making a point conceptually valid if properly elaborated. But in context he was implying that Mendelssohn could not understand him because he was a Jew and had therefore missed the historical moment of Christian revelation.

[54] Fichte himself unwittingly acknowledged their shared monism and the latter's source of ambiguity in 1787, when arguing that neither subjective idealism (his position) nor naturalism (which he later attributed to Schelling) could each refute the other from their respective standpoints. He, however, made a plea in favor of his position, on the ground that it enjoyed moral superiority. Fichte (1994), § 5. GA I:4, § 5. The whole paragraph is relevant.

monism is best reflected in his idea of what constitutes a historical event, as developed in his Phenomenology and concomitant Logic. This is the subject matter of the chapter. Ultimately, however, it is in their *feel* for humanity, or, in other words, in the religion they each espoused, that the differences between Fichte and Schelling, and between these two and Hegel, are best manifested. Accordingly, Chapter 6 concludes by reverting to feeling, but feeling which is in principle already reason.

CHAPTER 2

The Nature of "Nature" in Contention

"Our world is the material of our duty made sensible."

Fichte[1]

"The objective world is simply the original, as yet unconscious, poetry of the spirit; the universal organon of philosophy . . . *is the philosophy of art.*"

Schelling[2]

2.1   The Dispute in Context

The stage for Fichte's controversy with Schelling regarding the place of the concept of nature in a consummate philosophical system was set by Schelling's publication in 1800 of his *System of Transcendental Idealism*. Schelling had already published a number of works dedicated to the Philosophy of Nature.[3] It is difficult to make a simple statement about these writings, which to the modern mind might well appear a medley of wild speculations. For a brief but deliberately sympathetic description, one can say that Schelling's intention was to sum up, and bring to systematic order, what would otherwise have been a mass of empirical materials drawn from the sciences of the day. This was done by organizing such materials by means of imaginative constructs that, although governed by an internal logic and, in this sense, *a priori*, grew out of the materials themselves. The process, in other words, was not external to the materials but was allegedly

---

[1] *On the Basis of Our Belief in a Divine Governance of the World.* GA I.5:353.
[2] *System of Transcendental Idealism* (1800), Schelling (1978), p. 12.
[3] *Ideen zu einer Philosophie der Natur als Einleitung in das Studium dieser Wissenschaft* [*Ideas for a Philosophy of Nature as Introduction to the Study of this Science*] (1797); SSW I.1; English translation in Schelling (1988). *Erster Entwurf eines Systems der Naturphilosophie* [*First Sketch of a System of Philosophy of Nature*] (1799), in SSW I.3. No English translation is available.

carried out internally by the materials themselves; its *a priori* principles were themselves an *a posteriori* component of it.[4]

Schelling's Philosophy of Nature was a kind of cosmogony – not the kind of intellectual enterprise that would ordinarily have elicited much interest on the part of Fichte. But it did with the publication of the 1800 *System*, since there Schelling argued that a complete system of knowledge had to include two parts, both equally indispensable. One was a system of nature organized according to the overall paradigm of "it = it"; the other, a system of mind organized according to the counter-paradigm of "I = I." Each system internally gave way to the other at conclusion, and only together, in the medium of a unifying intuition that Schelling described as "artistic," did the two constitute a complete external revelation of the Absolute. This last was conceived, in typical Romantic fashion, as a living organism. In other words, Schelling was claiming that his Philosophy of Nature stood on a par conceptually with Fichte's *Wissenschaftslehre*; that in a complete system it provided the objective/theoretical part, as contrasted with the subjective/practical part that was the domain of Fichte's Science. And this was a claim that Fichte could not accept, for it entailed assumptions regarding nature, intuition, and the Absolute, which – at least on the face of it – were totally different from his.

We shall turn to this difference. There was another publication, also in 1800, that needs mentioning as also setting the stage for the ensuing controversy. Although not immediately concerned with nature, this publication nonetheless leveled accusations against Fichte's System that could have reinforced Schelling's claim that the latter failed to connect with reality objectively. The publication added urgency to the controversy and extra despondency on the part of Fichte.

I am referring to Kant's brief but incisive public declaration (*Erklärung*) in which the aging philosopher unqualifiedly repudiated all his self-professed disciples and their claims to be reforming his system.[5] Critical philosophy stood on its own, Kant declared; it had no need of intuitions or of special new standpoints. The repudiation was all-embracing, but it singled out Fichte's Science, which Kant declared to be nothing but a play of conceptual constructs, a logic rather than a science of the real. Fichte took this dismissal particularly hard. The young Jena Romantics were at that moment distancing themselves from Fichte. Nonetheless, their

---

[4] This is a theme that will acquire ever greater importance in the later Schelling, as we shall see in Section 5.2.
[5] Kant, *Erklärung in Beziehung auf Fichtes Wissenschaftslehre* (1799), in AA 12:371. English translation in Kant (1999), pp. 559–562: *Declaration Concerning Fichte's Wissenschaftslehre*, August 7, 1799.

original relation to Kant had been mediated by him. Fichte's own, on the contrary, had been immediate and direct. Being rebuffed by the master must have been especially hard.

To defend his *Wissenschaftslehre* against the charge of being just logic, and also to argue that the intuition on which it was based was, in fact, indispensable to all experience, thus became Fichte's pressing concern. However, the situation turned out to be complex. While defending himself before Kant, Fichte also had to fend off the charge of logicism coming from Schelling; yet his defense before Kant was based on precisely the notion of intellectual intuition, because of which Schelling (who had his own notion of it) was accusing him of never going past the sphere of subjective reflection. Clearly there was a deep conceptual problem shaping the complexity, and just as clearly the source of the problem had to be intellectual intuition.

The confrontation with Schelling regarding nature, only smoldering at the beginning, quickly came to predominate in Fichte's mind. Its place in a system of philosophy became for him the test of what one picked at the beginning of a system as its principle. The controversy was very likely at least instrumental in Fichte's altering the method of his Science soon after. Schelling also later did the same. While never repudiating intellectual intuition *tout court*, both philosophers ended up giving to it ever diminishing prominence.[6]

2.2 Fichte's Response to Kant

2.2.1 The Announcement of 1801 (Ankündigung)

How powerfully Fichte was affected by Kant's *Declaration* can be seen in his so-called Announcement (*Ankündigung*) of 1801,[7] in which he declared that nobody to date had understood his Science. He was therefore announcing the plan for a new exposition that would make it more accessible. This complaint about lack of understanding was directed at everyone around him – presumably also Schelling, whose name came up in context.[8] Indirect reference was also made to the *Clavis Fichtiana seu Leibgeriana*, Jean Paul's recent parody of the *Wissenschaftslehre* in which the latter was portrayed as an attempt to excogitate a real world out of the "I."[9] But the

---

[6] For Schelling, see Bruno (2013).

[7] Published in the *Allgemeine Zeitung* (1801), Beilage 1, pp. 1–4, in GA I.7:153–164. The critical edition refers to the text by its opening words, "Seit sechs Jahren." English edition in PR 85–92.

[8] PR 86; GA I.7:154.13.

[9] PR 88; GA I.7:158.20. Reprinted in Paul (2000). "Fichtean, or body-conjuring key." I presume that the "*geriana*" in "Leibgeriana" is from the Latin *gero*.

one author whom Fichte directly addressed was Kant, mentioning his claim that the *Wissenschaftslehre* was nothing but "pure Logic" and that "it was therefore futile work trying to ferret a real object out of it."[10] Fichte also cited Kant's comment, made in a different text, about "intellectual intuition," namely that a "non-sensible intuition of a stable subsisting something, [. . .] is nonsensical (*ungereimt*)."[11] In the face of these accusations Fichte countered by proclaiming in a tone just as declamatory as Kant's that, as a matter of fact, for him the *Wissenschaftslehre* was "in no way logic." "Indeed," he continued, "I ban pure logic totally from the region of philosophy. Intellectual intuition is for me not the intuition of anything subsistent. What it is, precisely because every intuition lies higher than the concept, does not allow conceptualization; one must learn what it is by having it [*daß man sie hat*]."[12] Intellectual intuition, so much denied by Kant, was where Fichte was making his stand so far as his Idealism was concerned.

Despite its alleged ineffability, in the Announcement Fichte said enough about intellectual intuition to give at least an idea of what he meant by the term. He said that at least since Kant one was obliged to distinguish between cognition based simply on concepts (which had been the cognition typical of philosophy prior to Kant) and mathematics, which, on the contrary, was cognition based on intuition. The distinction, however, necessarily involved the reflective cognition of a cognition (namely, the mathematical cognition) which is *ex hypothesi* intuitive. It followed that this reflective cognition had to be itself in some sense intuitive, for an intuitive kind of knowledge (as mathematical cognition was *ex hypothesi*) would have been accessible only to intuition. If there was *mathesis*, there had to be also a *mathesis* of this *mathesis*. And Fichte proceeded to extend the claim further. If there is any cognition by means of concepts – such concepts as we derive analytically from one another, or assemble together into new concepts – there must also be the cognition of this cognition. But how could this reflective cognition be certain that it is the cognition of the cognition that it claims to be unless this certainty were intuitive? Granted that we operate with concepts, whence do these concepts derive their cognitive power unless from an immediate intuition of which they are the reflective expression? Conceptualization and intuition are inherently bound together. Finally, in Fichte's own words,

---

[10] PR 89 (translation modified); GA I.7:159.18–19.
[11] PR 89 (translation modified); GA I.7:159.20–21.
[12] PR 89 (translation modified); GA I.7:159.23–160.3.

Since there has been talk of a critique of reason, of a cognition of reason, of reason as cognized, and the task of reason has become above all to cognize itself, and from that to establish how it might possibly cognize something outside it, it should have become clear that this reason grasps and conceives itself, not in something derived which, like the concept, does not have its ground within itself, but immediately in its own ground, in intuition: if philosophy is henceforth supposed to be reason's own cognition through itself, then philosophy can least be a cognition based on concepts; it must rather be based but on intuition.[13]

In brief, intellectual intuition was for Fichte the evidence that reason gains about its operations by the very fact that it performs them.[14] This evidence, just like the evidence that the geometer gains from spatial constructions by the very act of constructing them, is both immediate and infallible. And Fichte let it be known that his planned new presentation (*Darstellung*) of the *Wissenschaftslehre* would be based on precisely this coincidence of conceptual construction and intuition.

2.2.2 The Crystal Clear Report (Bericht)

The planned new *Darstellung* never came to light – at least, not in published form, for we have lecture notes for the years 1801/1802 dedicated to a new presentation of the *Wissenschaftslehre*,[15] about which more later.[16] True to his promise, however, Fichte provided a clarification of his Science that stressed its affinity to Geometry in a piece published in 1801 under the provocative title of *Crystal Clear Report to the Wider Public Concerning the True Essence of the Latest Philosophy: An Essay in Compelling the Readers to Understanding.*[17]

---

[13] PR 88; GA I.7:157.25–158.4.
[14] Fichte had first made this claim in his Review of *Aenesidemus* (1792); for details, see EPW 53–77.
[15] *Darstellung der Wissenschaftslehre aus den Jahren 1801/02*, in GA II.6:129–324. For the intricate history of these notes, see the editorial preface in GA, pp. 106–128.
[16] Section 2.5.
[17] *Sonnenklarer Bericht an das grössere Publikum über das eigentliche Wesen der neuesten Philosophie: Ein Versuch, die Leser zum Verstehen zu zwingen.* in GA I.7:185–268. The critical editors (pp. 167–181) give a detailed account of the raucous reception of the book. Object of special scandal was the supposed attempt at "compelling understanding." The decisive break with Schelling, already in the making, occurred at this point. In a postlude to the Report, Fichte encourages the would-be philosophers who still do not understand him to change profession and suggests lenses grinding as an option. The reference was of course to Spinoza, and nobody would have missed the implied dig at Schelling, who at the time professed to be a Spinozist. The general reaction was humorously captured by Karoline Schlegel in a doggerel that did not fail to find its way to the press: "Zweifle an der Sonne Klarheit / Zweifle an der Sterne Licht, / Leser, nur an meiner Wahrheit / Und an Deiner Dummheit nicht" ("Do doubt the sun's clarity / Do doubt the stars' light, / Reader, only of my truth / And your

It began with a reflection on experience in general. In everyday experience, Fichte argued, we are so completely given over to the things that fall within our conscious purview that we naturally identify reality with precisely these things. We forget our own engagement with them as if it were not itself anything real. Without this engagement, however – that is, without those same things being represented and remembered by us; without their being subjected to any number of conceptual adaptations that make them part of our conscious life – they would not exist for us. And it is possible for us to tear ourselves away from them (to bracket them as objects of direct attention, as we might say nowadays in a post-Husserl age) and make our own avowedly subjective engagement with them the new object of attention.[18] Of course, those things do not disappear for us as the result of this shift of perspective. On the contrary, they still are, as they already were, very much part of us, but now explicitly indexed *as existing for us*, or, to use Fichte's expression, which echoed Schelling's language at the time, as raised to a higher power (*Potenz*).[19] They are facts of consciousness (*Tatsache des Bewußtseins*).[20] We can also call them, so Fichte said, "experiences."

Moreover, when we are unreflectively absorbed in things, we presume them to be part of a world-system within which their physical composition is determined by factors inherent to the system itself. We also presume that these factors, even though normally unknown to us, are nonetheless all already present at any given moment, and, for the sake of bringing them to light, we excogitate hypotheses and theories as need be. Equally, when reflectively considering the same things as incorporated in our conscious life, we expect them to be – in the shape of representations, memories, sensations, or other mental products – all parts of a system of experiences from which they derive their special function in the life of consciousness. It behooves the philosopher, therefore, to seek the factors that go into the making of these experiences, just as we seek the causes of physical facts; and also to expect that such factors are all at work in any given experience even though their presence and their nature are still unknown to us. Just as the drawing of one segment of a geometrical line entails the capacity to draw all

---

    stupidity, doubt not" (my translation; I suspect that the doggerel is a play on Shakespeare's *Hamlet*, Act 2, Scene 2).

[18] Fichte says this in many ways – in one place that it is like concentrating, in the presence of a friend, on the friend's presence as friend, rather than being absorbed in the friend himself, forgetting oneself. GA I.7:14–19.

[19] See GA I.7:212–213; 243–244; 246, among many places.

[20] This was a common trope already the property of common-sense philosophy. Reinhold introduced it in critical philosophy. See di Giovanni and Harris (2000), pp. 2–50.

the rest even if the actual drawing is never completed, so also are we, by virtue of bracketing the otherwise naïvely direct apprehension of things, already in possession of a whole of internally diversified reflective knowledge. We have all the factors that go into the making of experience in one single glance (*mit einem Blicke*).[21]

We have, therefore, two systems at hand, one of physical facts and the other of facts of consciousness: a world-system and a system of experience. The two differ in two important respects. First, whereas we simply find ourselves engrossed in physical things, and naturally engage in the process of explaining them without any deliberate effort on our part, the move by which we tear ourselves away from this natural attitude of physical explanation and reflectively make such an explanation itself an object of explanation is one that has to be done deliberately, as a free response to an equally free demand. In the case of the *Bericht*, this was the demand that Fichte was making to his audience. Second, whereas in the process of physical explanation the connection between any physical occurrence and its supposed cause necessarily remains conjectural (for the connection depends for its ultimate consummation on an indefinite number of other yet undiscovered links), the situation is altogether different in the system of "facts of consciousness," as Fichte proceeded to elaborate at great length.

In both systems, he went on to say, the effective presence of all the factors that go into the making of a given fact must be presupposed. However, since it is *de facto* impossible to presume that one can ever trace all the lines of influence that lead to that fact, one must be satisfied with identifying the general laws that govern the unfolding of these lines, thus providing, though only in principle, the explanation for the fact. Specific to the world-system of physical facts, however, is that the first of such laws, or, for that matter, any such law, is only an abstraction: the only compelling evidence for it would consist in the actual exhibition of all the facts to which the law applies. But such an actual exhibition is in fact impossible; moreover, were it *per impossibile* to succeed, the law would turn into a mere declaratory statement of all the facts that it was supposed to explain. It would simply state rather than explain. In the system of the facts of consciousness, on the other hand, the first principle carries immediate

<hr/>

[21] GA I.7:229.13. If we were interested in the present forum in a detailed diachronic account of Fichte's development, we would have to note that, although in the *Bericht* Fichte still holds the standpoint of the I that he later criticizes, he is already anticipating his 1804 revised position, as we shall see (Chapter 3). In effect, Fichte is already saying that the pure I is but reason grasping itself as reason, or that intuition (*Blick*) is an operation of reason which, however, only exposes an incontestable evidence that transcends words. See GA I.7: 229; 237.15–19; 243.6–22.

and compelling evidence. Since consciousness is at issue, and since the success of consciousness consists in the subject-object identity achieved in it, this identity, or the attaining of it, must be the fundamental principle governing the whole system. But this identity is precisely what is achieved when, in response to a freely initiated demand, one overcomes one's fascination with the objectively given world and turns one's attention instead to one's own engagement with it. In this reflective performance, the object is the subject and the subject is the object – that is, the required identity is attained. This is not an identity that can be attested to in the way that one can attest to the presence of a physical object. It cannot be put into descriptive language but can only be obliquely expressed – intimated rather than indicated. Yet, *that* it has been attained is a fact of which, Fichte claimed, we can all be immediately aware. We have incontestable albeit only subjective evidence of it, because the identity is made into a fact by the very act by which we tear ourselves apart from the external world and make this act itself the object of interest. For this reason it is important that the system begin with a performance freely undertaken in response to a freely initiated demand. The *Wissenschaftslehre* – Fichte insisted – is a highly personal affair. Without the willingness to perform the reflection in which its evidence originates, the Science would not even get off the ground, let alone succeed.

According to Fichte, "intellectual intuition" is the immediate awareness generated by precisely this reflection – "immediate" because ultimately non-conceptualizable, yet such as to provide subjectively irrefutable evidence. When Fichte insisted, as he repeatedly did in the *Bericht*, that the truth of the *Wissenschaftslehre* depends on its ultimate success in providing a complete account of all the facts of consciousness, and that until such a completeness is achieved the *Wissenschaftslehre* remains conjectural, this limitation was obviously intended to apply only to the *Wissenschaftslehre* considered as system. It did not apply to its principles, or to the conclusions achieved at each stage of its development. The certainty that intellectual intuition provided for these was, though subjective, incontestable.

Because of this immediacy and infallibility of evidence, Fichte also made a lot of the affinity, already signaled in the *Ankündigung*, between *Wissenschaftslehre* and Geometry.[22] The *Wissenschaftslehre* is itself a kind of *mathesis*, so much so that a notational language in mathematical style – a "universal characteristic" of the kind that Leibniz had envisaged for language in general – should therefore be possible for it. Already in the

---

[22] See GA I.7:228ff.

Ankündigung Fichte had proposed eventually to attend to this task. Of course, there are differences between the two sciences, as Fichte admitted. There is no tablet on which to draw the *Wissenschaftslehre*'s objects as there is for those of Geometry.[23] Nonetheless, the intuition of the subject/object identity on which the *Wissenschaftslehre* was based was not unlike the intuition of the imaginary space which is the presupposition of Geometry. It was as if the intuition opened up a type of intellectual space within which, in a manner not unlike the way the geometer formulates theorems and constructs demonstrations, the practitioner of the *Wissenschaftslehre* progressively posits ever new facts of consciousness, each linked with the preceding on the ground that, without it, the latter would not be ideally possible. Both the *Wissenschaftslehre*-practitioner and the geometer are free whether to operate or not to operate within their respective spaces. However, upon making even one move within that space, they find themselves constrained by its inner structure: the force of the constraint is for them a matter of immediate awareness or intuition. They are *led*, in other words, along the lines of development preordained by their respective sciences – freely led indeed but led (*deducti*) nevertheless.[24]

For Fichte it was also instructive in another respect to reflect on the affinity between *Wissenschaftslehre* and Geometry. It is indeed legitimate to speak of a genesis of both sciences, since they both proceed from demonstration to demonstration in constructing their respective complete systems. It does not follow, however, that there is a *genesis* of the reality of which each is a progressive reflection (*Abbild*), namely consciousness in the case of the *Wissenschaftslehre* and imaginary space in the case of Geometry. This reality is already all there from the beginning. As Fichte had already said, all the conditions that make for consciousness in general, and hence for any occurrence of conscious life, must be present at once. The *Wissenschaftslehre* was not psychology. It was not concerned with how consciousness comes to be[25] but was simply a reflection by consciousness on consciousness that originated within consciousness itself. Reflection is an essential moment of all consciousness. One hits upon it as if on the spur of the moment.[26] For anyone to try to step outside it in an attempt at discovering how one gets to it would be like trying to jump over oneself.

The aim of the *Wissenschaftslehre* was thus construction, not reconstruction.[27] Fichte did not bring memory into play in this text. But he

---

[23] GA I.7:244.18–19.   [24] Fichte is playing on the Latin root of deduction," i.e., *ducere*, "to lead."
[25] GA I.7:249.28ff.   [26] *"durch einem glücklichen Einfall"* GA I.7:217.18–19.   [27] GA I.7:218

could have compared the *Wissenschaftslehre*'s work of reflective representation (*Abbildung*) to that of memory. In remembering a past event, memory
makes something to be present again which is otherwise already gone by. It
must do it, therefore, out of its own inner resources, as if hitting upon it by
a lucky incidence – in any event, by constructing it, not by copying it, since
the event is no longer there to be copied. Moreover, that the construction is
true to the original is made manifest only in the course of the construction
itself and by virtue of it, because – as just said – the event is no longer present.
The *Wissenschaftslehre* thus constructed: it did not re-construct. It was not
unlike a work of art[28] – one, however, whose product, once achieved,
presented itself as already having been there, on its own right.[29] It carried
its own immediate evidence. That kind of conceptual art was not, however,
suited to everyone. As Fichte said, one is born a philosophical artist, just as
one is born a poet. There is indeed an affinity, he added, between the
intuition that envelops both *Wissenschaftslehre* and poetic intuition.[30] For
this reason, undertaking the *Wissenschaftslehre* was, again, a highly personal
decision. But it was not a private affair, for the pure "I" which is at its
foundation is nothing other than reason grasping itself as reason. Hence,
though a personal matter, anyone engaged in the *Wissenschaftslehre* was not
doing a work that was just one's own; in principle it was everybody's.[31]

To the claim that the *Wissenschaftslehre* was just an abstraction that said
nothing about the actual (where by the "actual" one meant the things that
were the objects of direct experience), Fichte therefore replied that the
objection was like complaining about the demonstration of the workings
of a clock on the ground that at the end there was no clock in one's
pocket.[32] The objection was based on a failure to distinguish between
"science of knowledge," such as the *Wissenschaftslehre*, and *Weltweisheit*,
or a science of natural things: it was a matter of confusing a reflective model
of experience with a cosmogonic construction.

2.2.3   Fichte's Departure from Kant

Although Fichte's claim that science of science was not science of life *tout
court* was made in conversation with Kant, in doing so he was already
making a point against Schelling.[33] Nonetheless, Kant was the one Fichte

---

[28] The work of the *Wissenschaftslehre* was one of pure *erfinden*, pure fabrication. GA I.7:218.14–18.
[29] See GA I.7:248.30–249.8.   [30] GA I.7:243.4–29.   [31] See GA I.7:229.12ff.
[32] GA I.7:210.3ff. 58.
[33] GA I.7:247.31–34. Schelling claimed to have knowledge of the world (*Weltweisheit*), not just
knowledge of knowledge.

was addressing directly, and it is significant that there was a change in the *Bericht* from earlier presentations of the *Wissenschaftslehre* that actually brought it closer to Kant's idea of science. He still presented his Science as originating in the deliberate decision of an individual to perform a thought with the sole intention of reflecting on it simply as a thought-act. This was already the case at least as early as the First Introduction to the *Wissenschaftslehre* of 1797.[34] The personal character of this decision came through just as clearly in the *Bericht* as it did then. But the systematic stress was now on the rationality of the performance requested of this individual self: on the fact that the performance was a product of reason and that the consequences that followed from it were constitutive of reason's life. Fichte now rather spoke of the "I" in the plural, as "Iche" – the universal "I" itself being, rather, the first product of abstraction. The *Wissenschaftslehre*, in other words, was a science of reason rather than an egology, and, inasmuch as the issue of personal choice entered into it explicitly – as indeed it had to – it was a science of the conduct of individual selves motivated and governed by a rationality common to them all. By engaging in the work of the *Wissenschaftslehre*, one was doing a work which was not just one's own but in principle everybody's.

In this, inasmuch as the *Wissenschaftslehre* was presented essentially as a product of reason, it could have been taken as a version of Kant's Critique of Reason that, however, did not simply stop at reason's limitations. In both cases, still at issue was reason reflecting on its activities precisely *as reason*. This was, however, the full extent of Fichte's rapprochement to Kant. On the central issue of intellectual intuition, one might well have wondered whether Fichte was addressing Kant at all. Of course, Kant knew that reason was aware of itself, indeed self-critical, in its performances *as reason*. This is exactly what he meant when claiming that reason is autonomous or that its performances are norm setting, *a priori*. In this, Kant was still operating within the tradition of Descartes' *cogito*, albeit with the difference – a big difference indeed – that, mindful that existence is nothing but radically individualized, he could not accept the force of Descartes' *ergo sum* unless the *ego* that performed the *cogito* were filled with a content that made him or her an individual. For this reason, Kant had rejected Descartes's argument: it remained too formal to have existential value.

When Kant spoke of an intellectual intuition that he denied we had, the intuition in question was one that would have provided precisely the

---

[34] Fichte (1994), 6–9; GA I.4: § 1.

individuating determination, hence the existential value, that Descartes' argument needed in order to be effective. So far as Kant was concerned, such a content could be derived only from sense impressions. Whether he was right or wrong, the fact is that Fichte, in conversation with him on the issue of intellectual intuition, was equivocating. The intuition that he affirmed we had was not the one Kant had claimed we did *not* have. In fact, in stressing the purely reflective nature of the intuition, Fichte was playing into Kant's hands, for he gave evidence of the fact that his science was purely a work of reason – in this sense, therefore, a kind of logic.

Fichte was right in saying that "science of science" is not "science of nature." But the question was whether, on the strength of what he had said so far, he could ever perform the transition from "concept of the concept of nature" to "concept of nature." The question was not whether the demonstration of the workings of a clock should conclude with an actual clock in one's pocket. No demonstration can do that. It was rather whether the demonstration would have any existential relevance for the handling of clocks that fit in one's pockets. Fichte had bracketed for the purpose of the *Wissenschaftslehre* the direct apprehension of things: he had bracketed their being in themselves, their "otherness" with respect to thought understood in any robust sense. The question was whether in his system he could ever succeed in removing these brackets and return to direct experiences for the sake of saving their immediacy.

Not that Fichte had any doubt about the existential relevance of his Science. On the contrary, after the exposition of the nature of the *Wissenschaftslehre*, much of the rest of the *Bericht* was dedicated to an account of the benefits that would accrue to both individual and social life upon its completion and acceptance. But this only made the question just posed even more pressing. For Fichte gave every indication that all that was needed for the envisaged new life to be brought about by the *Wissenschaftslehre* was a thought-revolution; that the unbracketing of direct experience was, therefore, not needed. The determining event in the required thought-revolution was simply the recognition that our naturally direct engagement with external things is due to a forgetting (a sort of natural amnesia) of the fact that reason, and reason alone, is what counts for us as the real. The *Wissenschaftslehre*'s bracketing was thus only the dissolution of an otherwise natural illusion – no need, therefore, to undo it.

Where for Kant the natural illusion lay in believing that reason yielded objective knowledge, for Fichte it lay in believing that immediate experience did. Yet if Fichte's Science was not mere formal logic but yielded real knowledge – granted also that it did not revert to dogmatic metaphysics – what kind of knowledge was it? It obviously entailed a metaphysical commitment. Kant's transcendental idealism also did. It was, as we said, still that of classical metaphysics. But this was assumed only hypothetically, by default, and kept at bay by critical ignorance – exactly the ignorance that Fichte rejected by virtue of the intellectual intuition he posited. But, to repeat, what was the commitment regarding "being" that motivated his Science? This was the issue that remained unresolved in his reply to Kant and which his talk about "intellectual intuition," rather than clarifying, obfuscated instead. It was the issue that further worked itself out in his controversy with Schelling. It devolved into the question of how to understand the status of nature in a system of science – understandably so, for it is only in nature that the individualizing determination is attained that, as Kant well knew, is required for existence.

2.3 Fichte in Controversy with Schelling

In 1801 Schelling published an exposition of his *System* (*Darstellung*) which he amplified in 1802 (*Fernere Darstellungen*).[35] The *Darstellung* and the *Fernere Darstellungen* coincided chronologically with Fichte's already mentioned lectures of 1801–1802. The coincidence was more than just chronological. Albeit at a distance, Fichte and Schelling were carrying on a controversy that had begun at a more personal level in a correspondence initiated in 1800 and terminated with Fichte's publication of the *Bericht*, at which point any personal relation between the two men was irrevocably disrupted.

There were signs of tension from the beginning of the correspondence, despite the fact that the immediate occasion for it was Schelling's plan to found a scientific journal, for which he was enlisting Fichte's collaboration.[36] The plan, as transpires from the extant exchange of letters, involved navigating many personal intricacies, including keeping the Schlegel brothers at bay. The story makes for an interesting social portrait of the intellectual world of the day. Of interest to us, however, is that from the beginning Schelling had been keen to reassure Fichte that his Philosophy of Nature was in no way at odds with the *Wissenschaftslehre*; nor was his *System of Transcendental Idealism*, the work that had especially aroused Fichte's suspicions. Schelling's assurances, especially in view of the arguments on which he based them, did little to reassure Fichte. We know

---

[35] For publication details, see Section 2.4.
[36] For a historical account of this correspondence, see the editorial introduction in GA II.5:405–415.

from notes that the latter wrote in connection with the correspondence that the arguments had in fact the contrary effect of convincing him that Schelling had forged a philosophical path directly counter to his own.[37] Their eventual rupture was but fated from the beginning.

It is significant that each man gave clear evidence that he understood the other's position, yet based his objection to it on the very grounds that the other adduced in its defense. To start with Schelling, Fichte had objected to his Philosophy of Nature on the ground that it took nature as something found, indeed ready-made,[38] yet found according to laws which are not nature's own but in fact immanent to the intellect. It was as if, in being made the object [*Sache*][39] of consciousness, nature itself became consciousness; as if, in other words, nature was added to consciousness while consciousness was being added to nature. For Fichte, on the contrary, consciousness and the object were immediately united in the "I," which was at once "real as ideal" and "ideal as real." To make nature by itself an object of reflection, the "I" thus needed a "fine abstraction" from itself as consciousness in order to concentrate exclusively on the "real" side of its original "ideal/real" unity. By virtue of this abstraction, Fichte claimed, one could then construct a fiction that we call "nature in itself." In other words, just as the beginning of science required a bracketing of the natural attitude, so the beginning of the particular science of nature required the bracketing of precisely this original abstraction. But, it is important to note, for Fichte this bracketing of the bracketing did not amount to its removal. It represented rather a further reflective elaboration of the "ideal/ real" world of the "I." There was no relapsing into the natural attitude which, according to Fichte, was rather that of Schelling's science, since it began with an abstraction from the "ideal" side of the "I" and ended up turning consciousness into a fiction.

To this, Schelling replied that he had no difficulty accepting Fichte's original union in the "I" of ideality and reality, as well as the abstractions that Fichte prescribed for his sciences, be they of the ideal or the real. He accepted Fichte's analysis of the situation. The issue was not which was added [*zukommen*] to which: whether the *Sache* to consciousness or consciousness to the *Sache*, since both were at one in Fichte's "I." Indeed, Schelling also had no difficulty accepting the *Wissenschaftslehre* as a self-justifying science

[37] "*Bei der Lectüre von Schellings tr. Idealismus*," in GA II.5:416ff.
[38] "durchaus gefunden, und zwar *fertig* und *vollendet*," PR 42; GA III.4.:360.23. *Fichte to Schelling*, November 15, 1800.
[39] *Die Sache*, a German word not easily translatable with any single English equivalent. For comments regarding this term, see the footnotes to Chapter 6, specifically, Section 6.5.1.

complete on its own. Such a science could not, however, stand opposed to his Philosophy of Nature, for the two – this was Schelling's claim – pursued different interests. The *Wissenschaftslehre* proceeded logically and had nothing to do with reality. The issue separating Fichte from him was rather that Fichte's "I," unbeknown to Fichte, was in fact itself nature,[40] or, more precisely, that it constituted the highest form of nature, or that in its highest power [*Potenz*] nature had become conscious of itself. This nature was not merely found (Schelling insisted that his Philosophy of Nature was no mere empiricism) but actively *represented itself* as found. The abstraction with which the Philosophy of Nature originated was, therefore, an abstraction from precisely the subjective and intuitive activity that posited in self-consciousness the subject-object identity by virtue of which the "I" of the *Wissenschaftslehre*, and the *Wissenschaftslehre* itself, were first constituted. The *Wissenschaftslehre* itself never performed this abstraction; indeed, it refused to make it and therefore remained a purely logical product – as Kant had claimed,[41] even though Schelling was diplomatic enough to leave this unsaid. Once the abstraction was performed, however, there was left precisely the object of Schelling's Philosophy of Nature, namely an object subjectively (i.e., conceptually or manifestly) reconstituted as independent of the subject [*Subjekt-Objekt*]. This object was nature, of which, as Schelling did not tire to repeat, the reflective and philosophizing "I" is the highest potentiation.

The Philosophy of Nature, according to Schelling, thus constituted the theoretical part of Transcendental Idealism. The "I" with which this theoretical part concluded was in turn the principle of the ideal practical part ("the practical" as Kant had called it, according to Schelling) of the same Transcendental Idealism. This was the part in which nature was subjectively reconstituted as dependent on the subject. There was an antitheses between these two parts, since "nature" was conceived as both independent of the subject (in the first part) and dependent on it (in the second). This is an antitheses that was generated by the very abstraction with which the Philosophy of Nature originated but which – Schelling asserted – was finally overcome [*aufgehoben*] in the work of art. The Philosophy of Art was, accordingly, the third part of a System of Philosophy: "The sublation of the antithesis that was posited through that first abstraction yields an actually objective, as contrasted with a merely philosophical, ideal-realism (art); such

---

[40] "nichts anderes, als Natur ist," PR 44; GA III.4:363.12. *Schelling to Fichte*, November 18, 1800.
[41] AA 12:570; Kant (1999), p. 559.

a sublation occurs in the Philosophy of Art, the third part of a System of Philosophy."[42]

This is how Schelling had also stated his position in his 1800 *System of Transcendental Idealism*, where the two parts of the System balance each other, each leading to the other. In the present dispute, however, Schelling was in fact identifying his Philosophy of Nature with the System as a whole. He started from the lowest powers of nature and progressively made his way to Fichte's "I." This "I" was still part of nature. It was its highest potentiation, by virtue of which nature, in becoming conscious of itself, generated the antithesis between itself *as in-itself* and itself *as conscious of itself*. It thereby also set in motion the process of returning to an original intuition that would transcend nature both *as in-itself* and *as conscious of itself* and would thus issue in the kind of self-objectification that only art can provide. The problem with Fichte's Idealism was that it failed to recognize its place within the larger schema of Idealism; therefore it remained formal science exclusively.[43]

Fichte's retort was brief. What Schelling considered as subjectivity derived from subjectively-objective nature, that is, what Schelling took as Fichte's "I," was in fact "an **analogue** of our self-determination (nature, as noumenon) which we bring, through thought, to the (undisputed) creative work of the imagination." In other words, it was an imaginative idea (a noumenon) of the Kantian type. But, Fichte continued, "the 'I' [i.e., the "I" according to Fichte himself] cannot in turn be explained by what is otherwise explained *by* it."[44] In effect, according to Fichte, Schelling had mistaken the phenomenal product of reflection for reality and had then explained reflection by its own product: in this he was a dogmatist and a Spinozist.[45] Perhaps over-ingenuously, Fichte blamed himself for this mistake of Schelling. He (Fichte) had so far failed to explain his "system of the world as *intelligible*." He had not explained it adequately, and this failure also explained, he added, "why Schlegel and Schleiermacher chatter about their confused Spinozism, or the even more confused Reinhold does

---

[42] PR 45 (translation modified); GA III.4:364.8–13. *Schelling to Fichte*, November 19, 1800.

[43] "It [viz. *die Wissenschaftslehre*] is, as I see it, idealism's formal proof, hence Science κατ'ἐξοκήν. What I however want to call philosophy [as contrasted with *Wissenschaftslehre*] is the *material* proof of idealism. In this proof Nature is indeed to be deduced with all its determinations, in its objectivity, in its independence, not however from the I which is itself objective [i.e. already part of Nature], but from the I which is subjective and engaged in the very act of philosophizing [*subjectiven und philosophirenden*, that is, Fichte's kind of "I"]." PR 44 (translation heavily modified); GA III.4:363.27–33.

[44] PR 48 (translation modified); GA III.4:404.26–405.3. *Fichte to Schelling*, draft of a letter.

[45] That he was a dogmatist is said explicitly only in the notes Fichte wrote for himself. GA II.5:414.1–2.

about his Bardilism."⁴⁶ By this "intelligible world" Fichte clearly meant one contained within the realm of reflection. As he wrote to Schelling:

> The *Wissenschaftslehre* or Transcendental Idealism [is] a system that operates within the circle [*Umkreis*] of the subjective-objectivity of the "I" as a finite intelligence, that is, within the circle of an original limitation of this "I" through material feeling and conscience: a system which might indeed be capable of deducing, within this circle, the sensible world in its every detail, but one that does not in any way presume to venture into an explanation of that original limitation.⁴⁷

This was Fichte insisting again, as he had done in the *Bericht*, that the *Wissenschaftslehre* was phenomenology. It could display nature in itself as an idea excogitated *a priori* according to reflective requirements (i.e., as an intelligible world) and could also characterize it as a factor felt internally as constraining thought *externally*. In no way, however, could it explain how this constraint arose from nature considered by itself, independent of the reflection that gave rise to the idea of it in the first place. *Wissenschaftslehre* was not psychology, nor, for that matter, metaphysics. Schelling's Philosophy of Nature was totally contrary to Transcendental Idealism. In his personal notes Fichte summed up the difference between Schelling and himself playing precisely on this point:

> [Self-consciousness] may well be treated as a form of *Being* [as it is by Schelling]; but I say that all Being is only in connection with a *Knowledge*. He retorts: no, all knowledge is a form of *Being*. [. . .] He thinks of Nature as an activity which is checked through another and thereby first produces appearance. But on the contrary, *Intelligence* is a power that grasps [*ergreifende*] and checks [*hemmende*] itself through itself: this is the true opposition. This he [Schelling] cannot ever produce out of nature: not ever an "I."⁴⁸

The opposition between nature and mind that, at least as Fichte saw it, Schelling posited as generated within nature but as also resolved therein, Fichte posited instead within the mind alone, within the circle of its inner resources. It was generated there by virtue of reflection and resolved by virtue of intuition. The critical editors of the Correspondence remark that by accusing Schelling of dogmatism and Spinozism Fichte was unwittingly

---

⁴⁶ PR 48; GA III.4:405.4–11. *Fichte to Schelling*, draft of a letter. C. B. Bardili was the proponent of what came to be known as "logical realism." Reinhold converted to it when, after 1800, he repudiated first Fichte and then any form of Kantian idealism. Fichte had just received a long letter from Reinhold, including an excerpt from Bardili, explaining the system. See di Giovanni (2006).

⁴⁷ PR 48; GA III.4:405.12–18 *Fichte to Schelling*, draft of a letter.

⁴⁸ GA II.5:414.13–415.13. Citation highly redacted.

also rejecting *avant le temps* his soon to come Identity Philosophy in which Schelling quite openly sided with Spinoza. This is a fair comment.[49] It must, however, be kept in mind that in the current discussion Schelling was not advocating simple identity between system of nature and system of mind. The transition from the one to the other was in fact mediated by a *tertium quid*, an extra third term that only the creative artist apprehended intuitively. This was a mediation already present in the System of 1800.

The *tertium quid* was of course Spinoza's substance, nature and mind being its two attributes. This no doubt made a Spinozist of Schelling, and Fichte was perceptive enough to recognize the fact. But Fichte failed to note that the difficulty Schelling was laboring under without apparently appreciating its gravity was caused by Spinoza's monism. Indeed, it would have been caused by any form of monism. This is the difficulty of deriving multiplicity out of the presupposed One. He equally failed to note that he, too, was affected by this difficulty. For the "true opposition" which he claimed to be the product of an intelligence "grasping [*ergreifende*] and checking [*hemmende*] itself through itself," was for him a fact only ascertained *ex post facto*, never at point of origin. This origin, no less than the emergence of Schelling's nature and mind, had to remain unspoken, shrouded in intuition, because it was projected into an extra space that transcended the presumably derived space of reason, in which alone distinctions and oppositions have a place. The original intuition remained ambiguous, just as ambiguous as the monism to which it allegedly provided access. Everything depended on how one interpreted the intuition's import, and by the very fact of interpreting it one way or another one no longer was in the position of addressing the other on its own terms. Misunderstanding was the rule.

As we said, Fichte and Schelling both subsequently altered their method of doing science. Fichte further capitalized on an ontological quietism he had in fact already announced when insisting that the *Wissenschaftslehre* is not explanatory (a quietism, we shall see, that had nothing to do with critical ignorance).[50] Schelling populated with imaginative/ideal constructs the extra-rational space he had presupposed inhabited by the Absolute, as only a philosopher at once prophet and artist would dare doing. Hegel proceeded to populate the same space with reasons, in effect abolishing it. But first we must see how the Fichte/Schelling controversy farther worked

[49] It must be kept in mind that Schelling later complained regarding the title of "identity" attributed to that system, a title for which he claimed he was only incidentally responsible. HMP 120; SSW I.10:107.
[50] In Chapter 3.

itself out in Schelling's public presentation of his System and in Fichte's public lectures, both in the years of 1801/1802. The private controversy between the two had only been a rehearsal.

2.4   1801/1802: **Schelling's Presentation of His System**

The original motivation for Schelling's *Darstellung* was to clarify his position in response to C. A. Eschenmayer's criticism of his earlier works on the Philosophy of Nature, a criticism which, very much in the spirit of Fichte, stressed the primacy and irreducibility of thought with respect to nature. It was also to bring his position more closely in line with Goethe's, whose speculations on nature had strongly influenced him. It was only too natural, however, that, especially as expanded in the *Fernere Darstellungen* of 1802, the work would set itself up in direct opposition to Fichte's Science.[51]

Schelling's System defies condensed exposition. It unfolds, like Spinoza's *Ethics, more geometrico*, in full mathematical paraphernalia – principles, propositions, corollaries, proofs, explanations – all of which makes a summary impossible. But it is possible to extract the idea that motivates the System and governs its development. Four terms are key, drawn from classical metaphysics but assuming special meaning in the System itself. The first is *Wesen*, for which "essence" is a fair translation,[52] provided one keeps in mind that, in the present context, the term assumes the added meaning of "substance." Schelling's "essence" carries existential connotations: it is something that can stand on its own and on which anything else depends for its subsistence. "Form" defines, on the contrary, the *what* of this something that stands on its own. Schelling normally associates *Wesen* with the "real," the "objective"; "form," with the "ideal," the "subjective." But it is important, initially, to take the two concepts in their broadest possible

---

[51] *Darstellung meiner System der Philosophie* [*Presentation of my System of Philosophy*], originally published in *Zeitschrift für spekulative Physik*, 2.2 (1801), in SSW I.4. *Fernere Darstellungen aus dem System der Philosophie* [*Further Presentations from the System of Philosophy*], originally published in *Neue Zeitschrift für spekulative Physik*, 1.2 (1802), in SSW I.4. (English translation of *Darstellung*, and of an extract of *Fernere Darstellungen*, in PR, by Vater and Wood.) This journal (*Neue Zeitschrift*) had been established with the purpose of publicizing Schelling's philosophical physics. C. A. Eschenmayer (1768–1852) was a notable exponent of speculative physics at the time. His critique of Schelling's position had appeared in the previous issue of the *Neue Zeitschrift*, and Schelling had replied in the same issue with an appendix in which he also promised a fuller reply in a new exposition of his system. This exposition appeared in the following issue. It is clear, however, that replying to Eschenmayer was certainly not Schelling's only motive behind the piece. The latter's title was clearly an indirect reference to Fichte.

[52] As Vater and Wood normally translate it in PR.

meaning, for, as we shall see, the distinctions of "real/ideal," "objective/subjective," occur in the System only as derived. The distinctions need "construction" – a term about which more will also be said momentarily. A third term is *Sein*, "being," best definable in the present context as the determination, or the content, that accrues to *Wesen*[53] because of its "form." The distinction of "universal" and "particular," as used by Schelling, falls within the domain of precisely "being." The fourth and final term is "nature," which Schelling apparently uses in accordance with its Latin etymological meaning of "what something is born to be."

So much for the general meaning of the four terms. They can be summed up in one proposition by saying, quite in general, that something standing on its own (*Wesen*) behaves at it does (*Natur*)[54] because of the being-determinations (*Sein*), whether universal or particular, that accrue to it by virtue of its form (*Form*). And their meaning can further be illustrated by showing how, together, they constitute the conceptual scaffolding for the idea of a living organism. An organic being is a kind of *universe*, in the sense that, despite the presence in it of an otherwise amorphous matter, it nonetheless succeeds in informing this matter by making it *its being*, that is, the medium of its self-contained substance (*Wesen*). The otherwise dispersed matter is thus made to coalesce into several organs, each discharging a specialized function within the organism; each, therefore, existing *for* the organism. To be *for* the organism is precisely their nature. The organism, accordingly, becomes *versed* in a variety of ways: on this account, it is a complex entity. Nonetheless, each organ would not be an *organ* were it not in *essence* the organism *as such*, the whole of it: any difference between it and any other organ is, therefore, only quantitative, that is, in no way affecting the organ's *in-itself* that must rather be, as just said, the organism *as such*. In this respect, the organism persists as a simple substance, but only existentially speaking, for when it is a matter of describing *what* it is, this must be done in terms of the organs' determinations, whether taken in general or particularly. Each of these organs, for their part, acquires a specific being of its own only by contrast with all the rest, for, to repeat, *in-themselves* they are, one and all, the same *Wesen*. But, precisely because each is the whole *Wesen* undividedly, in this contrast each also tries to attain for itself the same self-containedness of the organism of which they are otherwise only figurations. Consequently, they each potentially compromise

---

[53] I use the German term to avoid committing myself to either "essence" or "substance," both of which are possible in all instances, but each not necessarily the best choice in some.

[54] *Natur* makes only a fleeting appearance in *System*, but will assume crucial importance in the Freedom Essay, as we shall see in Chapter 4.

the integrity of the organism. The power of the latter lies in resisting this centrifugal tendency.

More important, however, and the reason why the organism can be taken as the model for a universe of being, is that the organism is self-contained in the strong sense that, when taken from the standpoint of its *being*, that is to say, of the many organs that determine it in particular, it can be said to *precede itself*. For, although such organs make up its *being* (they constitute *what it is*), they in turn would be nothing apart from the organism's self-identity, which grounds them *existentially* and which they are *essentially*. The organism is thus self-creating, the ground of its own *being*, truly *causa sui*. Accordingly, Schelling calls it *secundum Existens*, as contrasted with the *primum Existens*. The latter is the primordial *being* of which Schelling's System is intended to be the exposition. Its ground is the primordial *identity*, of which the self-containedness of any organic structure (the *secundum Existens*) is only a particularized and derived form. The challenge for the interpreter of Schelling is to understand how the stated four key terms enter his System at the very beginning, that is, at the level of this *primum Existens*, where *being* is immediately grounded in original *identity*. Schelling also refers to this identity as "the Absolute," clearly the counterpart of Spinoza's *substance*.

On the face of it, Schelling's first move is plain enough. Since the Absolute, as truth requires, is One, the conceptual distinctions expressed by the four terms cannot apply to it, except ideally, that is, from the standpoint of someone who operates in the medium of concepts. From such a standpoint, that is, granted that one must thus make use of the distinctions, one would have to say that, in the Absolute, *Wesen* and *Form* are one, each equally the other. The Absolute *is* precisely the identity of the two, essence and form. If we thus define the *Wesen* as "identity," its *Form* would be conceptually expressed by the formula "A = A," where the " = " sign signifies the *indifference* of the two hypothetically introduced terms, A & A. "Indifference" is an all-important concept for Schelling. It denotes a conceptual space that Schelling repeatedly compares with the imaginative space of Geometry, because, just like the latter, although not in itself exhibiting any particular determination, it nonetheless makes the introduction of determinations possible – points, lines, and planes, in the case of Geometry. Moreover, with respect to geometrical space, although with the introduction of determinations the space becomes distributed *in extenso* into a potentially infinite numbers of figures, its spatiality (i.e., the "part-outside-part" that makes it what it is) is nonetheless totally present in every figure:[55] it

---

[55] This is also Kant's argument for why space/time must be intuitive and not conceptual. KrV B40.

makes the figure's limits at once possible yet indifferently replaceable by any other. The same applies to the identity which is the essence of the Absolute when informed by the "A = A." It might best be termed negatively as a not-non-identity,[56] an *indifference* to determination that makes the two terms (A & A), when introduced, at once possible yet each equally replaceable by the other, since the essence (*Wesen*) of the distinguished terms is none other than the identity of the Absolute.

This is not to say that such distinctions can therefore be introduced, and annulled, *ad hoc*. This is certainly not the case in Geometry, which is a science precisely because its constructions, and the theorems associated with them, build upon each other progressively, in each case systematically adding limitations to space as such, but at the same time also disclosing further possibilities of particularized determination. The same goes for Schelling's *System*: it is a science because it is a "system." Accordingly, the first distinction that Schelling introduces in the Absolute's otherwise indifferent being is precisely that of "thought" and "being" (this last now determined in opposition to "thought"), obviously the counterparts of Spinoza's attributes of "thought" and "extension." Each is essentially the same *Wesen*; anything said in terms of the one is equally determinable in the medium of the other. This first distinction opens the space for the further distinctions, already alluded to, of objective and subjective, real and ideal, universal and particular. Other distinctions are methodically made to follow from these, as well as further terms, some of which describe the dynamics by which the whole process of determination unfolds. "Potency" is a case in point. It stands for the degree to which, within a presupposed equilibrium of opposed terms, one term assumes preponderance over the other (i.e., becomes more "potentiated"),[57] and thus generates the need for equilibrium to be redressed. Other terms, such as "gravity," "light," cohesion," "matter," "universe," "individual" (this last the counterpart of Spinoza's *modus*), stand rather for renewed starting points, new and more determinate forms of the original identity that in turn open the space for further ever new sets of distinctions. Schelling's constructions range over magnetism, electrical fields, voltaic batteries, chemical elements, terrestrial forms, animal brains – in short, over the whole scientific knowledge (or mis-knowledge) of the day. Included are criticisms of some current popular theories, with Newton singled out as especially wrong-headed, while Goethe, on the contrary, is held out as a paragon of speculative acuity.

---

[56] My term.   [57] Schelling's own term.

Much of this material is repeated from Schelling's *System of Transcendental Idealism* and his earlier treatises on Nature. This is the part of Schelling's work that resists summary. But we need not dwell on it. More to the point for our purposes is the question that, although not voiced, has in fact been pending since the first mention of Schelling's Absolute. It is the same question that can be raised, and has been raised, to Spinoza; no less to Parmenides, or, for that matter, to any monist. If reality is essentially One, where is the warrant for introducing distinctions with respect to it, as monists in fact invariably do? How can Parmenides tread a "pathway of appearances" after he has traversed that of "truth"? Or Spinoza present his simple substance under an infinite number of attributes[58] and an indefinite number of modes? Or again, granted that for Schelling *Wesen* and *Form* are identical in the Absolute, how can he then proceed to develop a whole system of determinations of the Absolute in a space (Being) that only the non-identity of the two would make possible?

This line of questioning is both inevitable and compelling. And one must give credit to Schelling for not having hesitated to raise it himself, and for having given to it the one answer that would have been consistent on his monistic assumptions.[59] In short, the questioning cannot be met because it has no meaning. This is the short answer. It needs expanding.

Suppose, as a start, that one asks of any apparently singular thing why it is the particular being that it happens to be. In that case, one would have to refer the thing to other equally singular things, only by reference to which it acquires its particularizing determination. The same question, however, can equally be raised for each of the singular things to which the first is referred, and, inasmuch as one refers these to others for their respective determinations, these too would have to be included as factors in the determination of the first, in effect diluting any content specifically belonging to it. And suppose that one extends this referral process *in infinitum*, as one would logically be bound to do: the net result would finally be the total dissolution of that content – the dissolution, that is, of the first thing's presumed particular determination but equally of the content of the subsequently introduced things, for they too are subject to the same infinite process of external referral. The argument demonstrated, according to Schelling, what should have been apparent from the beginning, namely

---

[58] "Thought" and "extension" are the only two known to us.

[59] I am generating one single line of argument basing myself on *Fernere Darstellungen*, §§ II and IV, in SSW I.4:361ff., 392ff. These are the extracts translated in PR 206ff.

that singular things, *as particulars*, are nothing on their own. They lack an in-itself; *per se*, they are a *nothing*. But one does not ask of a nothing why it is *there*. At best, one can ask why one might have been deluded into believing that it is there.

This is Schelling's negative argument. There is in his text, however, also another, positive, line of reasoning. Suppose that, when raising the question of the why of particularity, one proceeds, not *in extenso*, as just done, but *in intenso*.[60] That is to say, rather than relating a thing to everything else as the source of its particular determinations, one can try to identify *what*, on the contrary, a thing might have in common with something else, ideally with everything else. One can try to identify, in other words, the "what" that constitutes whatever "in-itselfness," or whatever subsistence, a thing ideally has of its own. This is exactly, as Schelling says, what scientists do when they seek to establish the laws of phenomena, obviously in the belief that these laws, and not the singular events that they explain, are the truth of reality. Schelling could, of course, point to his own systematization of natural events to make this point about scientific procedure. But the most telling statement of what he means, and the best clue to the nature of his idealism, can again be gathered – as is often the case at this stage of his thought[61] – from his comments regarding Geometry. In Geometry, Schelling says, what counts as truly real are not the triangular or round things that we find in nature and draw on a chalkboard for pedagogical purposes. Rather, the truly real are the ideas of triangle or circle that geometers conceive on the basis of their postulates about space and display in their full determination by means of the appropriate theorems. The "in-itself" of geometrical entities, Schelling says, is to be sought in these ideas, just as, when it comes to physical nature, it is to be sought in the laws that the scientist constructs. In the face of such ideas and laws, the singular things that common sense believes provide the touchstone of reality are in fact demoted to a nothing.

Both lines of argumentation lead to the nothingness of the individual things of common experience. The second strikes a positive note nonetheless, because, while asserting this nothingness, it at the same time points to where the "real" is to be found. Here is where Schelling's "intellectual intuition" and his method of "construction" come into play. As Schelling

---

[60] This is a terminology I am introducing to sum up Schelling's otherwise dispersed argument. According to Paola Mayer, this is the Platonic side of Schelling. Mayer (1999), p. 192.

[61] Even though Schelling recognizes that Geometry still belongs to the sensible domain; for philosophy proper one must transcend Geometry as well. See PR 261, note 289: *Schelling's note*; SSW I.4.369, note 1. This insistence on Geometry later fades away, as it does also for Fichte.

says,[62] "intellectual intuition" is normally taken to be something mysterious, even occult. In fact, nothing could be farther from the truth. And the clue for this is again drawn from Geometry. The latter is possible as a science only because its practitioners, in drawing their points, lines, and surfaces, do so in an imaginative space of which they must have an original, immediate intuition, even though *that* they have such an intuition, and *what* the intuition is an *intuition of*, is something of which they become explicitly aware only in the process of informing it by actually constructing their figures. The same applies to knowledge in general. It would not be possible unless, in consciousness, there were for the scientist the intuitive presence of a primordial and absolute being, of which, just like space for the geometer, the scientist is not explicitly aware except in the actual process of informing it by determining it conceptually. "Construction" is precisely this process of informing and thus of objectifying. Schelling insists (with silent but nonetheless obvious reference to Fichte) that construction is in no way a proof or deduction,[63] whether logical or dialectical. Nor, for that matter, does the traditional analytical/synthetic distinction apply to it in any relevant manner. Rather, construction is *demonstration* understood in its Latin root of *monstrare*,[64] that is, as *exhibiting*. In science, demonstration is a matter of making true being *manifestly* present. As Schelling puts it, construction is an activity that stands between the singulars of ordinary experience and the universality of being. It is a process of idealizing singulars, of reducing them to a mere *precipitate* (*as singulars*) while at the same time manifesting the universal being which is their true reality (*as idealized*). What ordinary experience takes as *real* reality is in fact but an irrelevant leftover, like the precipitate in a chemical reaction.[65]

But what about the first distinction of *Wesen* and *Form*, without which there would be no question of a space for the idealizations of otherwise merely illusionary appearances of reality? Here Schelling becomes more voluble and also less transparent. All depends on what one packs into "intellectual intuition." One can take it as the source of a knowledge which is absolute *as knowledge* only because it recognizes that the Absolute of

---

[62] PR 261, note 289 (Schelling's note); SSW I.4.369, note 1.

[63] This is an unspoken, but obvious, reference to Fichte's Science, in which a lot is made of deduction.

[64] According to Vater and Wood, Schelling got the term form the English (PR 264, note 321).

[65] See PR 220ff.; SSW I.4:404 to the end of § IV. This is one of Schelling's more extensive statements of the method of construction. See also Schelling's note, PR 257, note 174; SSW I.4:167, § 95, note 1. The Spinozism of Schelling's dialogue *Bruno*, which immediately followed, is already apparent in these texts.

which it is the knowledge is ineffably other than it. The conceptual constructs it generates are directed at the world of appearances: because of their unavoidable subjectivity as constructs, these, too, are only appearances of truth. The space created by the distinction of *Wesen* and *Form* is thus purely negative, in the sense that it negates the same distinction that it makes possible. It is like a night whose darkness absorbs even the world of ideas where the scientist seeks truth.[66]

One need not stop, however, at this negative view. Intellectual intuition can also be taken as the immediate recognition that *Form* is nothing except the *Wesen*'s own *Form*. It is not the case that there is an absolute knowledge on the one side, and the Absolute outside it; on the contrary, the knowledge of the Absolute is identical with the Absolute's knowledge of itself. On this intuition, the question of the whence of the space between *Wesen and Form* has no meaning, for the *Wesen is this space*: to talk of form, of ideas, or of things, in other words, is in fact to speak of the Absolute. And if one were to press the question and ask whence the origin of the talk in the first place, then one would have to revert to the point already made regarding the nothingness of singular things, since also the talk is an instance of such things. Any question regarding it of a "whence" has ultimately no meaning. There is no "whence" for a nothingness.

None of this is, of course, transparent in meaning. But it is, as a minimum, self-consistent. To let Schelling speak for himself:

> Only in the form of all forms is the *positive* essence of unity cognized, but this (absolute form) is embodied in us as the living idea of the absolute, so that our cognition subsists in it and it subsists in our cognition, and we can see in it as clearly as we can see into ourselves and view everything in a single light, in comparison to which every other sort of cognition, but especially sensible cognition, is profound darkness.[67]
>
> There is not an absolute knowledge and outside of this an absolute as well, but the two are one. [...] Philosophy's first cognition depends on identifying the two, on the insight that there is no other absolute except in form (in absolute evidence itself), and no other access to the absolute than this form, that what follows from this form also follows from the absolute itself, and [that] what subsists in the former also subsists in the latter.[68]

---

[66] I am glossing on PR 220; SSW I.4:403: "For most people see in the essence of the absolute nothing but empty night." I presume that Schelling has Fichte especially in mind here, to whose "crystal clear" report he has just referred. PR 219; SSW I.4:402.

[67] PR 220; SSW I.4:404.

[68] PR 220; SSW I.4:404. There is a mistranslation in the lines omitted in the quote. Schelling's point, which is obfuscated in the translation, is that there is another knowledge outside philosophy [*ihr*]

> Identification of form with essence in absolute intellectual intuition [or the insight that absolute knowledge is also a knowledge of the absolute][69] snatches the ultimate doubling [of the real and the ideal] away from the dualism it inhabits and establishes *absolute idealism* in place of the idealism that is confined to the world of appearances.[70]

Only in the context of this absolute idealism does the philosophical method of construction truly comes into its own. It is not a process of reflectively ferreting out thought-implications (as per Fichte) but of displaying Being as the Form of the Absolute, navigating over it as if, at first, over a chaos. But, "where at first the ambiguities of determinations and concepts of reflections" predominate – where, "one item can appear as real or finite on one side, but can be shown to be ideal or infinite on another, and vice versa"; or again, where, "in this fluctuating and living totality [in which] one factor plays with the other, like color in color, time in nature, space in history" – finally, "thanks to a construction carried to the point of totality which actually comprehends everything in everything, this almost divine chaos is exhibited in its simultaneous unity and disorder."[71]

But this ultimate construction would not be possible unless the intellectual intuition on which it depends for its evidence were not at once the philosopher's and the Absolute's. It is the Absolute itself who informs its own identity, and thus becomes cognizant of it *as Being*, but eternally, while the philosopher does the same, but progressively in time. At least, this is what Schelling apparently claims, at this point, however, shrouding his words in a religious imagery that hardly helps making his meaning transparent. With an obvious reference to the figure of the Christ[72] as God's eternal word, Schelling says that only in this figure did the Absolute step "forth *in his own shape* in the act of his self-intuitive cognition." And he proceeds:

> This eternal form [i.e., of the Christ], identical with the absolute itself, is the day in which we comprehend that night [i.e., the night of the self-contained identity], the light in which we clearly discern the absolute, the eternal mediation, the all-seeing and all-disclosing eye of the world, the source of all wisdom and cognition.[73]

---

which is also absolute but, unlike philosophy, is not, as knowledge, at one with the Absolute. Schelling has in mind non-philosophical knowledge.

[69] Schelling's note.   [70] PR 221; SSW I.4:404.PR 221.   [71] PR 219; SSW I.4:402.

[72] The name is not mentioned, but the imagery is clearly drawn from Christian beliefs.

[73] PR 221; SSW I.4.404–405. See also Schelling's important note to his text, PR 262, note 295; SSW I.4:391, note 1 (*Recapitulation*).

Whatever the exact meaning of such a passage, it is clear that, according to
Schelling, the light of this intuition in which the Absolute becomes self-
cognizant, and the philosopher cognizant of the identity which is the truth of
all things, has already shown through, albeit only in fragmentary form, in
past philosophies.[74] And it should be expected indeed that it would at all
time shine through "in some exceptional individuals in more or less universal
form,"[75] as Schelling says, obviously still playing on the figure of the genius
so important in the 1800 exposition of his Idealism. At any rate, the
statement of the monism of his own philosophy is uncompromising:

> It is essential that we understand [unity] in its strongest and genuine sense.
> [. . .] Our view is not just that opposites are generally brought to unity in
> some universal concept, for such a unity would again be of a merely formal
> sort, but that *substance* is one in all things that are ideally opposed, and that
> everything is identical, not by the external bond of the concept, but in inner
> substance and concept, as it were. What you cognize [. . .] are things not just
> figuratively one or one in concept, but truly *the same thing*, however
> different they may seem.[76]

2.5   1801/1802: **Fichte's Lectures on the *Wissenschaftslehre***

Fichte's lectures notes of 1801/1802 also played on the *Bericht*'s analogy
between geometrical constructions and the constructions of the
Wissenschaftslehre. There is no point dwelling on the analogy, since it
adds nothing to what Fichte had already said in the *Bericht* or, for that
matter, Schelling was saying in the exposition of his system. There is one
point, however, that deserves mentioning because it bears directly on the
possibility of a *Wissenschaftslehre*. In Geometry, knowledge simply *is*, that
is, it is knowledge that knows without knowing that it knows. In the
Wissenschaftslehre, by contrast, knowledge is knowledge knowing itself *as
knowing*, grasping itself as such in one single glance (*mit einem Blicke*)[77]
and, therefore, as a self-equal unity. It is as if, Fichte says, in this "knowledge of knowledge, knowledge externalizes itself, and places itself before
itself in order to grasp itself once more."[78] None of this amounts, however,
to a proof of the possibility of the *Wissenschaftslehre*. Such a proof, Fichte
adds, lies rather in the fact that the *Wissenschaftslehre is*, and this is a *fact* of

---

[74] PR 218; SSW I.4:401.
[75] PR 218 SSW I.4:400. Schelling will pose again as philosopher/prophet in the Munich address that
aroused Jacobi's indignation. See Section 4.1.
[76] PR 225; SSW I.4:411.   [77] GA II.6:139.11.   [78] GA II.6:139.25–26.

which anyone can become immediately aware simply by making the Science *exist for oneself*, by heeding to the instructions that Fichte had issued at the beginning of his first lecture, so that his hearers could elevate themselves to the abstractive standpoint of philosophy.[79] "§ 1 [of the *Wissenschaftslehre*]," Fichte says, "is its proof."[80]

Here again Fichte was insisting on the character of his Science as the product of a thought-deed, not of any reasoning process or any psychological fact. There was nothing new in this. The claim had already been made in response to Reinhold and the Humean sceptics. The novelty lay rather in the context in which it was being reiterated. Fichte was still in dispute with Schelling. The implication was that the *Wissenschaftslehre* was from the beginning, and had to be throughout, a product of reflection – and, in this sense, subjective. It had to remain within what Jacobi had called (but disparagingly) the "magic circle" of reflection. Whereas Schelling (with Fichte in mind) was saying that knowledge of the Absolute had to be also the Absolute's knowledge of itself, Fichte now made it clear that, while the *Wissenschaftslehre* was indeed absolute knowledge, it could not be "the Absolute."[81] The very addition of "knowledge" to the Absolute would qualify the latter's absoluteness, thereby falsifying it as Absolute: "The absolute is neither a knowledge, nor is it a being, nor is it identity or indifference of both [i.e., knowledge and being], but is through and through simply and solely the Absolute."[82] Science, therefore, could only begin from absolute knowledge, not from the Absolute, even though, as Fichte went on to say, it might well transpire in the course of the science that one has to *think* of an Absolute which is independent of knowledge. In that case, the Absolute indeed enters into science but only as a *form* of knowledge (i.e., as a postulate in Kant's sense), in no way as pure and for itself. All this was consistent with Fichte's more generalized claim that "being" entered the *Wissenschaftslehre* only as a form of knowledge – as its *real* form, a function of thought – never as absolute being in itself or as the material of knowledge.[83]

Fichte was attacking Schelling at a more personal level as well. In the Introductions to his Science of 1797,[84] he had said that only an individual's personal interest in freedom would ultimately sway the individual to accept the *Wissenschaftslehre*. In his lectures, as it transpires from the notes, he now also drew a parallel between knowledge of the Absolute and knowledge of freedom. One first becomes aware of the latter immediately, only in the freely undertaken performance of the abstraction by virtue of which the

---

[79] GA II.6:140.6–14.   [80] GA II.6:140.13.   [81] GA II.6:143.20–22.   [82] GA II.6:143.25–144.2.
[83] GA II.6:260–261.   [84] The first Introduction, § 4. In Fichte (1994).

Wissenschaftslehre originates. Both free performance and *Wissenschaftslehre* therefore precede knowledge, which is rather their product. What we call "freedom" was for Fichte, therefore, just as unconceptualizable as the Absolute of which the *Wissenschaftslehre* was the science – a science of it indeed but only as if at an infinite and unbridgeable distance.[85] The being of freedom was thus known (known all at once, in a single glance) yet equally not known. True knowledge of it consisted in recognizing this fact; it was a knowledge that postponed its fruition *in infinitum*. There was no point, therefore, Fichte continued, in "playing out" (*spielen*) freedom's absoluteness in that of the Absolute – "in unconceptualizable being or in the unsearchable will of God."[86]

Schelling, of course, was doing nothing of the sort. Certainly, in the 1801/1802 exposition of his System, "freedom" did not come up as an issue at all. But in making his point, Fichte was reiterating the accusation he had leveled against Spinoza from the start, and against dogmatism in general, of which Spinoza was in his mind the most illustrious case, but which, in the present context, he was clearly directing at Schelling as well. The dogmatists, in making thought dependent on being, in effect denied freedom. In this, as follows from Fichte's principles, they demonstrated moral weakness. Schelling fell within the compass of this accusation.

Fichte had said in 1797 that philosophical discussions invariably tend to become personal, and emotionally laden, because an individual's philosophy is an indication of the individual's humanity.[87] The acrimony of his dispute with Schelling, whether carried out personally in private or impersonally on the surface in the public forum, seemed to confirm this estimate.

2.6   The *Unfug* of Intellectual Intuition

The same Promethean spirit of the age was clearly motivating both Fichte and Schelling but in opposite directions. Where Fichte conceived nature as an "other" that thought itself had to invest with meaning in accordance with moral requirements (thought had to construct it morally, in other words, and had to do it while testing its own autonomy as thought), Schelling, for his part, conceived his science as a reflective continuation of a process of self-construction on the part of nature by which the Absolute

---

[85] I say "as if" because, strictly speaking, there is no distance at all, nothing to be bridged. The distance is generated by the effort at conceptualizing.
[86] GA II.6:261.12–13.   [87] Fichte (1994), p. 19; GA I.4:434.

manifested itself and, in the medium of Schelling's science, finally became conscious of itself. Where Fichte gave moral witness, Schelling proffered divine artistry. This was a difference in attitude, in the norm-setting feel for nature, which the ambiguity inherent in the belief in a reality that transcended reason inevitably nurtured. That reality, whatever the name one gave to it, was at once all that nature manifested in particular yet failed to manifest in general. Nature, for its part, was accordingly either overdetermined, that is, always more than it appeared to be, and therefore always in need of artful presentation, or *per se* insubstantial and therefore in need of ideal support. This was an ambiguity which appeal to intuition did nothing to resolve because the intuition was itself affected by it; relying on it only made for miscommunication. There was room to speak of the *Unfug* of intellectual intuition, its "mischief," just as Fichte once spoke of the *Unfug* of Kant's "thing-in-itself."

In one respect, however, the two stood on the same conceptual ground and should have known that they did. For on their own *ex post facto* interpretation of the origin of their *de facto* attitude toward nature, for which they were providing the needed conceptual scaffolding, the event could not be *per se* rational, for reason itself derived from it. It had to be creative. The challenge lay in showing that it was not therefore arbitrary: that their respective sciences connected with, and saved, lived experience. Whatever the role that their dispute may have played in this, the fact is that, as we have repeatedly said, both soon altered the method of their sciences. Both played down intuition, the emphasis being rather on method. For Fichte, the challenge was of methodically leading his audience to recognize that in the attitudes with which they related to reality in their day-to-day experiences, and with which they perforce made their initial ascent to science, they already possessed the truth, indeed the whole truth. There was no need, therefore, either to bracket such attitudes at the beginning of their journey to science or, for that matter, to unbracket them at the end. It was rather a matter of understanding them for what they were and to begin, therefore, to live them again, in their full truth. In this, Fichte turned out to be, perhaps *contre soi*, a true Spinozist.[88] For Schelling, the challenge lay rather in pinpointing the one event in experience the sheer irrationality of which was itself witness to experience's origin in a ground that was more than just rational. That

---

[88] I say "perhaps" because, despite his constant rejection of Spinoza and Spinozism, Fichte must have known that in principle he accepted Spinoza's monism.

event was evil, a fact of experience with which Fichte, by contrast, did not seem to be particularly concerned. But neither had Spinoza. Granted Schelling's strong Spinozistic leanings, the move seemed indeed quite out of character. But was it? As for Hegel, as we have already suggested, he bypassed this whole problematic by staying within reason, and reason alone. In his case, *our* challenge is to show that he did not lapse into the panlogism of which he has been repeatedly accused. But first we must follow up on Fichte and Schelling.

CHAPTER 3

The Transcendental Spinozism
of the Wissenschaftslehre

"You should know that before the emanations were emanated and the creations created, a most supreme, simple light filled the whole existence."

Hayyim ben Joseph Vital[1]

"Thus away with words and signs! Nothing remains except our living thinking and insight, which cannot be shown on a blackboard nor be represented in any way but can only be surrendered to nature."

Fichte[2]

"I am relying here on your [power of] penetration; since language can in no way bring us to our goal."

Fichte[3]

"The man that hath no music in himself, Nor is mov'd with concord of sweet sounds, Is fit for treason, stratagems, and spoils."

Shakespeare[4]

3.1   Fichte's New Start

Fichte died in 1814. To the end, after his departure from Jena in 1800, he produced several versions of his *Wissenschaftslehre* which he presented to the public in a series of lectures held at various locations. These versions were never published in finished form. We do, however, have the lectures notes, posthumously published in more or less fragmentary form.[5] Fichte gave

---

[1] *The Tree of Life: The Palace of Adman Cadmon* (1784).   [2] SK 60; GA II.8, 94–95.
[3] SK 145; GA II.8, 296–297.   [4] *The Merchant of Venice*, 5.1.83–85.
[5] The decision to present his science only orally was made on principle. In the *Grundzüge* Fichte gave as a sign of the empty formalism of his present age its fixation on the written word that had given rise to a stream of publications and of publications on publications, none of them exhibiting serious

three such series in 1804, at Berlin – their notes normally referred to chronologically as WL 1804[1], 1804[2], and 1804[3].[6] These series are seminally important, for in them Fichte substantially reformed the method of his Science. This is not to say that he thereby presented the Science as a fully worked-out system, even if in mere outline. He never presented it completed. The *Wissenschaftslehre* remained for Fichte a work in progress to the end. In 1804, he only set down the outline of a foundational theory of being. In the following year, also in Berlin, he proceeded to demonstrate how such a theory applied to lived experience; how, in other words, it provided the basis on which to establish the principles of such localized sciences as natural theology, morality, and the doctrine of right.[7] These were sciences for which Fichte also gave concrete samples in the same period of time, in their case in published form: *Die Pincipien der Gottes-Sitten- u. Rechtslehre* of 1805 (*The Principles of the Doctrine of God, of Ethics, and of Right*),[8] *Die Anweisung zum Seligen Leben* (*The Way towards the Blessed Life*), and *Die Grundzüge des gegenwartigen Zeitalters* (*Characteristics of the Present Age*), both of 1806.[9] We shall return to these last two works in due time.[10] Our interest at the moment is in Fichte's foundational theory of 1804, specifically as developed in WL 1804[2].[11] There are many reasons for this interest. The very idea of a theory of being as Fichte presents in these notes – the same Fichte who had just insisted against Schelling that *being* can be the object of science only *as thought*, never *in-itself* – would itself motivate it.[12] The interest mounts considering that in WL 1804[2] Fichte also declared that he preferred realism over idealism, albeit a realism of a higher type than that of common sense.[13] He presented this

---

thought. What was missing was the immediate, living, challenge, that the spoken work provoked. Fichte (2008), pp. 71ff; GA I.8:263ff.

[6] From January 17 until March 29, from April 26 until June 8, and from November 5 to December 31. See Lauth (1980), pp. 9–50. WL 1804[1] and 1804[3] are in GA II.7. 1804[2] is in GA II.8.

[7] The lectures of 1805 are normally referred to as *Principien*. They were announced by Fichte as "lectures on the fundamental principles of the doctrines of the divine (of God) and of the internal and external law, (usually) termed natural theology, morality and doctrine of right" (Communication in the *Königlich privilegierte berlinische Zeitung von Staats- und gelehrten Sachen*, October 20, 1804, cited in Ivaldo (2006), p. 37.

[8] GA II.7.

[9] For a very instructive study of WL 1805 and its relation to WL 1804 and other Fichte's writings of the period, see Ivaldo (2006).

[10] Sections 6.2.1 and 6.2.2.

[11] There are two sources for the notes of this version, both printed in GA II.8, one in *recto* and the other in *verso*. The English translation is from the source in *recto*, which I follow as a rule. Variations are, as a rule, not significant.

[12] Janke (1970), pp. 304–305. Janke considers WL 1804[2] to be the key to Fichte's subsequent thought; the question "what is true?" becomes "what is truth?"

[13] For Fichte's acknowledgment of his preference for realism, see SK 130; GA II.8:264–265. Also, SK 136–137; GA II.8:276–279. See also this passage: "We will thus conclude entirely realistically: if being

realism by building on a model of being suggested by the same Spinoza he had just disparaged in his dispute with Schelling. This reliance on Spinoza was glaring. Indeed, as Fichte later said, "the best starting point for [a deduction of the content of the Doctrine of Science] is the system of Spinoza."[14] These were moves all atypical of the earlier Fichte. Had he undergone a conversion? This is unlikely. More likely is that in the course of his dispute Fichte realized that he was vulnerable to the charge of subjectivism and that the vulnerability was due to more than just a failure in exposition. He had of course been a realist from the beginning. In the interest, however, of containing his realism within the limits of transcendental idealism – in effect, of grounding it phenomenologic-ally while avoiding the "thing-in-itself" that was indeed a source of psycho-logical subjectivism[15] – he had grounded it on practical interests, as a matter of belief irresistibly yet still only subjectively motivated by the need to act. This was a subjectivism of a much more serious nature than the psychologism of so many of Kant's contemporaries, for it amounted to a denial that truth has speculative value. This was the flaw that made Fichte vulnerable to Schelling's attacks and which Fichte's lectures of 1804 were intended to remedy. It was a matter of grounding the *Wissenschaftslehre* speculatively while still containing it within the framework of transcendentalism. Schelling, in Fichte's view, had failed on this score. As we shall claim, Fichte turned out to be a most consistent Spinozist, even more consistent than Schelling.

But before turning to the text of WL 1804², we must further motivate the discussion by again taking our bearing from Kant. His transcendental-ism was based on the premise that being is known only to the extent that it is given in sense experience and is intelligently recognized as so given by virtue of criteria that the mind (i.e., intelligent life) establishes out of its inner resources, *a priori*. Experience is achieved in a judgment of recogni-tion, as just defined. This meant that the fundamental constraint that transcendentalism imposed on any theory of being was that it be in essence a phenomenology, a science of being *as appearing* or *as given*. The con-straint posed a twofold requirement. For one thing, the theory had to save the robust realism imbedded in *givenness*: it had to save the expectation that

---

cannot ever get outside itself and nothing can be apart from it, then it must be being itself which thus constructs itself [as against idealistic constructivism], to the extent that such construction is to occur. Or [. . .]: We certainly are the agents who carry out this construction, but we do it insofar as we are being itself, as has been seen and we coincide with it; but by no means as a 'we' which is *free* and *independent* from being [. . .]. In short if being is constructed, as in fact, it seems to us to be, then it is constructed entirely through itself" (SK 122; GA II.8:244–245).

[14] *Die Wissenschaftslehre; Vorgetragen im Jahre 1812*, GA II.13:35–189. Regarding this problematic relation, see Lauth (1978).

[15] As Reinhold and Schmid made clear. See di Giovanni (2005), section 2.3.

the given in experience be in some important sense independent of the one *taking it as* given. For another, the criteria of intelligible presence had to be existentially relevant; that is to say, they had to apply, substantially rather than just externally or formally, to the objective presence of which they measured the intelligibility. These were two aspects of the one problem of saving the meaning of "phenomenon" as an event, the reality of which consists exclusively in referring to a transcendent "other than itself" of which it is nonetheless the manifestation. As we saw in Chapter 1, the unknown "thing-in-itself" that Kant posited behind phenomena did nothing to resolve the problem. It only obfuscated it.[16]

As for Fichte, his position when in discourse with both Kant and Schelling early in the 1800s was still based on the move he had originally made to deal with the problem. It was an elegant move that capitalized on Kant's truly innovative insight regarding experience, namely that while in experience the subject is bound to its given content, it is not thereby merely passive with respect to it but, on the contrary, actively adjudicates what of that content is *truly* given. The subject does not merely "take it in" (*capio*) but takes it *as*, or *for*, what it is (*per-capio*). To this extent, the subject transcends the content or, as we said earlier,[17] introduces into experience an intelligible extra space which is autonomous. The subject is therefore as much performer as observer; indeed, more performer than observer, for it sets the norms of right observation. Kant himself had encapsulated this insight in the claim that there is no knowledge which is not, at the same time, the knowledge of itself *as knowing*; no consciousness without self-consciousness; or again, in the formal claim that all experience is accompanied by an "I think."

The early *Wissenschaftslehre* was based on this insight of Kant, distilled out of the still psychological notes that encumbered it in Kant. Fichte engaged in a thought-experiment. He posited a thought-act, a *Tathandlung* as he called it to distinguish it from a mere *Tatsache*, a "matter of acting" (probably best rendered in English as "thought-performance") as contrasted with a "matter of fact." The point of the experiment was to have thought think itself exclusively as thinking, in abstraction of whatever content it would otherwise be "the thought of." It had to be a purely reflective performance. However, despite the subjective certainty on the part of anyone performing the required thought-act that he or she did indeed perform it, and did so as an autonomous "I," the performed thought-act was never consciously grasped

---

[16] At least in the eyes of his contemporaries. Sigismund Beck might have been an exception. For a recent reappraisal of Beck, see Nitzan (2014).
[17] See Section 1.4.

precisely as intended but rather only as already objectified; to this extent, it was grasped as already determined (hence particularized) in contrast to the intended act. In terms closer to Fichte's own formulation, the moment consciousness set in, to the presumed autonomously acting "I" there stood opposed a "not-I" that consequently determined it, the two (the "I" and "not-I") thus assuming the particularized forms of the subjects and objects that constitute the actual factors of experience.

On the face of it, this result marked the experiment's failure. But that is not how Fichte saw it. For his intention from the start had been to capture conceptually what in his view was the defining feature of experience, namely the facticity (*Faktizität*) of its content – its incontestable presence that, precisely because it was *felt* as incontestable, demanded explanation. This feature was the source of the robust sense of realism that, in fact, accompanies all experience. Fichte's experiment was an attempt at capturing this realism at source, which it did – this is where its significance lay – by relying on the active aspect of experience, on the same autonomy of thought on which Kant had based his whole transcendental theory. This was in direct opposition to common sense, which instead based its realism on the passive receptivity of experience; even to Kant who, still hostage to common sense, assumed the "thing-in-itself" as the cause of sense phenomena. On Fichte's thought-experiment, it was *because* one tried to grasp thought in its purely reflective activity that its being *de facto* consciously found only as an object, as externally determined where one expected it rather to be autonomous, that its presence *as object* demanded explanation. And this was an explanation for which the principle was already at hand in the same intended thought-act that generated the need for it. Experience is significant only because one poses questions to it, expecting its objects to satisfy thought. This was Fichte's foundational thesis regarding experience.

Fichte's move, stated in Kantian terms, was the equivalent of positioning oneself between the "thing-in-itself" and the phenomena of experience by presiding over the derivation of these from the "thing" in this way but without trespassing the limits of experience. Fichte proceeded to develop a full system of experience accordingly, first theoretically, on the assumption that the objects of experience are the subjective representations of an independent reality that they seek to determine (precisely as independent) at progressively ever more sophisticated levels of reflection. This was an irreducible assumption, for it reflected the defining intentional character of all consciousness. Nonetheless, the attempt was *ex terminis* fated to fail, for it unavoidably took its position from within the limits of a subject. The failure necessitated a shift in standpoint, namely from theoretical to practical – a shift that occurred in Fichte's Science in the medium of "feeling." The new assumption was that the realism embedded in experience was practical in nature, for the need to seek an "other of thought" – that is, the need of a theoretical standpoint – was due in the first place to the resistance that thought *de facto* encountered in its attempt at thinking itself, an attempt that naturally flowed from its autonomy as thought. It was the attempt that generated the "other," not indeed in any physical sense but by bringing it into the scope of experience as a practical obstacle. It also determined it accordingly, precisely as the *other of thought*. To be such, that is, to be the by-product of thought-activities, was its exclusive meaning. It followed that the objects of the theoretical sciences (in effect, nature) were whatever they were only as defined with reference to thought's interests (in effect, as morally determined). For this reason Fichte could not accept taking nature, as Schelling did, as a legitimate starting point on its own.

This, as said, was an elegant move which, however, denied truth speculative value, and in this lay its flaw. Fichte had presumed that anyone could perform his thought-experiment. Certainly, anyone could be believed at least capable of it, could even be instinctively convinced to perform the required reflection. But there was, in fact, no irresistible warrant for the belief or irrefutable support for the instinctive conviction. Relying on intellectual intuition would not do, for, as Fichte knew, intuition is *ex hypothesi* ineffable; hence, that one is supported by it is itself a matter of subjective belief.[18] There was no *a priori* guarantee that the whole experiment that Fichte proposed, and the science he derived from it, were not mere epiphenomena, the illusionary products of natural forces over which there was no ultimate personal control. On the face of it, Fichte's moral humanism appeared just as heroic and admirable as that of Goethe's Prometheus. But Prometheus knew that his was illusionary; the heroism in his case lay in accepting the illusion as the lot of human beings and in living in the deliberate enjoyment of it as the illusion it was. Fichte, for his part, was no doubt aware of the possibility of illusion. He had implicitly acknowledged that much in 1797 by admitting that the *Wissenschaftslehre*'s idealism was based on personal commitment; that naturalism was not refutable *per se* but only to be rejected subjectively. This is what gave his humanism its specific character but was also made the source of its vulnerability. It was based on a decision to hold at bay, the very illusion that Goethe's Prometheus openly

---

[18] Fichte (1994), p. 49; GA I.4:466.

admitted and lived by. But the decision was avowedly subjective. In this, it was open to attack: was it truly heroic or just foolhardy?

The only way of muting the question was for Fichte to reclaim the speculative value of truth. What was needed was a standpoint that transcended both the theoretical and the practical. Schelling had attempted that much in the 1800 *System of Transcendental Idealism*. But the system he had constructed from the two standpoints extended over experience externally, connecting with it only at the point of Schelling's poetic intuition. What Fichte needed was rather a theory of being *as such* that, as in classical metaphysics, stood in relation to the content of experience as its *a priori*, informing it essentially. In some way or other, the *Wissenschaftslehre* had to make its start, like Spinoza's system, with *substance*. The challenge of WL 1804² was to present such a system without falling into the dogmatism of Spinoza's, instead containing the metaphysic it entailed within the limits of a phenomenology of being. The *Tathandlung* and its subjectivism disappeared in 1804. The genetic derivation of experience previously dependent on it now unfolded as if basking, so to speak, in the *light* of being.

3.2 Fichte's Realism

Fichte's notes are difficult. Nonetheless, the insight that governed them is clear. Fichte expressed it relying on such tropes as "light,"[19] "evidence" (*Evidenz*),[20] "insight," "reason," this last normally associated with "intelligible" and "intelligibility."[21] It lay in the recognition that there can be no rationality without reasonableness being presupposed; that rationality means operating immersed in a presupposed *light* that makes the evidence or the direct visibility of truth possible. Subjective appropriation of the truth must be nestled in this light at the very origin. It is not the appropriation that sets the conditions for the light (as Kant had it) but the light of the evidence that makes the reasonableness of the appropriation possible. Fichte's earlier insight that the realism of common experience depends on the active moment of experience, not the passive as is normally believed, still held valid. It was now, however, deepened by the further recognition that the activity in question consists first and foremost in giving oneself

[19] "Light" as a metaphor for the source of truth is as old as philosophy itself.
[20] The English translation renders *Evidenz* as "manifestness," a descriptively accurate translation. Its flaw, however, is that it drops the image of "visibility" (see the Latin *video*) which would have been obvious to any German intellectual using the Latinate *Evidenz* and which directly connected it with the image of Light.
[21] For instance, "*intelligibly*, or in reason." SK 117; GA II.8:232–233.

over to a self-revealing truth. One does not construct truth; rather, one organically grows into it, *genetically.*

I repeat, Fichte's notes are difficult and, as lecture notes go, often only fragmentary. Nonetheless, we should first allow Fichte to speak for himself, in a text that summarizes the results of his investigation up to that point. To wit:

> Along with the necessity that arose from this [viz., the subjectivism and the realism that stand opposed to each other, and cannot truly be defined without each implicating the other][22] to ascend higher and to master the facts [*die Fakta*] genetically, we turned our attention to what promised to be most significant here, [namely] to the in-itself, bound to the realistic principle, life in itself [Fichte has already identified the "in-itself" with *being* as self-enclosed, not in relation to *not-being*, but as *esse in actu*].[23] The in-itself manifests itself [*einleuchte*][24] as an absolute negation of the validity of all seeing directed towards itself [i.e., as subjective idealism]: that it constructs itself in immediate manifestness [*Evidenz*] or light: yielding a higher realism which deduces insight and the light themselves, items which the first realism was content to ignore [namely dogmatic realism]. A new idealism attempts to establish itself against this new realism [namely critical idealism with its subjective *a priori*]. We had to take control of ourselves and struggle energetically to contemplate the in-itself in its meaning [i.e., within the context of this idealism]. So, we believed we realized that this in-itself first appeared as a result of this reflection [i.e., the "control of ourselves"] as simultaneously constructing itself with immediate manifestness [*Evidenz*] in the light; and that consequently this energy of ours would be the basic principle and first link in the whole matter [i.e., the practical realism of Fichte's early WL].
>
> To this, [the higher realism Fichte has been presenting] boldly retorts: That's how you think, but how do you prove your claim? [Fichte is criticizing the earlier effort just described.][25] You can adduce nothing more than that you are aware of yourself [Fichte has already rejected the witness of immediate consciousness],[26] but you cannot derive thinking genetically in its reality and truthfulness, as you should, from your consciousness in which you report it; but, by contrast, we can derive the very consciousness to which you appeal, and which you make your principle, genetically, since this can only be a modification of insight and light, but

---

[22] See SK 109; GA II.8:214–215.   [23] See SK 116; GA II.8:228–229.

[24] Note the *Leucht* (light: a noun) in the *einleuchte* (a verb).

[25] I have altered the English translation which I find unduly cumbersome.

[26] "The science of knowing denies the validity of immediate consciousness's testimony absolutely as such and for this exact reason: that it is this [i.e. the idealism just rejected by Fichte]." SK 106; GA II.8:204–205.

light proceeds directly out of the in-itself, manifestness [*Evidenz*] in immediate manifestness [*Evidenz*].²⁷

As the inserted glosses indicate,²⁸ Fichte had not abandoned the earlier
transcendental standpoint based on subjective activity ("self-control") but
was only building on it, deriving it genetically. Glaringly new in 1804 was
that Fichte demanded of his auditors that they fix their attention on the
truth that manifests itself in experience, on its self-imposing *in-itself* by
which the auditors must have been already unconsciously permeated as
they found themselves spontaneously accepting in experience a given
position, as if driven by nature. Of course, just as in the earlier attempt
at grasping the original *Tathandlung*, this giving over of oneself to the light
of evidence entailed transcending the subjective limits of conceptualization. For the earlier Fichte – that is, from the standpoint of a subject simply
bound to subjectivity – this gave rise to a disconnect between subjective life
and objective truth; to an area of non-knowing that the earlier Fichte filled
with faith. It was a matter of negotiating this subject/object disconnect by
means of a process of always finite conceptual determinations that in
principle extended *ad infinitum* yet was at each step supported by immediate certainty. This, as we saw, made Fichte vulnerable to Schelling. Quite
different was the situation in 1804, for on Fichte's new assumption experience does not get underway without truth already manifesting itself in it.
Any area of non-knowledge can only be local or, if generalized, the result of
failing to recognize that one already *de facto* lives in the truth.²⁹ Or to put it
another way, whereas in the previous *Wissenschaftslehre*, the coincidence of
subjective certainty and objective truth was postponed *ad infinitum*
because of a presumed lack of objective evidence, in 1804 the coincidence
was there from the beginning. It was the superabundance of evidence – its
being necessarily already there – that stood in the way of its recognition and
gave rise to the illusion of non-knowledge.

The new standpoint required a new methodology. One can visualize
Fichte's strategy by imagining two circles facing each other at a distance in
tridimensional space. One circle represents the space of self-manifesting
light, or the One (for truth is One);³⁰ the other, the space of conceptually
determined experience, or the realm of the "here and now" of experience.
Now, inasmuch as one tries to bring the surfaces of the two circles to
coincide – in effect, to reduce the distance separating them by means of

²⁷ SK 118–119; GA II.8:235.35–237.23.   ²⁸ The glosses are all mine.
²⁹ Significant is that Hegel's Phenomenology begins with the same recognition.
³⁰ SK 23; GA II.8:9.7.

conceptualization (as historically one must begin by doing, Fichte included) – one discovers that the surfaces resist the attempt. The distance assumes the aspect of a gap intractable to any attempt at traversing it.[31] Fichte called the gap *hiatus irrationalis*: "irrational," not just because it cannot be traversed discursively but, more to the point, because its irrationality is itself the product of the attempt at both defining and relating its two sides conceptually. For Fichte this gap was, as he also called it, *die Lage des Todes*, the "place of death" – the abyss of reason (*der Abgrund der Vernunft*)[32] where, borrowing an image from the alchemy of the day, Fichte said the products of conceptual reflection are *precipitated* like a *corpus mortuum*. It is in this place that one finds all the products of common understanding that deaden experience.

Fichte had already encountered this gap in his earlier *Wissenschaftslehre* in the form, as we just said, of a disconnect between subjective certainty and objective evidence. The gap had been generated by the method of doing his science itself, still bound as it was to the economy of the concept. And Fichte had strategically accepted this gap, had even welcomed it, for the infinite task of crossing it that it posed, and the consequent discipline it demanded, in fact, validated the moral commitment that had animated his science at origin. Schelling, for his part, while *de facto* creating in his science the same conceptual gap, had rather treated it as if it were not there – as if, in construing a positive narrative about determinate being, whether based on nature or on the mind, he were at the same time narrating the story of the Absolute, the One underlying both nature and mind. These were the higher kinds of idealism and realism mentioned in the cited text to which Fichte was opposing his new realism.[33] The new strategy, as we shall see in greater detail momentarily, was to methodically retrieve from the abyss created by the *hiatus irrationalis* the conceptual products historically precipitated therein while explaining experience and to rethink them in such a way that, if one were just *attentive* enough, one would recognize in them the already present truth of which they were only the appearances. In a way, the method of repeatedly exposing the failure of any just attempted

---

[31] At play here is still Lessing's ugly ditch separating historical from eternal truths.

[32] The genitive is both subjective and objective. The expression is borrowed from Kant. KrV A613/B641. Schelling also uses the expression. SSW II.4:342; also, see SSW I.8, 163.

[33] Fichte concluded that "Consciousness," to which idealism gave priority of place, was "rejected in its intrinsic validity, despite the fact that we have admitted we cannot escape it. *We* absolutely, i.e., even in the science of knowing." SK 110; GA II.8:216–217. But Fichte is also keen to remind his auditors that there will be room for an idealism as part of a theory of appearance, as contrasted with truth. That will be the object of later reflections. See SK 106; GA II.8:204–205. Equally closely refuted was Schelling's kind of realism, which Fichte described as "objectivism." SK 109; GA II.8: 214–215.

objectification of the intended truth had also been that of the earlier *Wissenschaftslehre*.[34] Fichte could therefore say, in all fairness, that there was indeed continuity between the earlier and the present exposition of the science. But the goal and the context had changed. *Attention*, rather than action, was now the keynote. Where the earlier Fichte demanded of his auditors that they *perform*, the demand now was that they be *attentive*, for attention required their *active subjugation* to a transcendent presence which, although transcendent, was nonetheless immanently encompassing.[35] It was a matter of colluding with it. That was precisely the kind of existential attitude that insight into evidence called for. Fichte's auditors were to practice this attention *energisch*, vigorously.[36] The goal was to whittle away the distance between our two imagined circles progressively, until it was shown that the *hiatus irrationalis* was only an illusion.[37]

3.3 The WL 1804²

3.3.1 The Prolegomena: Lectures 1–5

The WL 1804² is comprised of twenty-eight lectures divided into three parts not explicitly marked out by Fichte but recognizable from their line of argument. The first five are clearly introductory.[38] They set the stage for the rest. How did Fichte make a start – one that differed from the *Tathandlung* of the earlier "I think"?

Fichte was aware that it would be existentially self-defeating to try to objectify conceptually the preconceptual evidence on which conceptualization depends for its truth. Any such attempt would necessarily result in the objectification of the intended truth, and by that token it would also falsify it. All science, including the *Wissenschaftslehre* must be a *Nachdenken*, an afterthought, the artificial construction of an evidence

---

[34] SK 119; GA II.8:238–239.   [35] SK 47ff; GA II.8:66–67ff.

[36] "If I ask you to think energetically, I am asking you that you be fundamentally rational." SK 89; GA II.8:164–165. Note that Fichte refers to "Light" also as "Reason."

[37] Among many other texts, SK 123; GA II.8:246–247. The gap is a function of the *We*, nothing in itself. Also, SK 124; GA II.8:248–249. One immediately thinks of Aristotle's *energeia*, denoting, as the concept did, life, force, act. But one wonders how much Fichte knew, or cared to know, about Aristotle. For Aristotle's reputation in the late German Enlightenment, see Section 1.2.

[38] Lecture 4 is the most important; it summarizes the previous three and makes a general statement regarding the WL's project and method. Lecture 5 is a repetition of Lecture 4 from a different respect. Fichte also goes at great length disavowing any blame if the audience has failed to understand him (presumably in Lecture 4). He might have heard complaints. The blame falls on the auditors.

which is already there.[39] The beginning must be made with an assumption, a determinate taking of position, itself historically conditioned, consistent with the special historical vocation motivating a given process of knowledge. Once the assumption is made, the consequences unfold from it mechanically, according to a conceptual logic that drives the whole process to its conclusion from behind (just as in Spinoza's system). For this reason, no "I" in particular can accurately be said to reach the said conclusions but an anonymous "We," or reason in general.[40] The mistake of past theories of knowledge was to take this mechanical necessity as the source of evidence, consequently ignoring the preconceptual light of evidence in which the conceptual process is nestled and of which it is, in fact, only a historical expression.

It was the *Wissenschaftslehre*'s vocation in 1804 to bring attention to precisely this evidence. Fichte's strategy was to present his auditors with a conceptual construct they would immediately accept on the strength of common sense – if not universal common sense, certainly the philosophical common sense of the day. He then asked them to draw the consequences that followed from it mechanically, by simple entailment. The real point of the exercise was, however, to have the auditors take note, but only indirectly (as if by a side glance), of the evidence in fact illuminating the process they were engaged in; consequently to invest the derived consequences with a significance they would not otherwise have for them. By the same token, the uncritically accepted starting construct also lost its original significance. Ultimately it was a matter not of adding or subtracting from the auditors' common experiences or common assumptions but of altering the auditors' existential attitude toward them.

But what more universally received assumption than that the truth is one? As Fichte put it in his lecture,

> Thus, truth is absolute oneness [...]. Let me say that the essence would [thus] consist in this: *to trace all multiplicity* (which presses itself upon us in the usual view of life) *back to absolute oneness.* [...] *All multiplicity* – whatever can even be distinguished, or has its antithesis, or counterpart – absolutely, without *exception.* [...] *Absolute oneness* is what is true and in itself unchangeable, its opposite contained within itself.[41]

---

[39] Fichte was harking back to Jacobi's claim about science in general. MPW 230.

[40] Cf. "Das formale Wesen dieses Wir oder Ich." GA II.7:190. Fichte does not draw any sharp distinction between the I and the We because it is their essence, the reflective consciousness generating them, which is really at issue, just as we saw in Section 2.2.3 that "reason" and "rationality," not any "egology," is Fichte's real concern. Cf. also SK 197–198; GA II.8:412–415.

[41] SK 23–24; GA II.8:8–9. Also: "The essence of philosophy [...] consists in reducing all manifold (which nonetheless still impinges on us in the common view of life) to absolute unity" SK 23 [translation modified]; GA II.8:8–9. Schelling was given to accusing Fichte of plagiarism. One can understand why.

In this spirit, Fichte therefore began with a construct historically associated with Spinoza and Kant; significantly with both at once. He proposed for his auditors this formula as the general schema of experience:

$$A\bullet \Rightarrow D\&S \Rightarrow x, y, z.^{42}$$

The A was a "no-thing," but was posited simply as standing for the absolute truth instinctively assumed to motivate all experience. This truth was just as instinctively assumed to consist in a One, but a One that immediately translated itself into a Many. The interplay of this One and its Many was at the core of all experience and historically stood, in one way or other, at the basis of all philosophical positions. The • had to be imagined as the point at which the transition ($\Rightarrow$) from the one to the other originated; Being and Thought (D&S, *Denken und Sein*) were the first multiplicity, an original division that in turn translated itself ($\Rightarrow$) into the more particularized many of x, y, z.

All this had, of course, historical precedents. The A stood for both Kant's "thing-in-itself" and Spinoza's substance; the D&S, for Kant's *a priori/a posteriori* and Spinoza's attributes; the (x, y, z), for the subject matter of Kant's three Critiques and for Spinoza's modes. But such historical references, however factually important, were not the essential point. Indeed, Fichte went on to ask of his auditors that they abstract from the content of their knowledge altogether and rather fix their attention on what, despite the variety of that knowledge, made it *knowledge* – on the quality of that knowledge *as knowledge*, or (to gloss), on the intelligibility in which it was realized. If his auditors succeeded in this abstraction, they would have already gained a genetic insight into the A of the proposed schema – into the nature of the "oneness" that lay at the ground of Kant's transcendental system, and no less so of the dogmatic of Spinoza. Yet both, Spinoza and Kant, had simply passed over it in *Nachdenken*.[43]

---

[42] The diagram is first introduced in Lecture 2 (SK 30; GA II.8:26–27) and is expressed in various forms throughout the lectures. The two manuscripts available to us, *SW* and *Copia*, reproduce them differently. My version is based on the one found at the beginning of Lecture 4. SK 40; GA II.8:52–53.

[43] "All philosophy should grow out of knowledge (*Wissen*) which is in and for itself. Knowledge, or evidence which is in and for itself, is genetic. The highest appearance of a knowledge which no longer is its inner essence, but only expresses its external existence, is factual; and, since it is nonetheless still the appearance of *knowledge*, it is factual evidence. A factual evidence, be it even absolute evidence, remains something *objective*, alien, self-constructing, but not constructed by evidence, hence unexplored in its innermost, the kind which a weary speculation, doubtful of its own force, calls unexplorable. Kantian speculation ends at its highest pinnacle with the factual evidence of the insight that, at the ground of the sensible and suprasensible worlds, there must nonetheless lie a principle of union, hence a principle genetic through and through, one which simply creates and determines both worlds. This insight, quite

Fichte therefore instructed his auditors to make a further move. He asked them to place themselves in thought at the • of the proposed schema, where the transition (⇒) to the first disjunction (D&S) occurred. They had to place themselves at precisely that point, oscillating (*Schweben*) between oneness and manyness, without resting at either.[44] Clearly, Fichte was asking them to abide by Kant's critical injunction that, in explaining experience, they did not step outside it. That's what it meant to stay at that •. What it did not mean, however, was that they would thereby be in a position of recovering the stated transition, still from inside that oscillating movement but, as if intuited on the side of the A in the manner of dogmatic realism (of which Fichte had accused Schelling) or reflectively constructed on the side of the D&S, as in idealism. Either way, the irrational gap between A and the D&S, which was Fichte's goal to dissolve as illusionary, was generated. Instead, one had to insert the transition in the • with no remainder, annulling the transition as anything outside it. Only in this way would his auditors be overtaken by the insight into the true nature of A's transcendence. When viewed as the factor internally motivating the whole of experience, that transcendence was none other than the self-justifying nature of knowledge itself; the originative evidence that, like light, had nothing but itself as the source of its presence. It was the evidence to which one finds oneself already beholden even as one begins to reflect on why one accepts something as true.

Fichte's way of making the point (obviously with Kant and his own earlier subjective constructivism in mind) was to say that "truth creates itself by its own power. It is not we who do the knowing or intuiting, but the knowledge and intuiting that work themselves in us."[45] This was Fichte's way of overcoming the formalism of Kant's *a priori*sm by reinterpreting it as a form of life, a way of existing normatively. As he said: "[L]

correct in itself, could have occurred to [Kant], however, only because of the law working undisputed (*absolute*) but unconsciously in his reason, [namely, that] one should stand firm at absolute unity, recognizing it as the absolute substance, and deriving everything changeable from it. This insight remained for Kant only factual; its object, therefore, unexplored; for he let that fundamental law of unity work on him only mechanically, without himself taking hold of it again in his knowledge – in which case the pure light would have dawned on him, and he would have arrived at the W.-L." [my translation] GA II.8:42–44.

[44] Dieter Henrich offers an illuminating examination of the term *Schweben* in Fichte's earlier work. The term has two equally important senses: on the one hand, *Schweben* denotes the freedom of the one who *schwebt*, the freedom from any fixed state; on the other hand, *Schweben* denotes a double inclination, a wavering between two directions. Henrich's example is that of a "sea gull flying against a light wind." Henrich (2003), p. 212. Note that Fichte played with this idea of oscillation from his earliest reflections on Kant and attributed it to the imagination which he took at the time as the matrix of all human experience.

[45] SK 48; GA II.8:68–69.

ight's absolute, inner life is posited; it exists only in living itself and not otherwise; therefore it can be encountered only immediately in living and nowhere else."[46] His request that his auditors position themselves at the • was thus only an exhortation that they take hold of themselves existentially; that they submit themselves to the discipline of attention, where "attention" meant – to repeat – their active letting themselves be absorbed into an evidence which, in fact, had already taken hold of them. This was the postulate behind the whole new Science of Knowledge. It had to be further developed with a theory of truth and a subsequent theory of phenomenal existence.

3.3.2   The Theory of Truth: Lectures 6–15

Fichte let his auditors know early in the lectures that there would be much repetition in his exposition.[47] The same point would be made repeatedly, but each time with a different purpose in mind. Indeed, much already said by way of introduction was now repeated, in particular, the request that one position oneself at the • between A and D&S, so that, in the oscillation between the two, one might be overtaken by the insight into the oneness that had, in fact, motivated the conceptual construction up to that point. The repetition was itself part of the oscillation. That the motivating oneness was not itself anything objectifiable *per se* – that, on the contrary, it had to be imagined more like a light, or an intelligible space within which objects would be made to appear – constituted the postulate behind the theory of truth now to be presented. But, we should let Fichte speak for himself:

> I hope nobody assumes here that the act of assuming the distinction between A and • is actually grounded in an original distinction in these things, independently of our thinking. Or, in case someone is led to this conclusion by the previous factical ascent with which we had to begin, he will recover from this idea if he considers that in A and • he thinks only the oneness which, according to him, should be unconditionally one without distinction within itself, since he could not think the object except by virtue of the distinction; that he thus expressly makes his thinking as thinking the distinguishing principle. But the validity and result of this product of thought expressly surrenders and dies in relations to the thinking itself. With it at the root, its products A and • are also doubtlessly uprooted and destroyed as intrinsically valid. Thus away with words and signs! Nothing remains except our living thinking and insight, which cannot be shown on

[46] SK 80; GA II.8:142–143.   [47] SK 48; GA II.8:68–69.

a blackboard nor be represented in any way but can only be surrendered to nature.

We *intuit*, I say, that it [oneness] rests neither on A nor in •, but rather in the absolute oneness of both; we intuit it unconditionally without sources or premises. *Absolute insight* therefore presents itself here. Pure intuition, pure light, from nothing out of nothing, going nowhere. To be sure, bringing oneness with it, but in no way based on it.[48]

Here everything depends on this: that each person correctly identifies with this insight, in this pure light; if each one does, then nothing will happen to extinguish this light again and to separate it from yourself. Each will see that the light exists only insofar as it intuits vitally in him,[49] even intuits what has been established. The light exists only in living self-presentation as absolute insight, and whomever it does not grasp, hold, and fix in the place where we now stand, that one never arrives at the living light, no matter what apparent substitute for it he may have.[50]

Needless to repeat, there was no way of letting this light show forth except in the medium of constructions that would in fact, only objectify it and consequently obscure it. The task, therefore, was to replace the schema of experience conceptually constructed at any point with further constructions that, though never manifesting the light as such, would nonetheless ever more reflectively and explicitly manifest *themselves* for what they were, namely only constructions. In this way, Fichte's auditors could let themselves be overtaken by the intuition animating their experience at source.

---

[48] SK 60; GA II.8:94–95.

[49] Note how it is the light which is the source of intuition; the latter has no subjective source.

[50] SK 60; GA II.8:96–97. As presented in Lectures 6–8. Here is another representative text: "That the light lives absolutely *through itself* must mean: it splits itself absolutely into S [being] and D [thinking]. But 'absolutely through itself' also means 'independent of any insight and absolutely negating the possibility of insight'. Nevertheless, [...] light splits [for us] into S [being] and D [thought]: consequently this split *as* such no longer resides in the light, as we have hitherto believed, but in the insight into the light [i.e. on our side]. What then still remains? The inward life of the light itself, from itself, into itself, through itself, *without* any split, in pure unity; a life which exists only in immediate living and has itself and nothing else. 'It lives'; and thus it will live and appear and otherwise no path leads to it. – 'Good, but can you not provide me with a description of it?' Very good, and I have given it to you; it is precisely what cannot be seen, what remains behind after the completely fulfilled insight which penetrates to the root; it is, therefore, what is to [*soll*] exist through itself. 'How do you arrive at these predicates; that it is unseeable – i.e. what is not to be constructed from *disjunctively* related terms such as being is from thinking and vice versa; that it is what is left over from the insight [. . .]?' Clearly, only through *negation* of the insight [on our part]: all these predicates, therefore, with the most preponderant at the top, [i.e. that of] the absolute substance, are only negative notes, dead and null in themselves. 'Does the system, then, have its origin in negation and death?' Not at all; it rather pursues death to its final stand in order to arrive at life; this lies in the light which is at one with reality, and reality arises in it; and this whole reality as such, according to its form, is absolutely nothing more than the *graveyard* of the concept: the concept which would have tried itself at it." I have edited, and in two instances corrected, the English translation. SK 71; GA II.8:120).

Required at the moment was to focus attention at the & joining the D&S in the original schema.[51] At a purely factical or analytical level of reflection, joining and disjoining are mutually dependent. Joining presupposes already disjointed terms. Such terms, however, would not be significantly disjointed if they did not tend, on their own, to collapse together. The point of disjoining is precisely to keep them apart. With reference to Fichte's schema, the & thus entailed a qualitative commonality of D and S, or a "what" common to both which, however, neither term realized absolutely. If either did, the other would be absorbed into it, and the &, whether as joining or disjoining, would lose meaning. Each term had to be thought as indeed *qualitatively* determined by the common "what" but, as the scholastics used to say, only *secundum quid*: in a certain way or to some extent. The D and S thus doubled each other,[52] as if mirroring each other, but at a distance which they each bridged from their respective side only *quantitatively*, in the form of particular d_1, d_2, d_3, etc., and s_1, s_2, s_3, etc., respectively. Together, moreover, they doubled their common "what," the ground of their commonality – this also, however, at a distance corresponding to the distance separating them. To the extent that each was *not* the other quantitatively, it also was *not* (also quantitatively) the factor common to both.

All this was entailed by the &. If one remembers that D and S stood for *Denken* and *Sein* ("thought" and "being"), it is easy to see that the insight thus obtained was, factically presented, the same as had motivated Spinoza's schema of being: substance (the transcendent yet common "what"), attributes (thought and extension), modes (the quantification of the attributes). The next step was to present the synthesis of these elements that in Fichte's schema (just as in Spinoza's) had so far been indicated surface-like from "inside out" so to speak. It was a matter of adding the subjective dimension that all the Romantics had missed in Spinoza yet had been unable to remedy without lapsing into subjective idealism. What was needed was a renewed attempt at genetic construction. In this, as also in the subsequent attempts, Fichte's main concern, obviously in view of his own earlier position, was to keep clear of the idealism which he considered a product of consciousness, not of Spinoza's realism which he instead accepted while rejecting its dogmatic form.

Fichte proceeded to introduce a number of categories, each conveying the kind of intelligible presence (*Evidenz*) his auditors must have been

---

[51] I am redoing Fichte's argument which, otherwise, would simply have to be repeated *verbatim*.

[52] SK 117; GA II.8:235.13. The "doubling" is lost in the English translation: "*Wiederholung und Doppelung*."

already beholden to when willing to accept, but simply as a matter of common sense, the schema Fichte had proposed to them; and equally willing to dissect it analytically as Fichte had done for them. They had been beholden to it unaware: now they were in position to retrieve it reflectively. The first was *das Bild* (the image). Why image? Because it directly expressed the "doubling" that in the case of the "joining/disjoining" of the & rather needed conceptual sorting out to be brought to light. An "image" is nothing except what it images; this last is at once an *other* of it yet *at one* with it.[53] There is no resting in the being of the image as anything by itself; on the contrary, any presumed determination must be already superseded in order for the image to be itself *as image*. Fichte had earlier asked his auditors to place themselves at the point •, oscillating between D and S. The problem was that they might have believed that in this they were the ones responsible for the oscillation, that is, that Fichte was asking them to enact a subjective performance. This was the delusion that the introduction of "image" dispelled: the oscillation was *in the image*, a movement that had, in fact, anonymously antedated all their efforts and on which they had depended unaware.

The second category was "projection" (*Projektion*). This should not be understood in the sense of either Husserl's "intention" or Heidegger "thrownness." Fichte was, rather, playing on the image of a presence that, like light, expands outward, thereby creating a lit space where things can visibly appear yet in this expansion stays with itself. In language more akin to the neo-Platonic tradition, it was a presence immanent in emanation and emanating in immanence.[54] The intelligible space it created was the condition for the possibility of two more categories – the "through" (*das Durch*)[55] and the "by" (*das Von*), the latter understood in the sense of authorship. Together the two parsed the determination of yet another category which they presupposed, namely the "through-one-another" (*das Durcheinander*). They presupposed it as directly expressing the back-and-forth movement of the "image," a movement that had no remainder but was rather exhausted in its own mobility. The "through" and the "by" translated the scholastic *per se* and *a se*, both defining characteristics of Spinoza's substance. But whereas in Spinoza the *perseitas* and *aseitas* followed from the substantiality of substance, for Fichte, on the contrary, it was the *perseitas* and *aseitas*, which

---

[53] See SK 63; GA II.8:100–101.

[54] A thing that projects *jets out*, while remaining itself in the *jetting out*. This is the raw image at work here.

[55] "The existence of a '*through*' announces itself here as completely absolute and *a priori*, in no way grounded again on another real existence that preceded it." SK 88; GA II.8:162–163.

betokened the self-imposing presence of evidence, that made the substantiality of substance intelligible at source. Only because of that presence, in which any individual knower was absorbed unaware from the start, did the knower look for such starting points in experience as "substances." The "substance" of dogmatic realism was only a precipitate of that original intelligibility, the *caput mortuum* of mere facticity.[56]

On the face of it, Fichte was piling up images upon images, avoiding argumentation. But, in fact, his method of construction was internally regulated. Granted that the task was to bring to evidence the intelligibility that motivated all experience, Fichte had simply reflectively identified those minimal components of it that – albeit still factically but *self-consciously so* – nonetheless made that intelligibility manifest to anyone existentially ready to see it. He had not displayed the Light at its source *for itself*, or the intuition that presumably went with it. That would have been impossible. But he nonetheless should have succeeded in making his auditors capable of taking note of the Light – indirectly or, to repeat, in side view. And the test of his success lay in the difference of attitude he had instilled in them regarding the content of experience, as if they could now see it with different eyes.

How to define this new attitude? Surely not in terms of any subjective factor on the auditors' part. That would have been subjective idealism. Rather, it had to consist in the way the content of experience presented itself to their regard anew, engaged their attention, even absorbed them. It had to present itself precisely as "appearance," the category with which this section of Fichte's lectures conclude. The content of experience is phenomenal existence. But why so? The simple answer is that, if not already factically parsed as "thing" and the "appearance thereof" in the manner of ordinary thinking, "appearance" is the internally fully articulated instance of the doubling of being that all the prior constructs already entailed. What made it different, however, was that in this case it was explicitly presented as leaving no remainder outside the doubling itself, none of the *hiatus irrationalis* that, like an irreducible surd, haunted common sense – and classical metaphysics no less. Appearance was for Fichte the medium supporting all the hitherto introduced constructs. It manifested them all at once. Only because Fichte's auditors had been immersed in the logic of its internal structure from the beginning – unwittingly, of course – had they been able to follow their master's genetic quest.

---

[56] In the alchemy of the day, *caput mortuum* was the nonactive leftover of a chemical reaction – a precipitate, in other words.

Positing "appearance" at this point thus constituted the synthetic step by which Fichte could all too naturally mark his transition to the subsequent theory of phenomenal existence. He had genetically deduced the very realm of phenomenality that Kant had instead simply assumed at the head of his critical theory of truth. He could therefore legitimately see himself as once more taking up Kant's transcendental project but without the common-sense facticity that vitiated it – in effect, without the *corpus mortuum* of the "thing-in-itself." It was a matter now of grounding the basic components of experience by genetically deriving them from this posited realm of phenomenality, in general.

Before following Fichte in this further quest, two comments are in order that highlight how innovative Fichte was with respect to both Spinoza and Kant – in the first comment, with respect to both Spinoza and Kant; in second, with respect specifically to Kant.

As to the first, on Fichte's terms one could say that the phenomenal realm of experience is an "image" of the Absolute, whether understood as Spinoza's substance or Kant's "thing-in-itself," without thereby claiming to have traversed the gap that necessarily separates the "Absolute" and its "image" on either Spinoza or Kant's terms. Fichte had referred to this gap as a *hiatus irrationalis* simply because, on his own terms, it was not truly *there* but was rather the product of factical delusion.[57] It was the place, therefore, where conceptualization perished and conceptual obscurity reigned – the graveyard of the concept (*die Lage des Todes*), or the concept's death at root (*Tod in der Wurzel*),[58] to use Fichte's favorite expressions. On Fichte's precise sense of "image," however, no such gap arose, for, as we have seen, "image" stood for a doubling which, while maintaining within it the disjunction separating the two terms doubling each other, did not leave any remainder of either term outside the doubling itself. The Light, the intelligibility of its evidence, was not identical with experience, yet had no content except as found in experience. The task that Fichte was now undertaking was to show how Light's otherwise ineffable presence within the latter nonetheless informed it.

As for the second comment, Kant distinguished between "understanding" and "reason," famously assigning to each different functions – to the understanding, that of knowledge, but limited to the *mere* phenomenal; to reason, that of mediating the gap between

---

[57] See SK 123; GA II.8:248–249. See "A major portion of our task is to demonstrate the genetic principle of this irrational gap, which so far we have presented only factically, whose validity we have denied, but without our being able to dispense with it." SK 124; GA II.8:248–249.

[58] SK 111–112; GA II.8:220–221; see SK 144; GA II.8:294–295.

phenomena and the "thing-in-itself" but only *ideally*, in effect, only formally. Fichte kept the distinction, but in a different sense altogether. The understanding had to do with the phenomenal but the phenomenal inasmuch as it was unavoidably *precipitated* as factical and, as such, in need of being genetically led back to its source. Reason was precisely this source. Fichte repeatedly referred to the Light as reason[59] and to the intelligible life it made possible as rationality. Reason and rationality were the factors that made the content of experience intelligible in the first place: *materially* intelligible. This, in principle, was how the Light informed experience: it made it *normative*, that is, internally ruled.

3.3.3 The Theory of Phenomenal Existence: Lectures 16–28

(1) Fichte warned his auditors that this second part of his lectures would be more difficult than the first.[60] It was easy enough, in the first part, to start from certain given facts of experience, factically accepted, and, abstracting from their empirical content, arrive at the principles that must have motivated their acceptance in the first instance – the factor, in other words, that made them evident. This was the way of ascent completed in Fichte's previous lectures. Things were not as easy in the way of descent now to be undertaken, where the principles so far ascertained *in abstracto*, on factical starting points, had to be seen, rather, as informing the structure of experience internally; indeed, as even giving rise to, and containing, the unavoidable facticity of the starting points. Such a facticity had to be seen as itself a *fact of reason* rather than a mere surd of experience. In principle this had already been done in the transition to the third part of the lectures with the introduction of "appearance." Its internal structure summed up all the categories hitherto introduced. The task of this third part was to repeat the second but explicitly in the medium of "appearance." And for this one had to expect much richer and consequently more complex genetic constructions than the theory of truth had required.

The transition to this part clearly implied a tacit criticism of Kant's transcendental deduction, Kant's attempt at bringing the *a priori* to bear upon actual experience. The criticism that Fichte was also directing at his

---

[59] SK 136; GA II.8:276–277.
[60] This third part of Fichte's lectures, from 16 to 28, divides into three subsections, which Fichte, however, does not advertise until Lecture 22. The first subsection, from Lecture 16 to 19, derives "experience"; the second, Lectures 20 and 21, does the same for knowledge, and the third, Lectures 22 to the end, does it for the *Wissenschaftslehre* itself. These divisions are tentative. Fichte himself is not very specific. See SK 162–163; GA II.8:334–337.

own earlier *Wissenschaftslehre* was, however, not as tacit. In the first four lectures, attention was given to "a new and higher kind of idealism"[61] that had indeed historically come on the scene (clearly an allusion to his own earlier idealism). This had also been an attempt at returning to appearances on the basis of an original *a priori*, which in its case was the thought of a self-thinking I. Also in its case, there had been the attempt at saving the realism of common experience which it reintroduced on subjective practical grounds. The assumption was that action necessarily requires commitment to belief in its effectiveness, even in the absence of theoretical evidence justifying it.[62] This commitment was encapsulated in a *Soll* ("ought"), understood in the very specific sense of an authoritative decision (a *Machtspruch*) not to be held back in action by an otherwise irreducible surd of experience.

Not so in the context of the realism Fichte now advocated – a realism for which, significantly, the leading category was also the *Soll*, now, however understood in a completely new sense. It no longer carried moral meaning[63] but instead defined the nature of appearance as a selfcontained event carrying with it, its own norm of development. "In its *innermost essence*, a 'should' is itself genesis and demands a genesis."[64] A being that *should be* is one whose presence is effectively already at hand (it cannot be ignored) but which depends for its realization on conditions that, although still undetermined, when determined must be so from within the norm set by it.[65] In essence, the *Soll* was thus an expectation of rationality which would not, however, have been commanding except for the Light that shone through experience and made Fichte's auditors sensitive to the expectation. Only in this broader sense, if at all, did the *Soll* still connote the earlier typically Kantian meaning of imperative.

As parsed by Fichte, the *Soll* resolved itself into two levels of necessity. One was hypothetical, as expressed in an "if . . ., then . . . ," the template for the *Soll*'s possibly infinite series of realizations. This series made up the content of appearance, its *being*. It was the counterpart of the d_1, d_2, d_3, etc., and s_1, s_2, s_3, etc., that quantified the distance separating the D and S in Fichte's original schema. The difference was that the transition from one

---

[61] SK 135; GA II.8:274–275 (translation slightly modified). See also SK 138; GA II.8:280–281, where this idealism is claimed to be completely annulled.

[62] The architectonics of the system apart, Fichte was repeating Kant.

[63] This does not mean that it would not carry it in more localized contexts of the revised *Wissenschaftslehre*.

[64] SK 155; GA II.8, 318–319.

[65] This is my attempt at summing up in one sentence Fichte's intricate exposition.

term to another, from d_1 to d_2, or s_1, s_2, was now internalized to the d's or s's. The sequence followed necessarily, albeit by an ever more determined conditional or hypothetical necessity. But just as the D&S disjunction, and its quantitative expansion, presupposed a "qualitative oneness"[66] that transcended both the D and S and their quantifications, so hypothetical-ness (*Problematicität*) presupposed the immanent, yet ever transcendent presence of a necessity that was categorical. This was the second level of necessity.

What did the *Soll* add to the being of appearance, Fichte asked? It added to it its being *as being* – as carrying with it, in other words, its own validation. Appearances were not simply *there*: they carried internal evidence.[67]

It was probably because of the introduction of the *Soll*, carrying as it did long-standing Kantian connotations of being a product of reason, where "reason" was however understood as a subjective faculty of thought, that Fichte devoted in these first four lectures so much attention to refuting idealism. Jacobi also, despite his professed realism, came in for criticism.[68] Jacobi had dismissed philosophy "as a whole" (as if philosophy could exist at all without being "a whole," Fichte complained)[69] by denigrating it as mere "re-construction." But, Fichte pointed out, there could not be a "*re*-construction" without there having been a "construction" in the first place. The idealists had located this original construction in subjective thought. Fichte now located it in appearance itself. Appearance, as a "should-be," as something that came on its own, unannounced, so to speak, but carrying its own validation, constructed itself. As Fichte had done from the beginning, he was asking his auditors to actively let themselves be absorbed into this self-construction.[70]

At the beginning of the lectures, it might have seemed that Fichte's genetic method of doing science meant transcending actual experiences in order to bring them to their transcendent origin. Indeed, much abstraction had been required so far in the lectures, especially in the first part. But, as it now became increasingly clear, the whole point of the transcending was to return to the immediacy of phenomenal existence in which Fichte's auditors had hitherto lived their lives. But, they now saw this existence (with a seeing itself inscrutable) as, in fact, permeated by Light. It carried in its very phenomenality, the *a se* and *per se* (the *Von* and the *Durch*) hitherto

---

[66] SK 145; GA II.8:296–297. [67] SK 148; GA II.8:302–303. [68] SK 138; GA II.8:282–283.
[69] SK 139; GA II.8:284–285. [70] SK 148; GA II.8:302–303.

attributed to Light reflectively, now, however manifested to Fichte's auditors with existential immediacy.[71]

(2) Nonetheless, this insight had still been attained on the basis of starting points only factically assumed in experience, and this was not enough to see the Light permeating the latter internally.

> Being is something living from itself, and through itself, absolutely self-enclosed and never coming out of itself, as we grasped clearly at the end of what we called the first part [i.e., in the *Soll* as the structure of appearance . . .]. In brief, the task of deducing *appearances* (as we have so far labelled the second part) is entirely the same as completely proving the stated sentence from being (*esse*).[72]

Fichte's auditors had to recognize this structure of appearance in their lived being (their *to be*); they had also to recognize it in the various constructs by which they had hitherto factically parsed their ordinary ways of life, thereby deriving them genetically. In effect, one had to perform this work of genetic derivation existentially at five levels of experience. Fichte routinely referred to these levels collectively (and not just in these lectures) as the *Fünffachheit* or "fivefoldness" of experience, namely sense, legality, morality, religion, and science,[73] even though it is not at all clear whether in the present lectures he ever went past "sense" and "legality."

Fichte's exposition is especially difficult at this juncture. Nonetheless, one can recognize the basic moves. For one thing, his auditors were requested to become aware of the fact that the process of knowing in which they had hitherto engaged, that is, the very knowledge that constituted their being (*esse*) at the moment, was itself an appearing, the first and most immediate instance of Light's appearance. As they pursued the internal logic of the "if x, then y; but x, etc.," they were acting out with their very being the interplay of hypotheticalness and categorial necessity that defined appearance as a *Soll* – or better, the interplay was being acted out in their being. They had hypothetically posited the *Soll*, as requested to them by Fichte, that is, they had done it arbitrarily, with the same contingency that characterizes any appearance. Yet, in so doing, they had been overtaken by the necessity of a presupposition to which they had committed themselves by the very fact of doing the positing as requested.

[71] SK 146; GA II.8:298–299.
[72] SK 167; GA II.8:346–347. The parts referred to are of the third part of the whole series of lectures.
[73] At least, as stated in the *Anweisung* (367; GA I.9:104–105). Fichte is not very specific about this "fivefoldness" or "quintitude" in these Lectures.

They might have believed themselves to be acting arbitrarily. In fact, they were displaying a necessity already at work in them. Like an appearance, or, more descriptively, like the *Soll* which they were thereby exhibiting genetically,[74] they were living an interplay of necessity and contingency. This was the structure of their *esse* precisely *as lived*. And, if the question arose as to what made the difference between their *esse* in general and their *knowledge*, the reply was simple: an extra degree of intensity. The difference was purely existential. It was a matter of being the manifestation of light precisely *as appearance*. The reflective "as" defined the difference. One could understand why Fichte had made attention, and the need to think *energisch*, the leitmotif of his lecturing. What had begun as an external schematization of experience had now been turned into an examination of one's way of existing, each factor in the original schematization drawn in, so to speak, to the one point of their personal existence.

Fichte's auditors *were* knowledge; they could now see themselves as an "I" – an "I" in general, of course, the carrier of all knowledge. It remained to be seen how they were *Wissenschaftslehre*.

Here Fichte's text is more than just more difficult; it verges on the cryptic. The difficulty lies in that, while demonstrating how, by being the carriers of knowledge in their very existence, his auditors were also the science of that knowledge (at least in attitude), Fichte also genetically derived the possibility, even the inevitability, of the idealism of his earlier *Wissenschaftslehre*, together with the pragmatic realism that was its logical counterpart. This was precisely the idealism, and the realism, that had to be annulled so that his auditors would gain insight into how true science of knowledge was already *with them*. The two issues – genetic derivation of the earlier idealism and genetic derivation of the desired present realism – tend to get confused in the text. Nonetheless, it is clear that for Fichte the possibility of the earlier *Wissenschaftslehre* arose the moment knowledge historically became the object of reflection, and the warrant was therefore at hand for distinguishing between *derived* knowledge and the *genesis* thereof. But the distinction inevitably turned out to be relative, a circumstance that led to the positing of a knowledge that was self-generated, in contrast to knowledge as derived (or as *being*); by positing, in other words, the *genesis of genesis* itself, or *self-genesis*. This is where the "I" of Fichte's early *Wissenschaftslehre* came on the scene – a self-generating performance that at the same time established the possibility of a "not-I" (*being*). But a gap separated performative act and resulting being, which

---

[74] SK 163; GA II.8:298–299.

gave rise to the opposition between subjective idealism and dogmatic realism. Fichte conceded, perhaps in defense of his earlier stance, that in that historical context one could not have avoided being an idealist, even despite one's predilection for realism. But the vocation of the current *Wissenschaftslehre* was precisely to mediate idealism and realism – in effect, to neutralize the gap between the two that had reappeared as a variant of the earlier factical One/Many gap.

It was clear, therefore, that the idea of a "self-genesis," such as directly led to Fichte's earlier idealism, and of a merely "it" (the "not-I" that was the logical counterpart of the self) had to be annulled. Here are Fichte's key texts:

> That in the higher knowing a principle is presupposed for absolute self-genesis means that inwardly and materially this higher knowing is *non-self-genesis*. Yet it does not *not* exist, rather it exists actually and in fact; thus [it is] positive non self-genesis, and yet is *immanent* and is *itself* an *I*, because this is its imperishable character, as absolute. What else is negated besides genesis? Nothing, and to be sure this is negated positively; but the positive negation of genesis is an enduring *being*. Thus, knowing's absolute, objective, and presupposed *being* becomes evident in this higher knowing, hence directly genetic, as it has previously appeared merely factically.[75]
>
> Yet, in contrast to an absolute self-genesis, which is annulled as absolute by the addition of a principle,[76] the immanent knowing that never can get outside itself for just that reason can never appear as self-genesis but only as the negation of all genesis. Here, therefore, there is a necessary gap in continuity of genesis, and a projection *per hiatum* – but here presumably not an irrational one. Rather, it is [a projection] which separates reason in its pure oneness from all appearance, and annuls the reality of appearances in comparison with it.[77]

The texts, no doubt, are difficult. One can nonetheless recognize their intent. Fichte was methodically annulling[78] distinctions introduced by virtue of the factical logic of experience and thereby gaining insight into the presuppositions that made them possible. These presuppositions had to be gained by direct insight, that is, through vital thinking, even though, once put into words as was inevitable, they became statements like any other. But the insight persisted. It did by virtue, and in the medium, of the higher *esse* attained by Fichte's auditors because of it. The insight made for a new life-form. At issue for the auditors at the present juncture in their process of self-enlightenment was a disjunction between *self-genesis* and

---

[75] SK 158; GA II.8:324–325.   [76] As the new *Wissenschaftslehre* does, I gloss.
[77] SK 158; GA II.8:324–327.   [78] "Deconstructing" is the term I have occasionally used.

being for which Fichte himself had been historically responsible but which he had just genetically derived in the quest to further deepen the insight that had already been gained. But the disjunction played into the hands of subjective idealism. Fichte now annulled it, along with the idea of self-construction associated with it. Light had no need to construct itself; it was simply *there*, or better, it always was *already* there, manifested by the very facticity of being which, *as facticity*, begged for enlightenment: "The positive negation of genesis is an enduring *being*."[79] The distinction between immediate being and the source of its immediacy persisted. But it was not an irrational gap. The rational, the intelligible, was to be found in *being*. The doubling of the two was without any remainder.

For this reason, Fichte could say to his auditors that the knowledge they lived in their *esse* was *Wissenschaftslehre*. For the same reason, he could also say both that this *Wissenschaftslehre* was the product of conceptual art and that it nonetheless had ordinary knowledge as its counterpart.[80] The *Wissenschaftslehre* oscillated – but reflectively, in this sense artificially – between idealism and realism, mediating the two by, in fact, superseding both. This is what Fichte's auditors had been doing by attentively following his lectures. But they would not have been able to do it had they not have already done the same in their day-to-day experience, but unaware and *in extenso*, by constantly reforming their judgments, accepting yet at the same time also transcending what at each instance was for them a mere given. They had now summed up this ordinary experience into a single insight by the discipline of conceptual art. They were in the position, therefore, of henceforth living it all the more intensively.

3.4 Fichte's Transcendental Spinozism

This was at Lectures 21/22. Fichte had attained the goal that had eluded Kant: demonstrating the effective presence of an *a priori* in experience. He had, at once genetically demonstrated the possibility of a *Wissenschaftslehre* and of ordinary knowledge as its counterpart. In the lectures that followed, Fichte proceeded with his descent to actual experience, genetically deriving phenomena otherwise normally taken as starting points of any science of experience. "Certainty," which constituted the phenomenal "I," came in for consideration; so did "representation," "knowledge," "lawfulness,"

---

[79] SK 158; GA II.8:324–325.
[80] The clearest statement of this is only in Lecture 37: "Our continuing task is to show that, if transcendental knowing (= existing of absolute knowing) is to arise, then another, ordinary knowing must be presupposed." SK 190; GA II.8:396–397.

"drive"; finally the very "union of knowledge and life." The derivation consisted in recognizing in these phenomena, the already established principles; by the same token, however, also in further annulling their facticity as first postulated. As principles, they were now *lived*. They were factors in a self-validating life-process that owed its validation to an internal principle which, just because it was *a se* and *per se*, could never be captured in itself. In this sense, but in this sense alone, the principle remained ever transcendent. With respect to it, the moments of the process necessarily lacked truth, that is, they were *mere* appearances; yet, precisely in their phenomenality, they gave testimony to both the principle's effective albeit ineffable presence and to the self-containedness of the process that the principle made possible, and of which they were only passing moments.

This is how close Fichte stood in 1804 to the *Bericht* of 1801, yet also totally distant from it. In 1804, just as in 1801, the *Wissenschaftslehre* was a matter of "bracketing" the natural attitude we spontaneously assume toward the objects of experience. But in the *Bericht*, as in all the earlier presentations of the Science, the bracketing was done all at once, in a single and deliberate stroke of reflection. In 1804, on the contrary, it was more a matter of reflectively dwelling on elemental positions held in that attitude, progressively demonstrating their genesis and thereby also displacing them as anything original. It was more of an *emendatio intellectus* than a sudden conversion. But the result was the same, namely there should not have been the need of a bracketing in the first place, for the natural attitude that called for it lacked truth essentially; it was the product of a kind of amnesia, the forgetting of what our phenomenal existence is the *appearance of*. In 1801, however, and earlier as well, what was forgotten was the I = I. This is what made the *Wissenschaftslehre* vulnerable to the charge of subjectivism. In 1804, it was rather the light that, shining from the transcendent *a se* and *per se* and itself invisible, was the source of the incontestable evidence of the present.

In 1804, for those sufficiently illuminated, to live their phenomenal existence was at the same time to partake in another eternal life. What Fichte required of his auditors was a kind of ontological quietism: the awareness that the Absolute was with them; had indeed always been with them; they only needed to be engaged in the present to reside in its truth. In substance, Fichte was already saying this much in the *Bericht* or in controversy with Schelling when insisting that the *Wissenschaftslehre* was phenomenology and nothing but phenomenology: it made no metaphysical claim. But in the context of the discussion of the time, this meant that Fichte's Science did not step outside the circle of reflection, and this again made it vulnerable to the charge of subjectivism. Paradoxically, now that the metaphysical commitment that animated it was in the open, so too was the full meaning of the earlier claim that the Science was but phenomenology.

In Fichte's mind, of course, everybody *de facto* already lived in the truth simply by being engaged in their phenomenal existence.[81] But to know that one did meant partaking in that truth more intensively – *energisch*. This already required assuming a special religious attitude. In this 1804[2] series of lectures, religion did not come up as a theme of discourse in any extensive way. It did so in a series published in 1806, to which we shall turn in due course. It had also already come up in 1805, in another series of only public lectures,[82] but only as part of Fichte's more general task of establishing the principles of the particular sciences of nature, right, morality, and religion. These were principles that he had already established in 1804, but only in the context of his overall theory of phenomenal existence. In 1805, he took up the subject matter of these particular sciences as *de facto* phenomena, leading them to their already established principles from the ground up, so to speak – determining them historically.[83]

It has been said that in WL 1804[2] Fichte restored the foundational insight of a theological tradition that Kant had interrupted, developing a theory of absolute truth understood as the absolute unity of being as purely *in itself*.[84] This is true in the sense that in the 1804 lectures, Fichte revalidated the realism of Spinoza, but it would certainly be a misunderstanding were it understood to mean that Fichte had reconnected to the past tradition bypassing Kant, as if Kant had not effectively interrupted it once and for all. Fichte never abandoned Kant's transcendentalism; he never ceased to operate except within the limits of experience. His Science was indeed a phenomenology from beginning to end.[85] The schema with which he had set his genetic derivation of experience in motion was clearly Spinozistic in inspiration. But it was equally Kantian.

---

[81] "[L]*ight's absolute, inner life* is posited; it exists only in living itself and not otherwise; therefore it can be encountered only immediately in living and nowhere else." SK 80; GA II.8:142–143.

[82] Normally referred to as *Principien*. For this, see Ivaldo (2006).

[83] But still abstractly. The strictly historical treatment of right/morality, history itself, and religion, came elsewhere. It is noteworthy that, while Fichte acknowledged the need for a philosophy of nature, he never expounded one, perhaps because he would have had to depend for its content on Schelling's works on the subject or, more likely, because Fichte was simply not interested in the subject. For this, see Ivaldo (2006).

[84] Barth (2004), pp. 352–356, as cited in Janke (2009), p. 286.

[85] This comes through also in 1804[1], and in *Die Tatsache des Bewußtsseyn* 1810/1811. For the latter, see di Giovanni (2007).

The paradox is that it was both only in appearance. In essence, it was neither. Yet in being neither, it made Fichte a Spinozist *and* a Kantian in a much more profound sense than either Spinoza or Kant would have been able to appreciate.

The schema was not a statement about being *a se* and *per se* but a construct drawn from the philosophical common sense of the day, nothing "metaphysical" in any dogmatic sense. We have seen how Fichte proceeded to develop it analytically, at each step, however, annulling the new constructs that were thereby achieved, for, in their ways they all reintroduced the *hiatus irrationalis* between truth and its appearance that classical metaphysics had made irreducible but which Fichte rather wanted to demonstrate as illusionary. His Science was truly, as we said, an *emendatio intellectus*. It led his auditors to a vision of the truth *sub specie æternitatis*, a vision that could not be expressed in words; nor, for that matter, was there any need for so expressing it. The point was to live it. That, in effect, was what "ontological quietism," as we called it, meant for Fichte.

But this is still to speak in theoretical terms. More to the point is the pervasive existential attitude, the "feeling" in Fichte's robust sense, that amounted to this quietism *as lived*; the attitude, in other words, that for Fichte would color anyone's experience *ab origine*, even if the right pedagogical and social conditions were not at hand to make it apparent. These were the conditions that Fichte fought for his life long, in writing and action, always with religious and political fervor, at times with dire personal consequences.[86] Certainly the feeling had nothing to do with the heroism of Goethe's Promethean *Mensch*, committed as this Man was to live an avowed illusion as if it were not such. Nor would it be anything like the eschatological fervor of Fichte's *Mensch* of 1800, committed as this was to ensure that what might be an illusion would, in fact, not be such. Neither attitude would fit the Fichte of 1804. For the appropriate attitude we must rather turn again to Spinoza. "Bliss" (*Seligkeit*) is the right name for it, the *gaudium* (inward joy) that comes with *amor Dei*.

Lessing's Nathan perhaps illustrated the feeling best, because of the equanimity he displayed before the atrocities the Christians had inflicted on his family, still proclaiming despite them the perfection of all things.[87] *Sub specie æternitatis* evil ceases to be anything real. The problem is that not everyone would be ready to accept this consequence as a sign of true

---

[86] To the end, Fichte was a Jacobin.
[87] Act 4, Scene 7, lines 659ff. For Hegel's break with Lessing, see di Giovanni (2010).

humanism. Schelling, for one, began his 1809 *Essay on Freedom* with a stinging condemnation of past philosophers because of their inability to save the reality of evil. Schelling was a self-professed Spinozist, just like Fichte at that time, rethinking his relation to Spinoza. Whether he succeeded in this saving while still adhering to Spinoza's monism is the question to consider next. To note at the moment, however, is that, where this monism fostered ontological quietism in Fichte, it fostered a superabundance of ontology in Schelling. As on the issue of nature, monism still worked its ambiguity.

CHAPTER 4

Schelling's Prophetic Spinozism

"But, what kind of questions, O son of Dionysius and Doris, is the one you brought us: *What is the cause of evil?*

In fact, we are born with the thorn of this question stuck in our soul, and he who does not pull it out will never genuinely desire to partake in truth."

Plato[1]

"And can living philosophy be anything but history?"

Jacobi[2]

"What we call understanding, if it is real, living, active understanding, is really nothing but *regulated* madness. Understanding can manifest itself, show itself, only in its opposite, thus in what lacks understanding."

Schelling[3]

"Considered objectively, mythology is as it presents itself: *actual theogony*, the history of the gods. Because, however, actual gods are only those for which God lies as the ground, the final content of the history of the gods is the production of an actual becoming *of God* in consciousness, to which *the gods* are related only as the individual productive moments."

Schelling[4]

4.1 Schelling in Confrontation with Jacobi: On the Positivity of Philosophy

Schelling outlived all his philosophical opponents. He died in 1854, at the remarkably advanced age (for those days) of seventy-nine. By that time, his bitter dispute with Fichte at the early turn of the century lay long in the past.[5] So did the issue that had caused it. Schelling's philosophical output had

---

[1] *Epist.* II, 313 af.   [2] MPW 239.   [3] SSW I.7:470.   [4] HCI 137; SSW II.1:198.   [5] Chapter 2.

subsequently so quickly diverged from Fichte's, whether in style of expression, form of thought or content, that soon no common ground was left for even the possibility of a dispute between the two, let alone constructive dialogue. On two scores, however, the two men proceeded after the dispute in directions that in appearance at least ran alongside. For one, in 1804 Fichte had quite openly made Spinozism the leading problematic of his Science, as we have just seen. In this he seemed to have taken a page from Schelling's book. Schelling himself, for his part, while still pursuing his Spinozism, had by 1809 nonetheless altered his philosophical idiom altogether, like Fichte also adopting a more phenomenological method of exposition. This was clearly the case in an essay on human freedom he published in that year, to which we shall momentarily turn in detail.[6] As for the second score, apart for a few minor writings, this essay was Schelling's last publication. Just like Fichte in 1804, but for a much longer period of time, he thereafter presented his philosophy orally, in lecture courses for which we fortunately have a truly massive fund of manuscripts.

But otherwise, by 1809, the year of the just mentioned essay, Fichte was not Schelling's most obvious concern. The essay looked more like a reply to Hegel's recently published *Phenomenology of Spirit* (1807) than to anything by Fichte. Hegel was the one who soon became the most formidable of Schelling's opponents, and the one Schelling came to resent most.[7] In 1809, however, Jacobi, not Hegel, was still the opponent. This was the Jacobi who had brought Spinoza to the center of philosophical discussion in 1785; had subsequently accused Kant of Spinozism, hence of pantheism and fatalism; and had done the same confronting Fichte during the turbulent years of the French revolution. In 1810–1811, in the context of a full-blown Romanticism, he repeated the same accusation against Schelling, his colleague at the time at the Bavarian Royal Academy in Munich.[8]

The confrontation that ensued was bitter and, no less than the pantheism controversy of 1785, had widespread social repercussions. It was the

---

[6] *Philosophical Investigations into the Essence of Human Freedom and matters Connected Therewith.* EHF; SSW I.7.

[7] But Schelling outlived him. He did so not only chronologically (Hegel died a premature death in 1831) but, more important, culturally as well. In 1841, when Schelling was called to take up in Berlin the chair of philosophy that Hegel had vacated with his death, the royal rescript appointing him included the clear mandate of redressing the spiritual and political harm previously caused by Hegel's philosophizing. This is how far things had gone since the turn of the century. Schelling's ascent to Hegel's once chair occurred in a climate of cultural and political turmoil that was marking the end of whatever there was still left of the Enlightenment, of which Schelling and Hegel had both been the inheritors. It was also marking the end of the early Jena Romanticism, of which Schelling was the last representative but which Hegel had opposed from the beginning.

[8] For details, see di Giovanni (1995), the introductory study.

occasion for Goethe's final break with Jacobi, with whom he had otherwise been an intermittent, yet long-standing friend. Nonetheless, in his 1833–1834[9] Munich lectures on the history of modern philosophy, Schelling gave a fair overview of Jacobi's philosophical contribution that would still stand up to present historical analysis.[10] He also pointed to one aspect of Jacobi's early thought which in his estimate already presaged the positive philosophy that had long become the hallmark of his thought. The 1809 essay was an early example of precisely this kind of philosophizing.

According to the overview, Jacobi had conceded to the rationalists of the Descartes/Leibniz type that the knowledge their science provided was the only one possible on the basis of conceptual abstractions. "No other philosopher," Schelling said, "had conceded so *much* to pure rationalism [. . .] as Jacobi. He really surrendered his weapons before it."[11] For Jacobi, Spinoza represented the highest and most conceptually honest form of precisely this rationalism. But (according to Jacobi, and Schelling agreed) the way of conceptual abstraction necessarily led to a view of reality in which all things happen mechanistically; where individuality, and the freedom that goes with it, is a mere epiphenomenon. Jacobi, however, yearned for personalism; above all, for a relation with God in which the latter would stand for more than just a causation principle but would rather be for Jacobi *his* God, a Thou before whom he would find validation as an I. Yet rationalistic metaphysics, because of its conceptual presuppositions and the method these dictated, fell short of this. Jacobi had therefore also posited, side by side with this supposed scientific knowledge, what could only be called – since the title "knowledge" had been preempted by science – "non-knowledge." Jacobi himself called it so. It was, however, a non-knowledge of a peculiar type because, *as* non-knowledge, it nonetheless had truth value. It brought the non-knower into connection with a reality that transcended sense-experience and could not therefore be attained by way of abstraction based on such experience, as in classical metaphysics. This explained Jacobi's claim that "a God which could be known would not *be* a God at all," a claim that Schelling took to imply that God was the supreme negative, essentially non-being.[12]

"Belief" was another term that Jacobi had used for this non-knowledge. And in principle Schelling would have accepted it. For belief was something mediated.[13] It was a desire for knowledge that recognized itself as not satisfied by what conceptual abstraction yielded. It recognized the negativity of the

[9] Might also be 1836–1837.
[10] HMP 164ff; SSW I.10:165ff. The appraisal was repeated but in shorter form in the 1841–1842 (1842–1843?) lectures. See GPP 171ff; SSW II.3:115ff.
[11] HMP 166; SSW I.10:168.   [12] HMP 171; SSW I.10:175.   [13] HMP 177; SSW I.10:182–183.

latter but, precisely for that reason, was dedicated to transcending it in order to attain the positive satisfaction it actually desired. Rather than eschewing the work of the concept, belief was mediated by that work. But, in the Enlightenment climate in which the early Jacobi operated, he had been attacked for the use of the term. He had been accused of fideism, consequently of irrationalism.[14] And Jacobi, bowing to this pressure, had hit upon the stratagem, which Schelling found disingenuous, of replacing "belief" with reason – where by "reason" he, however, meant immediate feeling.[15] According to Schelling, this move marked a second stage in Jacobi's intellectual course. It was a disastrous move, for understood in this way as feeling, reason amounted to no more than a vague form of what Schelling also called "substantial knowledge" – that is to say, the immediate apprehension of reality as already *all there*, inactive, exactly in the way it also was for rationalistic metaphysics. Although the issue was of course not in Schelling's mind, this feeling had nothing to do with Fichte's notion of it, nor, for that matter, with the feeling of the Jena Romantics, both of which clearly were mediated phenomena. It was, rather, the counterpart of Enlightenment reason. And this, according to Schelling, ran directly counter to Jacobi's own demand that God be apprehended as a living God to whom one could relate as an agent.

In an effort at fending off the accusation of irrationalism, Schelling said, Jacobi went so far, when preparing the collected edition of his works, as to ask the readers to replace "reason," wherever in his earlier writings he had criticized it for yielding only abstractions, with "understanding," which had rather been, as he now realized, the effective instrument of past rationalistic metaphysics.[16] To the negativity of the latter the readers had to oppose the positivity of a science based on the immediate intuition of reality. This was a science which reason alone, now, however, understood as "feeling," would yield – as if, Schelling complained, one could produce positive science *tout court*, in a hurry, with a simple seeing, without the negative work of the understanding. Whereas the early Jacobi had recognized the superiority of the understanding's negative work of conceptualization above the vagueness of a reason dealing only in abstractions, he was now reversing the order of the

---

[14] As it could easily have been done because in German "faith" and "belief" are both rendered by *Glaube*.

[15] HMP 169ff; SSW I.10:172ff.

[16] This is quite correct. Jacobi did this in 1815, in the preface to the second edition of the *David Hume* which was also the introduction to the just undertaken collection of his works. He edited the text of the *David Hume* accordingly, obfuscating it in many ways. This is the edition that became canonical in the literature. The current English translation (MPW) includes the original edition, referencing the 1815 alterations. Jacobi was being disingenuous in claiming that he had left the text untouched except for minor details.

two, placing reason above the understanding. The net result was that the positive science Jacobi now proposed was only the counterpart of the rationalistic metaphysics he had originally opposed and still opposed. He had accused that metaphysic of nihilism because it was ultimately empty of content. But his new positive science, despite the appellation "positive" attributed to it, was no less empty. Thus, if Jacobi had disarmed himself before rational metaphysics at an early stage, he had later colluded with it at a distance, trading on the vagueness of reason as now understood by him to convey the impression that it reached beyond the realm of the sensuous, while in fact it remained bound to it.

Serious positivity, Schelling argued, was, on the contrary, an achievement. It required self-assertion, and this required, in turn, the laborious overcoming of the moment of abstractive negativity which was nonetheless essential to an adequate analysis of experience. Jacobi had failed on this score. Yet Schelling still saw him as presaging his own positive philosophy, the same he was advertising in his Munich lectures, in one crucial respect. For the God with whom Jacobi wanted to have a personal relationship had to be individual; for this reason, he had to be in significant connection with the empirical. He had to be historical, in other words, and the early Jacobi had explicitly said that much. "He had recognized," Schelling said,

> the true character of all modern systems, namely that they [. . .] offer only a tiresome [. . .] knowledge in which thought never gets beyond itself and only progresses within itself, whilst we really desire to get *beyond* thinking, in order, via that which is *higher* than thinking, to be redeemed from the torment of thinking. Thus the earlier Jacobi. In his earliest writings he had even used the expression "historical knowledge".[17]

To be sure, in context "historical" had meant for Jacobi the external authority of Revelation,[18] whereas the issue for Schelling was to recognize this authority as *internal* to history, for reason was itself, *as* reason, historical in character. What this meant we shall have to see. In his review of Jacobi, however, Schelling's point was that the early Jacobi had rightly associated significant knowledge with the empirical and the historical.

One could not take history seriously, however, without taking nature just as seriously. Here is where Jacobi had again failed according to Schelling, this time because of a Cartesianism that affected him personally

---

[17] HMP 167; SSW I.10:168–169. Schelling was right in this. "And can living philosophy be anything but history?" This is the question Jacobi posed to Moses Mendelssohn in 1785. MPW 239.

[18] MPW 230–231. In context, Jacobi's implication was that Mendelssohn could not understand him because, being a Jew, he had missed the historical moment of Christian revelation.

and made him recoil before nature as if in panic. Jacobi had been educated by the Cartesian mathematician Le Sage, of Geneva.[19] Just as Goethe had said that he was personally unable to think of nature except as alive, Jacobi could not think of it except as an inanimate mechanism, as Le Sage would have impressed upon him.[20] Thus, besides the fact that in Schelling's estimate his own philosophy had at no time been one of simple *identity* but had always included the moment of negativity, what also transpired from his review of Jacobi was that its defining mark, the one that best qualified it for the title of "positive philosophy," was rather the foundational role that the idea of nature played in it. In these 1833–1834 Munich lectures, after reviewing the transcendental idealism of Kant and Fichte, and before turning to Hegel, Schelling offered the exposition of another system which had followed upon Fichte's but which, as he said, was totally independent of it. This was patently his own system. The exposition included elements that pointed back to his early essays on the philosophy of nature; an account of the interplay at all levels of existence of the ideal and the real that recalled the system of transcendental idealism of 1800; and other elements that clearly indicated Schelling's current special interest in the historicity of reason. The exposition recapitulated the historical procession of Schelling's thought up to the time of the lectures but did so in the form of a seamless conceptual narrative. It is significant that Schelling called the system thus expounded *Naturphilosophie*, Philosophy of Nature. Equally significant is that, in the course of the exposition, he had occasion to object to the title of "identity system" that was being given to his idealism.[21] As he said, he had personally used that expression once, and

---

[19] HMP 173; SSW I.10:176–177. MPW 279ff.

[20] In point of fact, if Schelling had carefully consulted Jacobi's dialogue *David Hume* in its original edition of 1787 – that is, before Jacobi obfuscated it in 1815 by surreptitiously amending the text in accordance with his new concept of reason – he would have noticed that Jacobi, precisely because of his need for individualism that forced him to the empirical, had defined reason as a form of life, such as could be had by all living organisms in various degrees of perfection. See MPW 301.

[21] It is commonplace to divide Schelling's opus into three periods – that of the early philosophy of nature culminating with the 1800 System of Transcendental Idealism; the Jena period of the Spinoza-inspired identity system; and, from *circa* 1809 to the end, the period of positive philosophy. These might be useful chronological signposts for the sake of exposition. And there is no denying that Schelling's philosophical idiom changed over time, as one would expect of any serious philosopher. Nonetheless, one lesson to be drawn from the 1833–1834 overview of Jacobi is that at no time was Schelling's philosophy one of identity *tout court*. The identity he defended at every stage of his intellectual journey was one that did not eschew the negativity of opposition; on the contrary, it required it in order for the identity to be a living one, not simply given but achieved. Nor, for that matter, was his philosophy based on an intuition that eschewed the negativity of the concept. On the contrary, as Schelling clearly argued in opposition to both Jacobi's early "substantial knowledge" and the latter's later "rational feeling," intuition without conceptual mediation amounts to nothing. In this, Schelling was not unlike Fichte and Hegel. This is made exceptionally clear also in *The Ages of*

only in the exoteric context of an introduction.[22] Yet the "designation had been badly interpreted and used by those who never penetrated into the interior of the system to infer [. . .] that in this System *all* differences [. . .] were annulled."[23] Nature, in other words, conceptually mediated to manifest its internal oppositions, had been from the start the theme of Schelling's system. It must also be the clue for understanding his notion of "positivity."

The same can be drawn from Schelling's exposition of theosophy, which he did in the same Munich lectures in conjunction with Jacobi, and later again, in the Berlin lectures of 1841–1842.[24] The extent to which Schelling might have been influenced by Jakob Boehme has been the subject of much discussion in the literature. The most extreme positions have been defended on the subject, not just regarding the significance of any possible influence but even regarding the time when, and the extent to which, Schelling read Boehme.[25] It is certain that in 1809 Schelling borrowed some of his imagery from Boehme; equally so that, like all the Romantics, he had a special predilection for this *primitive* German genius.[26] Nonetheless, despite these warm feelings, Schelling rejected theosophy, under which rubric he included Boehme, because it was based on what was at best "substantial knowledge," the same as Schelling had attributed to Jacobi. For this reason he treated the two in the same lecture. To be sure, there was in Boehme's theosophy the blind awareness that being is inherently active, creative. The same intuition had also motivated Jacobi. But because the awareness had lacked conceptual expression – had not been subjected, in other words, to the discipline of the negative – it had gone nowhere, in

---

the World (*Die Weltalter*). WA 117; DWA 115: "We do not live through intuitions. Our knowledge is a working piece [*stückwerk*]; that is, it must be produced piece by piece [*stückweis*] in sections and degrees, and this cannot occur in the absence of reflection." Translation modified.

[22] HMP 120; SSW I.10:107. Schelling's reference is to his *Darstellung meines System der Philosophie*, 1801 (*Presentation of my System of Philosophy*). SSW I.4:113.

[23] HMP 120; SSW I.10:107.   [24] More likely, 1842–1843. See GPP 87 (translator's introduction).

[25] For an overview of the various positions, as well as a balanced and reasonable assessment of the situation, see Mayer (1999), especially chap. 9: "Idealism, Human Freedom, and the Problem of Evil: F.W.J. Schelling."

[26] In the Berlin lectures Schelling took offense at Hegel's dismissive attitude toward him, justified by Boehme's apparent incapacity to rise above the grossly metaphorical mode of expression. Schelling admitted that Boehme, innocent of speculative language, had no choice but to stumble from image to image as he tried to voice what must have been a natural intuition, not unlike a drunkard unsure of his territory. But, Schelling pointed out, did not Hegel himself resort to metaphor at the end of his Logic when he says of the Idea that "it lets itself go" into nature? What was this "*Selbstentlassen*" but metaphor? And who could avoid metaphors? It was better, Schelling went on to say, to behave drunkenly when actually drunk than feign drunkenness when in reality in perfect conceptual control. This was, of course, a dig at Hegel, and a clever one at that. GPP 176; SSW II.3:122.

Boehme no less than in Jacobi. Theosophy simply repeated itself, piling up images upon images but never ultimately saying anything.[27]

This was Schelling's considerate judgment regarding theosophy:[28] "In its essence, theosophy [was] just as unhistorical as rationalism."[29] How reason might be historical and, in order to be historical, would have to be discovered in nature, turns out, again, to be the issue that provides the clue for understanding Schelling's "positivity." It must also be the issue with which to approach his Freedom Essay.

4.2   Of Evil and Its Cosmic Significance

Hegel complained about the barbarism of Boehme's imagery. The modern reader can be forgiven for leveling the same complaint against Schelling's, all the more so because his is coached in a pseudo-scientific language that makes it mystifying.[30] Moreover, despite his many complaints about the formalism of other systems of thought, Schelling unabashedly relied on formal categories, notably the modal (such as possible and actual), simply adding imaginative content to them. But was he not thereby incurring the mistake, for which Kant had given fair warning, of taking as universal determinations of reality conceptual determinations that are in fact only competent to determine reality in particular?

For the student of Schelling, these are troublesome issues. Nonetheless, Schelling must be taken seriously, if for nothing else at least because, unlike the whole classical tradition of metaphysics preceding him, he took seriously the reality of evil in human experience and the need to account for its possibility. Schelling was right when in his essay he complained about this past tradition. Leibniz and Spinoza, no less than Plato and the various traditions flowing from him, had all ended up denying the reality of evil. They had all reduced it to a case of finitude, of imperfection, that would be revealed as in fact contributing to the perfection of the whole when seen from the perspective of the whole – in fact, therefore, itself a kind of good.[31]

---

[27] For Schelling's criticism of theosophy, see HMP 179ff; SSW I.10:184ff. A more balanced position is found in *Die Weltalter*. Theosophy has depth but lacks the reflection of philosophy. WA 118; DWA 116–117.

[28] The issue of how Boehme might have inspired Schelling's positive philosophy is for our purposes therefore moot. For a sympathetic and valuable treatment of the issue, see McGrath (2012). For an older study, see Brown (1941).

[29] GPP 177; SSW II.3:125.

[30] For a sympathetic reading of Schelling, see McGrath (2014), (2017). For Schelling on intuition, see Bruno (2013), Snow (1996), Bowie (1993).

[31] EHF 35–40; SSW I.7:367–373.

Kant was an exception. In his last work on religion, in order to save the language of moral experience, he had postulated the presence in individual human nature of a principle of radical evil. This was a historical precedent that Schelling did not fail to note.[32] He, however, was doing something quite different from Kant's. For unlike Kant, who had simply postulated a principle of evil in human beings, Schelling was raising the issue of evil speculatively, just as was done in past tradition, inquiring about evil's constitution and its possible cosmic sources. In opposition to that tradition, however, he claimed for evil a positive content of its own *as evil*, since only on the strength of such a content could it stand opposed to the good seriously, as it did on the witness of experience. To deny this, according to Schelling, resulted also in denying the reality of freedom, for the latter, also if taken seriously in accordance with its common meaning, could only mean the capacity for *both* good *and* evil. This was precisely the meaning that past metaphysics had refused to accept because it undermined the assumption on which, according to Schelling, that metaphysics had been grounded from the beginning – the belief, namely, that reality is of one piece, hence lifeless, lacking the inner oppositions that would call for ever new creative efforts at reconciliation.[33]

Postulating the positive reality of evil thus stood for Schelling as the signpost of a truly positive system of thought in which freedom was the fundamental concept. He associated this system with true pantheism – very likely with Jacobi in mind, whose idea of pantheism he considered false, but also because pantheism, of all the systems of philosophy, appeared to be the one that excluded evil in principle. Accordingly, the 1809 essay opened with precisely a long disquisition on various past forms of pantheism and the failure of each to be true to its fundamental insight of the presence of God everywhere in nature. Spinoza's was singled out as one that was terribly flawed in form yet true in inspiration.[34]

But Schelling had already given an explicit and detailed account of what he meant by a true pantheism in his October 1807 celebratory address at the Munich Academy, "On the Relation of the Fine Arts to Nature,"[35] the same that caused his dispute with Jacobi. It is significant, for reasons we

---

[32] EHF 53; SSW I.7:388. We shall return to this precedent in connection with Hegel.

[33] This term (*Versöhnung*) is important because it is the leitmotif of Hegel's thought.

[34] EHF 20; SSW I.7:349. Spinoza is fatalist, according to Schelling, not because he places all things *in God* but because he places them there (the will included) as things mechanically connected with each other. His failure lies in his conception of being: the mistake is ontological. On this reading of Spinoza, see Heidegger (1985), p. 89.

[35] *Über das Verhältnis der bildenden Künste zu der Natur*, 1807. SSW I.7:289–330.

shall see momentarily, that the address includes a eulogy of Johann Joachim Winckelmann, the father of German historiography of art.[36] Winckelmann's merit, according to Schelling, had been to recognize that the beauty of a work of art lies in the balance it achieves between its generic nature, such as can be realized in a variety of particular forms, and the form that actually shapes the work's singularity. This singularity is the reflection of the age to which the work belongs; it is the work's "characteristic," as Winckelmann called it. Schelling agreed with this. Beauty consists in the balance of body and soul, of characteristic form and universal concept, by virtue of which the particular does not obscure the universality of the concept, yet provides for it the limit it needs for being realized. However, missing in Winckelmann's analysis, according to Schelling, was the factor that links the body with the concept and makes the artwork something alive. Winckelmann knew, of course, that the work somehow reflects nature. However, bound to classical art, Winckelmann had viewed nature *in* art, that is, only in secondhand format, mediated by already established historical circumstances. Its vitality was thus lost. The problem was to bring this vitality back to consciousness; to make explicit, in other words, the vital link that connects art to nature and a work's characteristic form to the concept.[37] This was Schelling's project.

Nature, as Schelling went on to proclaim in his address and repeated in the 1809 essay, must be conceived as self-creating and self-contained. It is "creating" since it is realized only in particular products of which there are infinite possibilities that it transcends *as particulars*. However, it is at the same time "self-creating," since each of these products repeats within the limits of its particularity the process of creatively realizing itself in which nature's vitality in general consists. In creating the products, nature only repeats itself. The result is that, even though one can, even must, speak of nature as a self-creating process in general, this process is nonetheless nowhere *actually* found except in the particular events in which the self-creating is repeated and is thus realized. There is no remainder (no *hiatus irrationalis*, in Fichte's 1804 language) between creative and created nature.

In the abstract idiom to which Schelling routinely resorted, the whole process can be said to be a universalizing that does not, however, leave the particulars it transcends behind.[38] Or again, it is a conceptualizing that remains immanent to the body it ensouls. This nature's self-creating

---

[36] 1717–1768. For the eulogy, see SSW I.7:296. That Winkelmann recognized the idealizing function of art but simply looked at nature in art without considering the point at which the latter connects with it, and thus still treated nature as something itself spiritless, see 295ff.

[37] See SSW I.7:293, 300.   [38] See SSW I.7:304ff.

process is the link that Schelling found missing in Winckelmann's account of the artwork. Art, of course, is itself a work of nature. There are infinitely many such products, differentiated by the extent to which the link between universal and singular, form and matter, soul and body, is active in them; to the extent, in other words, to which the linked sides do not fall apart, thereby obscuring the vital connection that otherwise holds a product to its source in nature in general. Finitude consists precisely in a deadening of ostensive nature due to this obscuring. Art was important in Schelling's schema of things because nature's process of self-exteriorization in a particular to which it nonetheless remains immanent is acted out in the determination of the artwork *explicitly*. In the work of art, therefore, nature does not just realize itself: it does so by revealing itself as thus realizing itself. Art plays out a revelatory function. As for the rest of the infinitely many products of nature, only as reflected in art do they acquire the self-totalizing unity that makes a cosmos of them.

The works of art are themselves also many and differentiated; the explicitness with which they each act out nature's process of self-realization itself admits of degrees. Schelling proceeded, first, with a history of nature's self-creation culminating in the human body and the emergence of art and, second, with a history of art in which its works are shown as reflecting at various stages of development the stages that nature itself goes through until finally revealing itself in art. The latter's highest form was attained when it became conceptual and its revealing function was therefore fully transparent.[39] And Schelling asked whether, and when, a further epiphany of nature in art would occur. Obviously pointing to himself in both the address and shortly after in the Freedom Essay, he envisaged a time when conceptual art would become fully transparent – would then turn into philosophy and, as philosophy, would find completion in a system. One can understand why Schelling would want to eulogize Winckelmann. In Winckelmann he saw someone who had been looking in the history of art, but unknowingly, for the kind of epiphany that Schelling now sought with open eyes.

In 1800, Schelling had relied on the intuition of the artistic genius for the vision of the unity that internally binds together nature and mind, body and concept. He now gave a content to this vision which he found manifested in art. Nature has two distinct yet inextricably intertwined

---

[39] The latest achievement of painting, according to Schelling, was the interiorization of Michelangelo's brute expression of power, such as was found in the works of a certain Guido Rieti (of the Bologna school, 1626–1686). See SSW I.7:321.

meanings. As the source of all things, it is God. As the totality of all things produced by God, it is, though not God *tout court*, nonetheless *divine*, for it is the revelation of God. It is God *as revealed*. Such was the defining formula of Schelling's pantheism. Jacobi was not slow in recognizing it for what it was.[40] This explained the title of the tract he published in 1811 *contra* Schelling: *Of Divine Things and their Revelation*, the first salvo in the dispute that followed.[41]

But how did this pantheism differ from Fichte's of 1804? Fichte and Schelling both denied any gap that needed traversing between the One and the Many or, in the language most suited to Schelling, between God and his revelation in creation. Imagining a gap between the two, or any remainder between them, was only due to consciousness's need to object-ify; hence to treat the two sides of the relation as "things." For both Fichte and Schelling, therefore, God was essentially a "no-thingness." The differ-ence (itself the function, as we said earlier,[42] of the ambiguity inherent in any monism) lay in how they saw this "no-thingness" working itself out on the side of creation; in the attitude, therefore, that one should assume with respect to the phenomena of experience; or again, in the way one felt God's presence within. For Fichte, this presence manifested itself in the dis-appearing of the phenomena as anything in itself. Essentially, these were disappearing acts; nature itself, therefore, just an idea. For Schelling, on the contrary, the same presence made them revelatory in the positive sense of being pregnant of content, always containing more (instead of less, as for Fichte) than what they immediately demonstrated. Where Fichte was led to ontological quietism, Schelling saw in nature the warrant for ontological exuberance.

This is an important point. It might not save Schelling from mystifica-tion; it does nonetheless allow for a logic to the mystification. It further elucidates the otherwise puzzling questions of why the positive and irredu-cible presence of evil in reality validated for Schelling the truth of his System? The answer is clear. Actual existence is singular. And since exist-ence is God's epiphany, the epiphany is most fully to be expected exactly where the singular detail is at issue, notably the historical detail which is the

---

[40] MPW 573, note 29.

[41] For details, see MPW 570, note 27. The tract, which expanded on a piece Jacobi had earlier produced in 1801, moved from a critique of the pietist author Matthias Claudius to an attack on Schelling. Revelation had to be historical but certainly not in Schelling's naturalistic sense. As Jacobi privately summed up for Goethe the point of his attack, in a note of 1808 prior to the tract's publication, Schelling's project of uniting Platonism and Spinozism was an impossible one. The very attempt was illusionary, the product of double talk (*Zweizüngigkeit*: a forked tongue).

[42] In Section 3.3.3.

product of freedom. But it is in the capacity for evil – actual evil – that this freedom is demonstrated, according to Schelling; so, too, therefore, is God's presence. There could be no existentially serious demonstration of such a presence without the serious occurrence of evil.[43] It was not just the devil who lurked in the detail according to Schelling; so did God, and he was there because the devil was there.

Another way of saying this is that God's creativity lay for Schelling in his transcendence with respect to any particular form of existence in which his presence is manifested. This is a transcendence which is reflected in the form by rendering it contingent, in the sense that it might have been otherwise than it happens to be and yet equally manifest God's presence – a circumstance which is not just a product of external reflection (as it would be for Kant) but enters as a factor into the inner economy of the form. It follows that, regardless of how self-regulated and self-contained in form an existent might be, there always is a remainder in it that makes it unexplainable to its own eyes, if it happens to have eyes. This remainder – call it "the irrational" – is itself an epiphany of God, indeed the most revealing of all, for it manifests God's freedom. It must be assumed, therefore, as imbedded in him even before reflected in his creation. In Schelling's context, the remainder had nothing to do with the *hiatus* that Fichte was intent on denying and that Schelling also denied. For Schelling it was instead the basis for the speculative account of evil which his System was finally able to provide.

As for this System, inasmuch as its appearing on the philosophical scene was a new event, and hence in its way itself a creation *of* God (where the "of" was both subjective and objective), that it was *as it was*, and in this manifested God *truly*, was ultimately an indemonstrable fact, no matter how internally rational the System was in itself. For its truth one had to trust the unique creative genius of the author. In this sense Schelling's position was nonetheless ultimately intuitionist, though not naïvely so. This made his pantheism unique. It was no doubt a variation on Spinoza's, but what it added to the latter was its uniquely prophetic character. Schelling's Spinozism was vatic.

[43] EHF 37; SSW I.7:369: "The ground of evil must lie, therefore, not only in something generally positive but rather in that which is most positive in what nature contains, as is actually the case in our view, since it lies in the revealed *centrum* or primal will of the first ground." Schelling goes on to criticize Leibniz, rightly so. Also, 38; 370: "Hence it is necessary that a kind of being be in evil as well as in good, but in the former as that which is opposed to the good, that which perverts the temperance contained in the good into distermperance. To recognize this kind of being is impossible for dogmatic philosophy because it has no concept of personality, that is, of selfhood raised to spirit, but only the abstract concept of finite and infinite."

4.3 The Indivisible Remainder

4.3.1 Parts One and Two of the 1809 Essay

Regardless of how much one stresses the internal logic of Schelling's System, it is not easy to dispel Heinrich Heine's judgment of 1835:

> In the year 1804 the God of Schelling appeared at last in His complete form in a work entitled "Philosophy and Religion."[44] It is here that we have in its completed form the theory of the absolute expressed in three formulas. [... But] along the path of philosophy, then, Schelling could proceed no further than Spinoza, since the absolute can be comprehended only under the form of these two attributes, thought and extension. But at this point Schelling leaves the philosophical route, and seeks by a kind of mystical intuition to arrive at the contemplation of the absolute itself; he seeks to contemplate it in its central point, in its essence, where it is neither ideal nor real, neither thought nor extension, neither subject nor object, neither mind nor nature, but [...] I know not what! Here philosophy ceases with Schelling, and poetry – I may say folly commences.[45]

Heine was wrong. Schelling was not a naïve intuitionist, and there was a logic to his position; there was on his premises a valid explanation for the poetic moment of his System. From his point of view, moreover, there was no problem about the narrative he wove in that System having existential traction, for it was woven over nature. The System was intended from beginning to end as a Philosophy of Nature; as such, while schematizing nature reflectively, it never abandoned the existential/empirical level of experience; or, at least, so Schelling believed. This applied in particular to conscious life, itself a phenomenon of nature but one endowed with freedom and the consequent capacity for evil. It therefore most explicitly reflected the internal life of God. But this life, just like any other phenomenon of nature, did not come about without precedents – did not come on the scene like a sudden burst of light, an *éclat*, as Fichte's *Evidenz* apparently did. Consciousness, according to Schelling, emerged out of the unconscious; had its existential preconditions there. Modern

---

[44] In spirit and content, a prelude to the 1809 essay. See Section 6.3.

[45] Heine (1982), pp. 151–152. Also, pp. 148–149: "Poetry is at once Schelling's strength and his weakness. It is here that he is distinguished from Fichte as much to his advantage and disadvantage. Fichte is merely philosopher; his power consists in his dialectic, and his strength in ability to demonstrate. This, however, is Schelling's weak side; he lives in a world of intuition; he does not feel at home on the cold height of logic; he stretches forth eager hands forwards towards the flowery valleys of symbolism, and his philosophical strength lies in the art of construction. But this is an intellectual aptitude found as frequently amongst mediocre poets as amongst the philosophers." Heine believed that Schelling had turned to philosophy because he lacked sufficient talent for poetry.

psychoanalysts have no hesitation imaginatively narrating the pre-conscious life of consciousness, trusting for the verisimilitude of their narrative on individual experiences regarding one's psychic life. In the narrative the individual should recognize the truth of precisely this life.[46] Schelling was doing something very similar, as his constant intertwining of the life of God and individual conscious experiences showed. In the unconscious (or perhaps we would better say "pre-conscious") the modern psychoanalyst sees a naturally induced play of psychic mechanisms; Schelling saw God instead. One need not accept his vision. But the point is that, on his presuppositions, his method was justifiable. The existential constraint for his narrative was none other than the phenomena of individual consciousness for which he provided a transcendental narra-tive based on their presumed pre-conscious past.

The key word here is "transcendental." Schelling was again following a course parallel to Fichte's; like the latter he was engaged in a transcendental argument. Granted a fact of experience, it was a matter of establishing its *a priori*, that is, the conceptually required conditions for its possibility. Fichte's fact, we have seen, was the binding character of evidence that governed all experience. To explain this binding character, Fichte had methodically resolved all content of experience into form, finally resolving the evidence itself into a freely assumed style of existence. Schelling's fact was, rather, the presence in experience of an irreducible moment of irrationality, of evil. For this he had to reduce rationality (the formal side of experience) to a more fundamental source of existence that rendered it inextricably connected with the irrational. That was the point of his narrative.

This narrative fell into six parts.[47] The first was an imaginary exposition of God's inner life that provided the basis for the possibility of evil, the subject on which Schelling then expanded in the second. The first part was where Schelling most obviously borrowed from Boehme's imagery, while at the same time also explicitly referring back to his 1802 System.[48] In the exposition, he used "God" in four different senses, without, however, explicitly distinguishing them but rather shifting from one to the other,

---

[46] This is the warrant for Jacques Lacan's, and more recently Slavoj Žižek's, psychoanalytical reading of Schelling. Žižek (1997); Dufour (1998).

[47] But only after the long disquisition on pantheism on which we have already commented (Section 4.2). The essay's text is continuous. All divisions are drawn based on content and are by no means set in stone. EHF, pp. 26–33; 33–40; 40–54; 54–58; 58–66; 66–70. Schelling's imagery is not always transparent and needs interpretation.

[48] See Section 2.4.

often imperceptibly. This was already apparent in the opening statement. To wit:

> Since nothing is prior or outside of God, he must have the ground of his existence in himself. All philosophies say this, but they speak of this ground as of a mere concept without making it into something real [*reel*] and actual [*wirklich*]. This ground of his existence, which God has in himself, is not God considered absolutely, that is, in so far as he exists; for it is only the ground of his existence. It [the ground] is *nature* – in God, a being indeed inseparable, yet still distinct from him. This relation can be explained analogically through that of gravity and light in nature. Gravity precedes light as its ever dark ground, which itself is not *actu*, and flees into the night as the light (that which exists) dawns. Even light does not fully remove the seal under which gravity lies contained. Precisely for this reason gravity is neither the pure essence nor the actual Being of absolute identity but rather follows only from its own nature or *is* [*ist*] absolute identity, namely considered as a particular potency. For, moreover, that which, relative to identity, appears as existing also belongs in itself to the ground, and, hence, nature in general is everything that lies beyond the Being of absolute identity.[49]

In one sense, God was for Schelling the self-grounded One, Spinoza's *causa sui*. But this sense apparently entailed two others, which brought into play the difference in nuances of meaning between the German "existence" (*Dasein*) and "being" (*Sein*). Whereas *Dasein* carries the connotations of "thereness," "standing there," and thus of "self-manifesting presence," *Sein*, by contrast, conveys a more static meaning, expressing a possibility rather than anything definitely present. In the cited text, Schelling was playing on precisely this difference. God as the One, the *causa sui* containing within itself the ground or wherewithal of its existence, could also be taken in a second sense simply as this "wherewithal" by itself, as a *causa* still prior to the *sui*; prior to any existence (including God's) emanating from it. Schelling imaged this *causa* as gravity, presumably because gravity, at least in the science of the day, is a force which, left unchecked, would collapse all things together, seal them into an indefinite identity of which one could only say "*ist*," and as such, therefore, would be non-revelatory, would shun the light. And light was the figure with which Schelling proceeded to characterize God according to a third meaning. To God as *causa*, Schelling opposed God as light, as "that which exists"; God as expansive, in other words, as differentiating itself from the ground to which it thereby adds an "of itself," the *sui* in *causa sui*.

---

[49] EHF 27–28 (translation slightly altered); SSW I.7:357–358.

Even in this opening statement Schelling was thus introducing into God the only dualism that he considered admissible.[50] It was admissible, despite the monism that Schelling nonetheless still professed, because neither of the two terms in the asserted duality exceeded the other, or, more precisely, neither was any the less the other in being itself. This was, of course, paradoxical, but Schelling's position depended precisely on the paradox. To be sure, neither of the terms in the duality could be reduced to the other. "Gravity," as Schelling said in his opening statement, "precedes light as its ever dark ground [. . .]. Even light does not fully remove the seal under which gravity lies contained." Nonetheless, the two simply repeat God in full, according to the first meaning of "the One," although each in a different register. And this was the point that Schelling proceeded to make in this first part, relying on a variety of metaphors besides the play of dark gravity and expansive light (the *ist* and the *da*). In one way or other, all these metaphors related to "becoming," the one concept, according to Schelling, that was "appropriate to the nature of things."[51] Becoming, however, could not be attributed to God as an unfinished process. God had to be conceived rather as a becoming that had fully become; that had no whither to attain, yet, in this complete state, still carried with it, superseded, the past of its becoming. Just as there was no light without its dark background, regardless of how fully engulfed such a background was in the light's effulgence, so there was for God no expansive *da* without the sealed *ist*.

Schelling also represented this play of sealed *ist* and expansive *da* on the analogy of desire and love. God, as just ground, is like an inchoate desire. To this extent, since desire seeks a "something other," there already is in God's otherwise inward gravitational pull at least the principle of an expansive force. But a desire that does not seek anything in particular can only be intent on itself, on satisfaction only for satisfaction's sake. Love, on the other hand, is a self-giving; it is effective as an expansive force because it is directed at specific objects. Light illumines differences; love creates them. But differentiation entails intelligence. God cannot be love, therefore, without being at the same time intelligence. Or again, he cannot give himself to himself in love without at the same time differentiating himself from himself, that is, without at the same time expressing himself in a primordial Word. In this self-differentiation, God does not ever leave himself behind. He nonetheless generates a space within himself, a space of reason that establishes the possibility of particular determinations of being,

---

[50] EHF 30, footnote; SSW I.7:359fn.   [51] EHF 28; SSW I.7:359.

such as would express in particular God's love for himself, which would otherwise be in general.

This last point is important because it introduces the fourth sense in which God was conceived by Schelling and also completes his account of the economy of God's inner life. God is creator. And his creation occurs precisely in the space of reason just mentioned, one in which the picture of God as dark ground and effulgent light – the two perfectly balanced with each other in a union of harmony – is translated[52] into a struggle between the two out of which a world of individual beings first makes its appearance (never stepping, however, outside God's inner life). Schelling compared this emergence of the phenomenal world to a birth. Like a birth, it was a painful event because of the resistance that the gravity of the dark ground posed to the coming to light of anything particular. Nonetheless, it was precisely this resistance that made possible the diversity of realized individuals. The particularity of each was due to the degree to which the harmony, which is perfect in God (in whom there is, therefore, no actual evil), is realized in it. And this degree depends in turn on the extent to which either the darkness of the ground or the effulgence of the light prevailed, at first in the struggle for an individual's birth and subsequently as reflected in the life of the born individual. Either individuals open themselves up to others in love – they make themselves shareable, divisible – or, alternatively, they seal themselves up, resisting the presence of the "other."

Since in Schelling's picture the human being occupies the center of the created world, this resistance amounts to *pride*. Pride is the product of a selfishness that stands opposed to love and thus throws the human individual off that center. It is in him an "indivisible remainder" – "indivisible" because it is impervious to differentiation and therefore rationalization – the irreducible leftover of the density of the dark ground that was in contention with the effusiveness of light at the birth of the world. This remainder is present, to some extent or other, in all creatures, the source of the irrational, the evil, that unavoidably affects their existence. It is also the factor, however, that made possible the emergence of the world out of the internal harmony of the One. By the end of the second part of his exposition of God's life, Schelling had thus made good on the claim he had already announced at the beginning of his essay. Evil is no mere lack, no mere negation. It is a positive factor in the economy of existence, "an unmistakably general principle everywhere locked in struggle with the good."[53]

[52] "Translated" is my expression.   [53] EHF 40; SSW I.7:373.

4.3.2   Part Three of the Essay

God's ground (*Grund*) was thus also the abyss (*Abgrund*) of reason. This, however, had been established only in principle. Schelling, by his own reckoning, had so far constructed only the possibility of evil, not yet proved its reality. This might sound counterintuitive, considering the positivity of Schelling's narrative. But one must remember that Schelling's narrative was transcendental, at least in intention. It established the possibility of a fact, the facticity of which had to be established independently. This was the purpose of the third part of the essay.[54] This is not to say that there was no argument in this part or, for that matter, that in the argument the principles that had only been hypothetically introduced so far did not come into play. On the contrary, here, if anywhere, Schelling gave his most vivid portrayal of the economy of God's life[55] – vivid because close to the facts of experience that Schelling elucidated by narrating them in view of that economy, thereby also investing the latter, so far established only as possibility, with existential validation.

In this schematization of God's life through experience (for this is what it amounted to), Schelling's intention was not to provide a phenomenology of individual evil actions but rather to demonstrate how evil "was able to break out of creation as an unmistakably general principle everywhere locked up in struggle with the good."[56] For this he relied on a multitude of (alleged) natural phenomena. He also went back to the ancient myth of the various ages of human history, which he took as true history, interpolating into it elements drawn from Christian soteriology. In its barest outline, Schelling's story went like this. God created because of love – a love that needed objective specification (hence reason) to be effective in its self-giving. Schelling had already said this. But, just as God's being in general required a ground, so did its love. And this ground was none other than God's own dark ground, without which the love would have been only an empty intention. It was there that love found the inchoate material out of which to elicit the well-formed world where it revealed itself but where it also found resistance. In countering this resistance, it was energized. In this respect, love depended on the weight of the dark ground for its actualization. Creation, as Schelling had already said, was the result of this contest of darkness and light, of indefiniteness and limit.

What Schelling thus described was a symbiotic process by which, on the one hand, as love forged ever more determined forms of existence, through

---

[54] EHF 40–54; SSW I.7:373–389.   [55] For instance, see EHF 41; SSW I.7:3373–374.
[56] EHF 40; SSW I.7:373.

these very forms evil also found ever more devious venues for manifesting its power for chaos; on the other hand, in the face of these recurrent irruptions of irrationality, love found renewed redemptive means. For this reason (and Schelling enlarged at length on the theme), despite all the laws governing nature, and the symmetry of nature's forms, "there [are in nature] contingent determinations only explicable in terms of an arousal of the irrational or dark principles in creatures."[57] Without this disruptive irruption of irrationality, a given life form would preserve itself in its current position indefinitely; in actual fact, however, it was repeatedly forced to restore itself to form. It was fated to be a *"perpetuum mobile* [something perpetually in motion]."[58] *Mutatis mutandis*, the same applied to historical events, where human perfidy called for the intervention of heroes and, at some point in the process, for the redemptive revelation of God in man: "and God must become man so that man may return to God."[59]

Here is a representative text, long but worth citing because it perfectly conveys the flavor of Schelling's story:

> As a thunderstorm is caused in a mediated way by the sun but immediately by an opposing force of the earth, so is the spirit of evil (whose meteoric nature we have already explained earlier) aroused by the approach of the good not through a sharing but rather by a spreading out of forces. Hence only in connection with the decisive emergence of the good does evil also emerge quite decisively and as *such* (not as it first arose, but rather because the opposition is now first given in which it alone can appear complete and as such), [just] as, in turn, the very moment when the earth becomes for the second time desolate and empty becomes the moment of birth for the higher light of the spirit that was in the world from the beginning, but not comprehended by the darkness acting for itself, and in a yet closed and limited revelation; and, in order to counter personal and spiritual evil, the light of the spirit in fact appears likewise in the shape of a human person and as a mediator in order to re-establish the rapport between God and creation at the highest level.[60]

No need to expound further, except for one more point with which Schelling concluded this part three, connecting it directly with the main theme of the essay, namely the essence of freedom.[61] Granted that freedom consisted in the capacity for good and evil, as Schelling had postulated from the beginning, how was this capacity to be understood in the context of Schelling's transcendental story of creation, according to which evil was

---

[57] EHF 43; SSW I.7:376–377.   [58] EHF 43; SSW I.7:376–377.   [59] EHF 46; SSW I.7:380.
[60] EHF 46; SSW I.7:380.   [61] EHF 48–58; SSW I.7:382–394.

no mere negation but something positive? Here Schelling reviewed all past positions, in a way agreeing with all, yet also transcending them all by reframing the point at issue. Schelling agreed, following well-trodden lines of argumentation, that freedom to choose good or evil was not just a matter of an original indifference to either, the resolution of which was inherently unpredictable because the choice was contingent. He granted that choice, rather, had to be necessary, and to this extent predetermined,[62] but not in the sense (to which Jacobi had been adverse)[63] of being the product of a mechanical concatenation of events, each a possible determination of being in general. This sense of necessity, however conceptually refined, remained hostage to empiricism. Rather, the necessity that was equivalent to freedom had to be understood as Kant and his successors did. The Idealists, according to Schelling, had been the first to come up with the right conception of freedom. Namely, that an individual was free in the sense that whatever he or she did, they did it indeed necessarily, but only because the deed answered to the law of the individual's inner nature – the law, in other words, that made the individual what he or she was, by virtue of which they therefore spontaneously wanted whatever they did, even when from an external point of view this was to their physical or moral detriment. That this was the case, according to Schelling, was a matter of experience.

But what was at the origin of the thus assumed highly individualized law? It had to be an event conceived not as an occurrence *of* being (for this would have entailed a slide into empiricism) but, on the contrary, as constituting being in the first instance, in this sense as escaping time, or as eternal. According to Schelling, Fichte had been the first to provide the schema for such an event with his idea of a *Tathandlung* – an act which, as directed simply at itself *as act*, thereby also created the intelligible space for a first determinate *deed*, and thus, in the context of Fichte's Science, a primordial, yet already determined, moral self. The idea was already implicit in Kant's idea of law *as law*, that is, of lawfulness for the sake of lawfulness in general. This was a reflective product of reason that totally altered the meaning of otherwise merely empirical objects, investing them with moral significance. But, according to Schelling, Kant had failed to make explicitly clear, as Fichte subsequently did, that with his idea of the law he had transcended the whole realm of being *as being*, placing it in a larger ideal context whence it originated.[64]

---

[62] "We too assert a predestination but in a completely different sense." EHF 52; SSW I.7:387.

[63] But Jacobi is not mentioned. Mentioned, besides Buridan and his ass, are Descartes and Leibniz, Kant and Fichte.

[64] For Schelling on Kant and Fichte in this context, see EHF 50; SSW I.7:385–386. Of course, this is not true. Kant knew exactly what he was doing. The concept of the law opened a new ideal space

Schelling was now taking a further step. The question again: What was at the origin of the highly individualized law that made individuals necessarily, yet freely, want whatever they chose to be? Where was one to look for the event? In Schelling's story of creation, it was all part of the primordial contest of dark ground and light instigated by the latter's need for self-revelation, in the course of which the harmony in tension between the two was parsed out into an infinite number of beings, each differing by the specific degree to which either of the principles predominated in it. So it was that, as human individuals first became conscious of themselves, they found themselves already committed to ("thrown into," one is tempted to say) a determinate lifestyle, as if there had been for them an unconscious life before the conscious that determined the latter, one that was their conscious task to bring to consciousness.[65]

To cite Schelling's text:

> Once evil had been generally aroused in creation by the reaction of the ground to revelation, man apprehended himself from eternity in his individuality and selfishness, and all who are born are born with the dark principle of evil within even if this is raised to self-consciousness only with the coming on the scene of its opposite. As man is now, the good as light can be developed only from the dark principle through a divine *transmutation*. This original evil in man, [. . .] although wholly independent of freedom in relation to current empirical life, is still in origin his own act [for it presides over the individuation of his being] and for that reason alone original sin.[66]

Schelling proceeded to say that Kant was led in his later investigations to postulate the presence in man of a radical evil because, although he had risen in theory to the idea of a transcendental act that determined all human existence *ab origine*, at the same time he had remained faithful to the observation of moral facts. By contrast, Fichte, who had indeed grasped that act speculatively, fell prey, on the contrary, to the formalism that had otherwise prevailed in Kant's moral theory. He had thus ended up reducing the evil that antedates human experience to a lethargy of human nature – in fact, therefore, ignoring the reality of evil. Schelling was now in the position, or so he believed, of raising Kant's postulate to the level of Fichte's speculative insight.

Schelling could have also said that in Kant, since neither reason (because *per se* infallible) nor nature (because *per se* innocent) made room for evil, the

---

that transcended phenomenal being. But Kant, unlike Schelling, did not mythologize such a space. It was a space of reason.

[65] See EHF 52; SSW I.7:386–367.   [66] EHF 53; SSW I.7:388.

postulate of a radical evil in man had remained theoretically unanchored, its possibility unexplained and unexplainable. Schelling's story of creation provided, on the contrary, precisely the theoretical anchoring for the possibility of evil. But the nagging question returns. Kant, whatever the shortcoming of his theory, had at least saved himself from inconsequence by not claiming that his postulate would explain anything in particular. It had been meant simply as a way of saving common experience: of doing justice to ordinary moral language when dealing with the day-to-day vicissitudes of human existence. The postulate had only pragmatic value. Schelling, however, was claiming much more, and was he not, in this, hopelessly jumbling transcendental argument, imaginative constructs, and empirical material, all assembled in a vision for which he alone possessed intuitive evidence? It all depends on how sympathetic one cares to be to Schelling. On a sympathetic note the answer previously given still stands. Experience was the witness validating Schelling's story. It is indeed the case that human individuals find themselves, when first reflectively aware of themselves, already caught up in a web of intentions, of past genetic and social decisions working themselves out in time. They find themselves already implicated in a vocation which it is their life task either to continue promoting with intent or to extricate themselves from, normally both. In Schelling's vision, this vocation consisted essentially in the revelation of God. This was the factor that gave his story more than just the pragmatic value of Kant's religious constructs; but also the factor also that one needed not accept, for it required an assent in faith, a commitment in trust to Schelling's insight.

4.3.3   The Rest of the Essay

The rest of the essay was dedicated to an elaboration of Schelling's vision of God's revelation. Part four gave the outline of a phenomenology of the genesis of good and evil and at the same time also a definition of what Schelling understood by religion. To cite:

> This is the beginning of sin, that man transgresses from authentic Being into non-Being, from truth into lies, from light into darkness, in order to become a self-creating ground and, with the power of the *centrum* which he has within himself, to rule over all things. For the feeling still remains [in the sinner] that he was all things, namely, in and with God; for that reason he strives once more to return there, but for himself, and not where he might be all things, namely, in God.[67]

---

[67] EHF 55; SSW I.7:390.

[The] radiant glimpse of life in the depths of darkness in every individual flares up in the sinner into a consuming fire.[68]

The true good [is] effected only through a divine magic, namely through the immediate presence of what has Being in consciousness and cognition. An arbitrary good is just as impossible as an arbitrary evil. True freedom is in harmony with a holy necessity, the likes of which we perceive in essential cognition, when spirit and heart, bound only by their own law, freely affirm what is necessary. If evil exists in the discord of the two principles, then good can exist only in the complete accord of the two.[69]

We understand religiosity in the original practical meaning of the word. It is conscientiousness or that one act in accordance with what one knows and does not contradict the light of cognition in one's conduct. An individual for whom this contradiction is impossible, not in a human, physical, or psychological, but rather in a divine way, is called religious, conscientious in the highest sense of the word.[70]

No less than Hegel, Schelling had no sympathy with the philosophers of feeling [*Empfindungsphilosophen*] who voided religion of all objective content. In this part of the essay, he went out of his way to criticize the Romantics' figure of "the beautiful soul," in ways which (as we shall see) reminds one of Hegel's *Phenomenology* of 1807.

But it was in part five, where Schelling raised the question of God's freedom, and in part six, where the issue was the vocation of the created world, that Schelling's vision came to completion. At the question whether creation flowed from God necessarily, Schelling revisited his account of the internal economy of God's life. That all things have a ground meant, as he had already said, that existence is the product of an order being impressed upon an otherwise chaotic base ("*Basis*," another of Schelling's words for "ground") that resists it. It resists it because, whereas the order would open up within it distinctions between "other" and "other" and thus inject light into the base, thereby also making possible the effusion of love, the base would rather be just itself. This, in effect, was what being chaotic meant: being impervious to otherness. But the point that Schelling now stressed was that precisely this imperviousness constitutes personality. An individual would not be seriously open to an "other" without at the same time being herself an "other," that is, without retrenching back upon herself. The life of personality is therefore a constant struggle for love despite the inherent selfishness rooted in the ground of all existence. But selfishness was for Schelling another word for evil. It also was a necessary condition for at least the created personality. And since Schelling conceived "personality"

---

[68] EHF 56; SSW I.7:391. [69] EHF 56; SSW I.7:391. [70] EHF 56–57; SSW I.7:392–393.

very broadly, dispersing it in degrees across the whole of nature, and did the same for evil, he could poetically evoke the image of a "veil of dejection that is spread over all nature, the deep indestructible melancholy of all life. Joy must have suffering, suffering must be transfigured into joy."[71] As for God, Schelling explained that the dark ground/light complexity in him is necessary for him to be a person, as God indeed is. Nonetheless, there is no evil in God, for in him the principle of light has totally contained the principle of darkness and, by the same token, has also appropriated its power, sublimating[72] it into infinite love. The dark ground does not confront it as an independent condition: "Even in [God] there is a source of sadness [because of the presence in him of the darkness of the ground]; not one, however, that can ever come to actuality, but rather one that serves only the eternal joy of overcoming."[73] Pride, in which moral evil essentially consists, lies in the belief that one can be like God, totally self-contained. But this, of course, is a self-delusional belief which can only be countered by submission to the universal order that light makes possible.

In this, Schelling was only repeating what he had already said, but more vividly, except for the one extra claim that God is a person, a "He," exactly as it was conceived in traditional theology or imagined by the common believer. This was the claim Schelling required for confronting the just posed question of God's freedom in creation. God, of course, had created freely – with a freedom, however, in which there was nothing arbitrary, for to reveal itself was of the nature of light. God could not *not* have created. In this, Schelling openly sided with Leibniz. Unlike Leibniz, however, but like Spinoza, Schelling also held that the actually existing world is the only one possible. It flows from God necessarily – not indeed *more geometrico*, as for Spinoza, but organically, as an existential outpouring consistent with a person's freedom. Leibniz had been wrong in thinking that there could have been worlds other than the present one; that the latter is only the best among all possible worlds; its necessity, therefore, only moral. And Schelling attributed this mistake to Leibniz's proclivity, common to all rationalists, to think of possibility abstractly. The other worlds Leibniz was comparing the present with were only products of reflection, void of determinate content. Nonetheless, Schelling could understand why Leibniz would have wanted to distinguish logical from moral necessity. He wanted to capture with the latter the feeling of gratuity that the presence of the created world elicits. This feeling is undeniable, but it is wrong to associate it in any way with the arbitrary and contingent. Rather,

---

[71] EHF 62–63; SSW I.7:399.　　[72] My word.　　[73] EHF 62 (translation rephrased); SSW I.7:399.

it was already captured, according to Schelling, in the phenomenon of freedom understood as a personalized existential outpouring.

Other consequences followed. There is no evil in God, whether considered as light or dark ground, even though evil emerges out of the internal economy of the divine life. Did God have prescience *ab æterno* of all that would happen in the created world? Of course. In this sense the Word was in God already a system. But how could God then be absolved from the charge that he is responsible for the evils in the world, since he knew that they would occur, yet let them be? For this, Schelling went straight back to Leibniz, albeit duly modified to fit his picture of God. To cite:

> If God had not revealed himself because of evil, evil would have triumphed over the good and love. The Leibnizian conception of *conditio sine qua non* can only be applied to the ground so that the latter arouse the creativity of the will (the possible principle of evil) as the condition under which alone the will to love could be realized. We have likewise already shown why God does not resist the [inchoate, chaotic] will of the ground or abolish it. This would be precisely as much as to say that God would abolish the conditions of his existence, that is, his own personality. Thus, in order that there be no evil, there would have to be no God himself.[74]

Accordingly, in the sixth and final part Schelling raised the question that had traditionally motivated all theodicy: "Will evil end and how? Does creation have a final purpose, and, if this is so, why is it not reached immediately, why does what is perfect not exist right from the beginning?"[75] The answer had already been given: "Because God is life, not merely a Being. All life has a destiny, however, and is subject to suffering and becoming. God has thus freely subordinated himself to this as well. [. . .] Being becomes aware of itself only in becoming."[76] The rest of the essay was dedicated to this final claim.

In effect, these last pages were a reprise of the beginning of the essay and, like the beginning, also a statement, now renewed, of Schelling's idea of pantheism. Skipping over the usual cascade of metaphors, and of Christian and pagan soteriological themes, Schelling's first step was to clarify how God as One stands with respect to God as ground and light. It now transpires that God, thus taken as at the origin of everything, including

---

[74] EHF 65–66 (slightly modified); SSW I.7:402–403. [75] EHF 66; SSW I.7:404.
[76] EHF 66; SSW I.7:404. It is remarkable how Schelling can sound like Hegel. As we shall argue in Chapters 5 and 6, also for Hegel being is whatever it is only by way of an achievement, that is, by becoming *it*. But the conceptual framework is totally different.

"being," has to be characterized as an *Ungrund*, a "non-ground," in the sense that his unity, since it cannot be committed to any determination in particular (which would compromise its originality), must be one of *indifference*. God was *ab origine* simply a *neither-nor*, out of which there broke out (just why and how Schelling never quite said) the duality of "being" (God *in-itself*, or as base or dark ground) and light or love.[77] This duality was not to be conceived as an opposition, for opposition would have detracted from God's oneness. On the contrary, the two simply repeat this oneness, each in its way but equivalently.

Whether this further note did much to clarify Schelling's earlier claim that all being requires a ground, or, for that matter, whether it absolved him of the charge that he was dealing only in abstractions, is doubtful. Nonetheless, it provided a smooth transition to Schelling's renewed narrative of the creation of the world – "renewed" in the sense of being further developed rather than modified in any significant way. Previously, creation seemed to be the product of a contest between the two principles of darkness and light. Obviously it could not have been unqualifiedly so, for contest entails opposition, and there was no opposition in God. In the narrative Schelling now offered, it was rather the symbiotic relationship of the two principles in God, previously only alluded to, that took central stage, as well as the fact that in this symbiotic relation the principle of light holds, though not ontic precedence, certainly pride of vocation.[78] The principle of light, or love, embraces the dark principle for its own purposes, even indulges it by providing for it the factor of "otherness" by virtue of which it ceases to be just a desire for existence in general but rather acquires determination, thus realizing itself as something singular. Only then, in this realization, does it become actual evil. Finite human personality, or, for that matter, the quasi-personality of prehuman nature, consists in this singular realization of the dark principle. Evil *is* finite personality.

At this point one could indeed begin to speak of a contest, as Schelling had done earlier. For, as he had already said, for each irruption of determinate evil there is a countering determinate realization of God – God as the infinite person who, in order to overcome evil, has in Christ even taken up sin upon himself. This is the contest of good and evil. It is definitely not

---

[77] EHF 69; SSW I.7:407.
[78] This is my gloss. I am trying to save Schelling from an inconsistency in his narrative. How could the two principles be equivalent in the economy of God's life, yet, in the process by which creation makes its return to the oneness of God, it is the principle of light (consciousness) that prevails at process-end, the dark principle being totally constrained by it? "Vocation" in the gloss is an apt word, for Schelling has just said that "all life has a destiny."

make-believe. Nonetheless, its outcome is decided from the beginning, for that there is a contest at all is due to love's intention to realize itself by letting evil do the same in the first instance; to this end it has even provided evil with the required source of determination. The contest's purpose is the final differentiation of good and evil: the translation into actual existence of the darkness/light duality. But how is the final victory of the good to be manifested? Judging from Schelling's use at this point of Christian imagery, it is achieved in a universal community of individuals who would indeed have been evil in their singularized existence, except that they have overcome their selfishness, consciously subordinating themselves to the effusiveness of love. In their consciousness, it is God's own consciousness that is thus realized. The original *indifference* to determinations in God-as-One (the *non-ground*) is thus repeated but in the medium of an *achieved* non-differentiation, such as is consummated in universal love and universal consciousness. The community of love that Schelling apparently had in mind was one in which the individual members, in loving one another, know that in them God loves himself.[79] It is also noteworthy that in the Fichte of 1806 the absorption of all individuals into a common consciousness would have been the upshot of a final universal enlightenment.[80]

As for the evil thus defeated by this final subordination of all to the Son of God, and also the Son's final subordination to God ("for even the *spirit* [the Son] is not yet the highest thing"),[81] Schelling claimed that "when it is entirely separated from the good, [it] also no longer *exists* as evil. It could only have been active through the (misused) good that was in it without its being conscious of it. [. . .] It remains behind as desire, as an eternal hunger and thirst for actuality, yet it is unable to step out of potentiality."[82] Thus reduced back to the dark ground, evil no longer stands in contradiction to God. Like Lucifer in Christian mythology (though Schelling did not refer to the myth explicitly at this point), evil exists as overcome, not in the sense of being finally revealed never to have in fact been evil but by being rendered impotent, precipitated into the depth of a hell where it remains contained, in its perverse way manifesting the power of God.

This, as of 1809, was Schelling's full narrative. One cannot not help noticing in it, if not an internal logical discrepancy (what would "logical" mean in this context anyway?), at least an artistic flaw. Since God, whether

---

[79] I am interpreting EHF 67–68; SSW I.7:404–405.
[80] We shall consider this 1806 text of Fichte in Chapter 6.   [81] EHF 68; SSW I.7:405.
[82] EHF 67; SSW I.7:404–405.

as One, or as light and dark ground, is such only in potency; since only in creation is he actualized in necessarily singularized existence, it would have made for a more internally consistent story if Schelling had avowed that only in creation does God literally *discover* what he has created, and thereby also reveals to himself what, prior to creation, he was only *in itself*. As the narrative stood, there was a disconnect between, on the one hand, the stress earlier in the essay on the contingent and irrational in experience, on the irrational remainder or irreducible leftover even in God's inner life of the dark ground's gravitating pull, and, on the other, Schelling's claim in part four that God's Word was a System from the start; that all that happens in creation is therefore predetermined and presciently known by God. The claim that the present world was the only possible one also did not fit well with the earlier narrative. To be sure, Schelling was right. Leibniz's "possible worlds" were the product of logical abstraction and therefore empty of content. Nonetheless, they stood for the kind of worlds that would have come to be if human individuals had made decisions in the past other than they had actually made. They might at least have had actual historical content. Although no longer existentially effective, these possible worlds were nonetheless witness to the fact that the same individuals were responsible for the present world. In this sense, although ineffective, they still were existentially relevant. They stood for the openness of the future, the unpredictability of the irrational remainder that, again as Schelling had stressed earlier in the essay, made for the melancholy of finite existence.

All this was negated by the traditional doctrine of predetermination and divine prescience with which Schelling concluded. This might have been a sign of how much Schelling was still beholden to past metaphysics or, perhaps, of a still abiding fear of straying too far from religious orthodoxy. Whatever the psychological motivation, Schelling apparently wanted to have it both ways: on the one hand, to do justice to the becoming of nature, together with the turbulence (evil included) that goes with it; on the other, to retain the pantheistic vision of reality as absolute One. The net result was the vision of a becoming that has already become, self-contained and attained. In this vision, however, the finite reality normally associated with nature is inevitably degraded to mere appearance – exactly in keeping with the formalism that Schelling decried in Kant and Fichte. After all, if one were to abstract in Schelling's narrative from all the imaginative constructs about the economy of God's life into which he in fact reflected the vicissitudes of human existence – by the same token, however, also eviscerated them as just human – would the universe that emerged at the end not look precisely like the well-ordered, preordained and self-contained universe that the Enlightenment celebrated but Jacobi rejected because it negated human personality? Schelling was still a rationalist in the classical sense but one in bad faith, for he was hiding the rationalism in bad poetry, as Heine thought.

But we are perhaps being unfair to Schelling. It is therefore important to take a look, however brief, at later works that took as their subject precisely the structure and content of historical reality.

4.4 Of "Past" and "Future"

Of interest now are two texts, both well known in the literature, that directly relate to the just noted flaw in Schelling's Freedom Essay. The first is *Die Weltalter* (*The Ages of the World*), a manuscript originally intended as three parts treating respectively "the past," "the present," and "the future." In its three extant drafts, however, the text never goes beyond the "past." These were drafts penned between 1811 and 1815. The second draft, which is our source, dates to 1813.[83] The second text is much later. It consists of Schelling's notes for a series of ten lectures delivered in Berlin, in 1842, as a *Historical-Critical Introduction to the Philosophy of Mythology: or The Grounding of Positive Philosophy*.[84] The first text, closer in time to the Freedom Essay, still pursued its metaphysical narrative. The other, at two decades distance, repeated the narrative but as evinced by myths. It is this juxtaposition of contrasting methods, as well as their temporal distance, that makes the two texts significant, both singly and in juxtaposition.

Regarding the first text, we do not know how Schelling would have treated the "present" and the "future" in the other two parts if he had ever got to them. But it made sense that, for the "past," he would have continued the *ab origine* narrative of the earlier essay. "The past is known [*gewußt*], the present is recognized [*erkannt*], the future is divined [*geahnded*]," Schelling declared in his opening statement.[85] The past, precisely because it was *past*, was already all there, hence in principle also already known. For this reason true science, or, more precisely, *achieved* true science, had to be, as Plato's dialectic had become at the end, simply history (ἱστορία), the narrative of what was *there* and was known to be *there*. But the problem lay in the fact that this knowledge is unconscious,

---

[83] Schelling (1997) for the English translation, cited as WA.

[84] We have already referred to it, in Sections 4.1 and 4.2. See Schelling (2007b) for the English translation, cited as GPP. This series was among the lectures Schelling delivered between 1841 and 1854. Kierkegaard, Engels, Bakunin, and Arnold Ruge were among Schelling's auditors.

[85] WA 113; DWA III.

locked up into the recesses of nature. For this reason, while Schelling could admire theosophy because of its closeness to nature, which made it so much richer than the empty abstractions of some philosophy or the effeteness of some art, he still rejected intuitionism as access to either true science or living art. Method was required to unseal the secrets of the past, and this meant that, in order to give way to science as ἱστορία, thought first had to engage in dialectical thinking.[86] Past methodology proceeded from the ideal, in order from there subsequently to reach down to the natural. Schelling's prospective method was the reverse: "beginning with the unconscious existence [bewußtlosen Dasein] of the Eternal [in material nature], science leads it [i.e., this existence] to the supreme transfiguration in a divine consciousness."[87] Intermediary concepts are essential to this process of transfiguration.[88] Here is where dialectical thinking plays its indispensable function.

This statement of Schelling's in the introductory pages of the draft was significant. It set the tone for the rest. It might well be that inchoate in Schelling's idealism there was a commitment to materialism (as there was in Spinoza's naturalism); also that Schelling might well have been influential for Marx.[89] Nonetheless, the fact remains that in this draft, no less than in the earlier essay, Schelling's foremost preoccupation was to reassert his pantheistic view of reality. Even when what was immediately at issue was the unconscious of nature, it was clear that the narrative was from beginning to end about God's presence everywhere.

Where, according to Schelling, had one to turn to unlock the secrets of the past? The answer, of course, was the essence of the human being (the same essence that Schelling had placed at the *centrum* of the universe in the Freedom Essay), for it is through this essence that humanity transcends itself and finds itself already in touch with the Eternal.

> Man must be granted an essence outside and above the world, for how could he, alone of all creatures, retrace the long past of developments from the present back into the deepest night of the past, how could he alone rise up to the beginning of things unless there were in him an essence from the beginning of times? Drawn from the source of things and akin to it, what is eternal of the soul carries with it a knowledge of creation.[90]

---

[86] See WA 117–120; DWA 116–118. Schelling is talking in general about the recent advances of science, where by "science" he obviously means his own philosophy of nature.

[87] WA 119 (I have replaced "presence" with "existence"); DWA 118.

[88] See WA 117–118; DWA 116.   [89] Frank (1989).

[90] WA 114 (slightly altered: "carries with it a knowledge of creation" instead of the translator's "has a con-science/con-sciousness [*Mit-Wissenschaft*] of creation"; DWA 112.

Hence, drawing on a supposed immediate experience of time, Schelling distinguished two principles in the essence of the human being (in the "soul") which he immediately proceeded to paint on a cosmic scale, in reality in general but above all in God:

> Whoever takes time only as it presents itself feels a conflict of two principles in it; one strives forward, driving toward development, and one holds back, inhibiting [*hemmend*] and striving against development. If this other principle were to provide no resistance, then there would be no time, because development would occur in an uninterrupted flash rather than successively; yet if the other principle were not constantly overcome by the first, there would be absolute rest, death, standstill and hence there would, again, be no time. But if we consider both of those principles to be equally active in one and the same essence, we will have contradiction straight away.
>
> It is necessary to conceive of these principles in everything that is – indeed, in being [*Seyn*] itself.[91]

The two principles – *Seyn* itself and the *Seyendes*; or being and existing-being; the inchoate and the explicit; the utterable and the uttered, the two united in the act of uttering[92] – were clearly the counterpart of the dark ground and light duality of the earlier essay. Schelling now took them to generate contradiction rather than just opposition. Like opposition, however, contradiction was also essential to life: "Only contradiction drives us – indeed, forces us – to action. Contradiction is in fact the venom of life, and all vital motion is nothing but the attempt to overcome this poisoning."[93]

But Schelling (perhaps with an eye to Hegel) was not willing to let contradiction have the last word, or in any way to be the governing principle in the economy of existence, no less than in the case of opposition:

> If activity in general or a particular deed or action were the First, then contradiction would be eternal. But movement never occurs for its own sake; all movement is only for the sake of rest. If all acting did not have the calm and restful will of the background, it would annihilate itself, for all movement seeks only rest, and rest is its nourishment or that from which alone it takes its power and sustains itself.[94]

As Schelling also argued:

> If we recognize contradiction, then we also recognize non-contradiction. If the former is motion in time, then non-contradiction is the essence of

---

[91] WA 122; DWA 123.   [92] Schelling shifts from image to image.   [93] English, p. 124; DWA 123.
[94] WA 133; DWA 132.

eternity. Indeed, if all of life is truly only a movement to raise itself up from contradiction, then time itself is nothing but a constant yearning for eternity. And if non-contradiction persists forever behind all contradiction, then it follows that something always persists behind and above all time that is not itself in time.[95]

Just as in the Freedom Essay, Schelling's main preoccupation was still to hold on, behind all oppositions or contradictions, to a fundamental union, one that could only be of indifference to the determinations that otherwise generated time. This union of indifference he now called the Eternal. Time was only its external manifestation. To cite again:

> In the unity – presently under consideration of being and existing-being – it is not even the case that one of these two is inactive; rather, both are inactive, for this is an inert opposition, or one in which the opposites are indifferent to each other. They are present as utterable, not even as actually uttered. For this reason, the principle of contradiction does not come into question; its application begins only when this unity comes to an end.[96]
>
> We can therefore say of *this* – which is supposed to express the opposition but does not – that it both is existing-being as well as being and yet *is not* [existing-being and being].[97]

Schelling elaborated the claim at length, at one point also divagating on the logical relations that obtains in a judgment between subject, predicate, and copula and between judgment, concept, and syllogism, using such relations as indicative of the internal economy of reality. However, whatever the tropes or the arguments, his intention was clear. It still was, as it had been for Schelling from the beginning, to defend his monistic vision of reality.

Accordingly, what Schelling referred to as "the great riddle of all times"[98] cropped up in the present draft just as it had in the earlier essay. Namely, the riddle of "how anything could have come from what is neither externally active nor is anything in itself," that is, the indifferent One which is the matrix of all differentiation. And the answer was still the same:

> [In Eternity] existing-being does not oppose itself to being and does not recognize itself in being. Being is, for its part, perfectly indifferent towards existing-being. But the more this composure is profoundly deep and intrinsically full of bliss, the sooner must a quiet longing produce itself in eternity, without eternity either helping or knowing. This is a longing to come to itself, to find and savor itself; it is an urge to become conscious *of which Eternity itself does not become conscious.*[99]

---

[95] WA 125; DWA 124.   [96] WA 128–129; DWA 128.   [97] WA 131; DWA 131.
[98] WA 135; DWA 135.   [99] WA 136; DWA 136.

However unconsciously, the will to creation for the sake of self-consciousness had to arise, and the stage was thus set for Schelling's further cosmic narrative. The being/existing-being opposition in the original essence, the first offspring of creation that lay deep in the human unconscious, was repeated in particularized form, first, with the emergence of nature, it took the form of a lack,[100] the blind hunger for the lost essence, and, subsequently, with the progressive satisfaction of this hunger, in ever more concrete forms of life. The process culminated in the human soul, with spirit,[101] which summed up all of nature and thus brought to consciousness nature's original essence. By the same token, the process also returned to the union of indifference that Schelling had called the "non-ground" in the Freedom Essay. It returned to it, however, in the form of a totality of otherwise opposing particulars, all absorbed into a universal system of necessary inner connections.[102] Spirit, while raising nature up to itself, at the same time brought the non-ground down to the *here and now*, thus realizing its supposedly original inchoate desire to become conscious of itself:

> For spirit – or the highest unity produced through its [the creative will's] desire – is by nature one with indifference or eternity. For this reason, spirit is not only the unity of opposites, as was assumed until now; it is at the same time the link between eternity and the life built up from below, a life that already presents itself ever more clearly as the instrument of eternity.[103]

There is no need to expound farther. Despite somewhat different language and a more complicated dialectic,[104] Schelling's narrative was still essentially the same as in the Freedom Essay. It included his account of freedom,[105] whether human or divine, which he repeated in a somewhat curtailed fashion, still emphasizing, however, that Eternity had seen "everything in the immediate ectype of its essence."[106] Schelling marked the boundary between the past and what followed precisely at the point where the Eternal finally attained awareness of itself as "being and existing-being," the event for the sake of which the whole process of creation has

---

[100] WA 139; DWA 137.   [101] WA 143ff; DWA 143ff.   [102] WA 144–145; DWA 144–145.

[103] WA 147; DWA 147. WA 153; DWA 154: "Spirit cannot pull this being of eternity to itself without thereby positing it as object in relations to the eternally-existing-being, thereby making a division in eternity and finally also moving that very innermost principle, the still concealed uttering of itself, to action."

[104] Schelling also adduces many details regarding the unfolding of creation, including a reflection on mesmerism and natural sleep, which Schelling takes to be not unlike the mesmeric (WA 158; DWA 160), and a distinction between the Lord and Wisdom (WA 164–165; DWA 167–168).

[105] WA 156; DWA 157.   [106] WA 155; DWA 156.

occurred.[107] He concluded with a comment that he apparently took to apply also to the human situation,[108] but which for him had cosmic significance in the first instance. As self-awareness came on the scene – be it of the Eternal, as just described, or of the individual human being taking the decision that would determine its whole life[109] – this awareness was *ipso facto* precipitated into the unconscious. It had to be so precipitated for the sake of life itself, which consists precisely in the laborious process of retrieving what had thus been concealed. In this, apparently, lay the future, according to Schelling.

But Schelling never went on to the "present" and the "future," as planned. So far as human experience was concerned, his parting comment did display, of course, much perspicacity. It is perhaps the case that repression is at the origin of everyone's life history; also that such a repression is unconsciously willed for the sake of living. This was indeed a claim that would have been perfectly acceptable if stated as applying to a *de facto* situation of the human psyche; if, moreover, the situation itself were left open to creative and therefore essentially unpredictable changes. It would also have been acceptable – if one was willing to play along with Schelling's narrative – to paint the claim on a cosmic scale, provided this was also done as *de facto*. But Schelling was saying much more, whether at the merely human or the cosmic scale – namely, that the repression was orchestrated *ab origine* for the sake of satisfying the Eternal's inchoate desire for self-utterance; also, that the repressed story about the Eternal (which included the story of every human individual as well) was already all written in the Eternal's ectype and only needed to be gone through piecemeal. But what kind of a future would it be in which, in effect, nothing truly new would ever happen? This was the jarring element in Schelling' narrative about time, another version of the flaw we found in the earlier essay regarding freedom. On the one hand, Schelling wanted to include a moment of finality in his monism (to differentiate it from Spinoza's); on the other, for the sake of the same monism (the postulated eternal rest), he undermined the seriousness of the finality by *a priori* foreclosing the "new" that would have kept intention and achievement truly apart. What remains to be seen is whether Schelling's postulated future might have in any way relieved this conceptual discomfort.

---

[107] WA 167; DWA 169: "We thus see everything ready for a decision, and for the Eternal, this last stage in which it becomes aware of itself marks the boundary between the past state and the one to follow."

[108] See WA 181; DWA 183.   [109] But was in fact predetermined on a cosmic scale.

4.5   The Creation of God

We might get a glimpse of this future in the second text, Schelling's 1842 lectures on mythology.[110] The aim of these lectures was clear. They documented "the creation of God," [111] where the genitive had to be understood in both a subjective and an objective sense. The lectures in fact picked up precisely at the point where, according to the unfinished earlier *Ages of the World*, awareness comes on the scene. On the one hand, the Eternal acquires objective shape; in this, it creates an "other." On the other hand, its subjectively inchoate desire for self-utterance is thereby also actively realized; in creating the other it therefore equally creates itself. At issue in the lectures, in other words, was God's self-creation. This explained why, although the gods of mythology were for Schelling clearly the objects of representations, they were not for that reason any the less active participants in the course of history; nor were the humans, the carriers of the representations, any the less beholden to them as real entities. The gods were not invented or in any way deliberately constructed. They emerged in the course of the history of human consciousness on their own, just like other natural events, according to laws to which consciousness itself was subjected.[112] To cite:

> The mythological ideas are neither invented nor voluntarily taken on. – Products of a process independent of thinking and willing, they were of unambiguous and urgent reality for the consciousness subjected to this process. Peoples as well as individuals are only tools of this process, which they do not survey, which they serve without understanding it. It is not up to them to elude these representations, to take them up or not to take them up; for they do not *come* to them externally, but rather they *are* in them without their being conscious of how; for they come out of the inner part of consciousness itself, to which they present themselves with a necessity that permits no doubt about their truth.[113]

The procession of the gods was still a continuation of the process by which nature, to use Schelling's typical term, is potentiated, thereby acquiring ever new and self-contained determinations. This was a process to which, in Schelling words, the gods were "fated."[114] Mythology was literally the becoming of the living God,[115] God's story:

---

[110] For an instructive study of the late Schelling, see E. A. Beach (1994).
[111] For a detailed discussion of the plan and composition of Schelling's late philosophy, and of its transmission, see Tilliette (1970), vol. 2, pp. 27–36.
[112] See HCI 89; SSW II.1:124–125.   [113] HCI 135; SSW II.1:194.   [114] HCI 134; SSW II.1:194.
[115] See regarding the God of Abraham, HCI 116; SSW II.1:165.

Considered objectively, mythology is as what it presents itself: *actual the-ogony*, the history of the gods. [. . .] Considered *subjectively*, or as according to its coming into being, mythology is a *theogonic process*. It is [. . .] a process in general, which consciousness actually completes, namely in such a way that it is obliged to tarry in the individual moments, and in the one following constantly hangs on to the preceding one, and thus experiences that movement in the proper sense.[116]

One must admire Schelling. In the lectures, he methodically detailed all the current theories regarding the origin and the meaning of myths, just as methodically rejecting them all on the general ground (as he elaborated for each) that their principles were *ad hoc* and rationalistic in intention. Hume, incidentally, repeatedly came in for criticism, at one point for displaying what Schelling thought an out of character rationalism.[117] Moreover, true to his avowed commitment to empirically ascertainable history, Schelling brought in as evidence for his arguments vast material drawn from a variety of religious traditions. Schelling knew all that there was to be known about myths at the time.

However, we cannot, and need not, dwell on this mass of details. Reduced to its bare minimum, Schelling's theory is easily stated. Since it had to be scientific, and since science excluded the importation of contingent hypotheses, the theory required *a priori* principles. And it was clear, even though Schelling never said this much explicitly, that the *a priori* was the internal economy of the Eternal as already developed in the *Ages of the World*, and even before that, in the Freedom Essay. The becoming of God in the medium of human consciousness occurred in three stages. Keeping in mind the distinction in German between *Geschichte*, or history as a course of events, and *Historie*, or the record of such events, one had to posit a first stage of *absolute* pre-history (*Geschichte*) at which consciousness was still dense, internally undifferentiated; where there could as yet not have been any issue of beginning or end, hence of time and becoming. A second stage, which Schelling designated as *relative* pre-history (*Geschichte*), was transitional. This was the stage at which there arose in the otherwise dense consciousness a first stirring of the idea of God. This idea accounted, according to Schelling, for what must have been the original monotheism of the human race. That monotheism had preceded polytheism was at the time the generally accepted view.[118] Schelling agreed. However, as

---

[116] HCI 137–138; SSW II.1:198.
[117] HCI 58; SSW II.1:79. The German philologist F. Creuzer was the only one whose theories Schelling praised for their insight.
[118] It was a belief essential to the Enlightenment rationalism. See Lessing, *The Education of the Human Race*, § 6.

generally accepted, the view was based on the belief that monotheism was the natural product of reason, and, since this reason stood unadulterated in the pristine mind yet unclouded by the pressures of natural needs, monotheism would naturally have originally been the possession of humankind in general. Polytheism was the result of the temporal degeneration of this presumed pristine reason. Schelling held the opposite. Original monotheism was natural in the sense, rather, of being pre-rational.[119] As monotheism, therefore, it was only relative – "relative" because the Oneness of the God that was its object remained undifferentiated, hence ineffective as a principle.

This second stage was for Schelling still pre-historical (*Geschichte*) but only *relatively* so, because, despite the fact that this stage still eschewed temporality, it must nonetheless have harbored (because of the idea of God stirring in it) the event (the *crisis*)[120] which first led to the dispersion of humankind into many *peoples*. This stage concurrently also led to the dispersion of the otherwise undifferentiated one idea of God into many particularized ideas.[121] Since this event, just like the first stirring in dense consciousness of the idea of God, itself escaped both time and comprehension,[122] it was not the object of the historical record (*Historie*)[123] that Schelling's contemporary philologists were busy compiling. Nonetheless, it was the event that inaugurated the temporal becoming of God in recognizable particular shapes. The second stage in the creation of consciousness that harbored it was thus "transitional" in the sense that, although itself pre-historical (both as *Geschichte* and *Historie*), it nonetheless gave rise to both *Geschichte* and *Historie*. This was the third stage, the truly temporal and historical becoming of God.

Polytheism thus was for Schelling not the deterioration of reason but its first product. And by "polytheism" Schelling meant first and foremost what he called "successive polytheism," that is, not just a plurality of gods but the historical fact that a system of such gods, each expressing some particular aspect of the Divine, would in time give place to another. He meant the transition from one system of gods to another that marked a new recordable age in the temporal becoming of both

---

[119] Schelling shared this view with Creuzer.
[120] In Greek "crisis" means both division and judgment.
[121] See HCI 91–93; SSW II.1:127–131. The whole of Lecture 6 is relevant.
[122] Schelling curiously says that it cannot "yet" be understood, as if it might be so understood at a later time and were not, rather, pre-sense. Schelling is constantly on the verge of setting up a *hiatus irrationalis* which he then tries to cross. See HCI 134; SSW II.1:192.
[123] HCI 147; SSW II.1:211.

consciousness and God. According to Schelling, it was only in this third stage, where reason was effective, that revelation,[124] such as entailed a subjective relation of God to an individual consciousness, was possible, or, for that matter, the possibility of a true monotheism was also established.

Schelling concluded his series of lectures by arguing for the relevance of his philosophy of mythology to religion, art, and science in general. But he prided himself especially on having finally established the philosophy of history that Herder had left unanchored on a truly scientific basis. He had done so by providing for it a starting point and, presumably, an end.[125] History was the temporal revelation of God's inner life: this was its immanent *a priori*. As for the meaning of mythology – the question that according to Schelling was uppermost in everybody's mind – this is what he had to say:

> How was it possible that the peoples of antiquity were not only able to bestow faith in those religious ideas – which appear to us thoroughly nonsensical and contrary to reason – but were able to bring to them the most serious, in part painful, sacrifices [? ... The answer is,] because mythology is not something that emerged artificially [e.g., by way of contrived allegorical explanation], but is rather something that emerged naturally – indeed, under the given presupposition, with necessity – *form* and *content*, *matter* and *outer appearance*, cannot be differentiated in it. The ideas are not first present in another form, but rather they emerge only in, and thus also at the same time with, the form.[126]
>
> The meaning of *mythology* can [thus] only be the meaning of the *process* by which it emerges into being.[127] [...] Mythology is not *allegorical*; it is *tautegorical*.[128] To mythology the gods are actually existing essences, gods that are not something *else*, do not *mean* something else, but rather *mean* only what they are.[129]

Whatever one might otherwise think of Schelling's cosmogonic super-structure, one must grant that his understanding of the nature of myth was impeccable. In this he stood head and shoulders above the rationalist philologists of the day.

---

[124] See HCI 100; SSW II.1:194. Creuzer had instead assumed that revelation was the source of the first, natural, kind of monotheism.

[125] See HCI 160; SSW II.1:229–230.   [126] HCI 136; SSW II.1:195.   [127] HCI 135; SSW II.1:194.

[128] Expressing the same subject, but with a difference (*Oxford Dictionary, sub voce*). Schelling borrowed the word from Coleridge.

[129] HCI 136; SSW II.1:196. See also, HCI 147–148; SSW II.1:212–213: "No single moment of mythology is the truth, only the process as a whole. [...] Indeed to this extent every individual polytheistic religion is indeed a false one [...] – but polytheism considered in the entirety of its successive moments is the way to truth and to this extent truth itself."

4.6 History As an Issue

I have repeatedly stressed how much Fichte and Schelling mirrored one another despite outward appearances and despite their different onto-logical agendas: how their method was equally phenomenological in character and equally intent on bringing to light the *a priori* of experience. And since the two were also equally motivated by an underlying monistic view of reality, their common problem was to demonstrate that, despite having to posit a distinction between the One and the Many, there needed not be an irrational gap separating the two: the One *was* the Many, and the Many *was* the One. However, where for Fichte the claim led to what I have called an attitude of ontological quietism, in Schelling's case it led rather to ontological exuberance – even enthusiasm (*Schwärmerei*), as the unsympa-thetic reader might say. This was a crucial difference separating the two, rooted in the ambiguity inherent in the very monism they shared; one, moreover, that affected their respective attitude towards history.

There is yet another point of contact between Fichte and Schelling that must be noted, the most fundamental. We said that for Schelling the story of God that unfolded across the ages in the succession of myths was fated from the beginning. It proceeded according to a predetermined logic internal to it that also determined the story of humankind, inherently bound as the latter was to the story of God. The story of the one was equally the story of the other. All this sounds worlds apart from anything that would come from Fichte. Yet Schelling was thereby making a point about experience, and about the place of the historical individual within it, that was not unlike Fichte's in 1804, except that at issue for Fichte was the commanding presence of "evidence" and his favorite medium of expression was the imagery associated with light. This is of course a significant difference. Nonetheless, the point they made about experience was the same. When one is engaged in it, one finds oneself already in the grip of a self-justifying objective truth to which one is committed even before being aware of being so committed. One finds oneself just as involved in the story of God, just as much already living the myths in which God has at any age become incarnate, as one finds oneself given over to the inevitabil-ity of "the evident" whenever and wherever the latter announces itself. The individual so engaged, moreover, does not come to exist as the individual she is except in the moment, and by virtue, of thus finding herself so engaged, whether as given over to God's life or to the light of evidence, in either case as the appearance of a process of being that has gone on anonymously *ab æterno*.

Whether for Schelling or for Fichte, this "finding oneself" amounted to the retrieval of an always already accomplished past, a retrieval that made up the history of humankind (such as was possible in a monistic system). For both, the retrieval culminated in their respective systems of philosophy. And it was in the contrasting attitudes toward history that these systems fostered that the difference in the conceptual method they pursued, and in the speculative motivation behind it, came most clearly to the fore. So, too, did the ambiguity rooted in monism. For Fichte, committed as he was to translating factical content into form (in effect, into idealizations with no ontological commitment *per se*), the point of history was to concentrate on the present situation where alone reality manifests itself in its full import. Schelling had complained about Fichte being indifferent to the reality of evil. This was not fair. There was no doubt in Fichte's mind about the presence of evils in the world. The reflections on the situation of his age that he presented to the public in the lectures of 1804–1805 were but a litany of such evils.[130] Nor, for that matter, did he fail to give a story about how they came to be what they were at the moment. But the point is that he was not interested in explaining the origin of evil. Explanation was not his remit. His attitude was rather that of a man who already lives the blessed life *sub specie æternitatis* and is therefore committed to bringing the whole of humankind to that state. The Fichte of 1804 had altered his method of philosophizing but in personal attitude was still the author of *The Vocation of Humankind* of 1800. The change in his method of philosophizing had only made him more personally consistent. He still was the consummate existentialist. Schelling's excursions into the history of myths were meant, on the contrary, as theoretically explanatory. They were a statement of God's mind. The irony is that the same Schelling who had repeatedly berated his predecessors for sacrificing the immediacy of existence to the reflection of the concept was the one who, in the end, let the march of the gods across the ages run roughshod over the vicissitudes of the historical individual. Schelling had no language (as Fichte, on the contrary, did) for the individual caught up in the existential dilemmas of the moment. Clearly, Schelling was still the adept of the rationalism Jacobi had preached against.

Yet, although pursuing directly opposite approaches to history,[131] Fichte and Schelling were drawing from the same source. The drew from the same

---

[130] "Characteristics [*Grundzüge*] of the Present Age," to which we shall turn. Section 6.2.2.
[131] The two approaches lead respectively to Sartre and Marx. But it is significant that Sartre could consider himself a Marxist.

towering figure of Spinoza. And, although the humanism that each approach inspired was, on the face of it, directly the opposite of the other, both were nonetheless equally exposed to Jacobi's same criticism. They did not do justice to the individual. But were such approaches true to actual history? It remains to be seen whether an altogether different approach was possible.

CHAPTER 5

Schelling, Hegel, and Positivity

"The principle by which God is defined for human beings is also the principle for how humanity defines itself inwardly, or for humanity in its own spirit."

Hegel[1]

"One forgives the individual who [like Jakob Boehme] staggers when he is actually drunk with intuition, but not one who [like the Herr Hegel] by nature is actually sober and only wishes to appear that he too is staggering."

Schelling[2]

"It is one of the profoundest and truest insights to be found in the Critique of Reason that the *unity* which constitutes the *essence of the concept* is recognized as the *original synthetic* unity *of apperception*, the unity of the '*I think*,' or of self-consciousness."

Hegel[3]

5.1   Hegel's Novelty

There was much rancor in the elderly Schelling against Hegel, his erstwhile disciple who had eventually overtaken him in eminence. In 1840, when Schelling had acceded to the chair in philosophy that Hegel had left vacant in Berlin because of his untimely death, he accused him of plagiarism; worse still, of having misunderstood and misconstrued what he had plagiarized. This is unfortunate. Under more serene circumstances it would have been clear that Hegel had in fact been moved by the same idea of factual necessity – of a historical *a priori* – that had motivated Kant from the start and had equally motivated Fichte and Schelling after him.

---

[1] Hegel (2006), p. 203; Hegel (1985), vol. 4a, p. 413.   [2] GPP 176; SSW II.3:122.
[3] Hegel (2010), p. 515: GW 12:17.36–18.2.

He had even provided the right speculative framework for it and the right method for building a whole system of thought on its basis. He had done so without incurring the formalism of Kant; also without making himself vulnerable to mystification or without reducing nature to a mere construct of reason.

In their different ways, Kant, Fichte, and Schelling had all subordinated reason to a source that transcended it, with the net result that, while reason indeed generated an intelligible space once it came on the scene, *that* there would occur such an intelligible space remained an unexplained fact. The *a priori* that reason's presence introduces in experience is thus affected by mere facticity. In the previous chapters, we have seen the strategies that the three adopted to deal with it: Kant by reclaiming superiority for reason in experience, but only ideally; Fichte, by evoking the right existential attitude; Schelling, by poetizing. Hegel's strategy, as it progressively took shape, turned out to be the opposite of all these. In essence it consisted in reclaiming for reason the originality and superiority traditionally attributed to it. It did so, however, by making reason itself the source of the facticity which, just as traditionally, was presumed instead as limiting it. The play of contracting ground and expansive love which Schelling painted on a cosmogonic canvas was seen by Hegel as instead constituting the life of reason itself as it weaves its way in the course of actual history. In this, Hegel was perhaps inspired by Schelling. He was also perhaps taking a page from Schelling's book by, like Schelling, considering the life of reason as continuous with the life of nature in general and its emergence within it just a moment of the latter. But, where for Schelling it was God's creative freedom that acted itself out in that emergence, for Hegel it was nature itself that, at that moment *as reason*, reclaimed its merely organic past and transformed it into a new universe of meaning. Reason was at the origin of the *Evidenz*, the intelligible light, to which Fichte insisted we should be attentive in experience. The difference was that, for Hegel, being attentive to this *Evidenz* was for reason to be attentive to itself. Of course, Kant had already said that reason is autonomous: it sets its own norms. And Hegel was indeed marking a return to Kant but in a different conceptual register altogether, stripped of the encumbrances from classical metaphysics that still affected Kant and affected Fichte and Schelling no less.

All this required, for Hegel, a new understanding of metaphysics and of logic, as well as a new philosophical method, new factors in his philosophical outlook over which he became clear only progressively. These all first came to a head in the *Phenomenology of Spirit* of 1807. We will turn to this text. But first, since when he was in Jena, where the Phenomenology was conceived and composed, Hegel thought of himself a Schelling's disciple, and there were no doubt continuities between his then mentor's vision of nature and his own, we must first consider such continuities. At issue is the nature of the positivity that later in life Schelling claimed had been the defining mark of his philosophy from the beginning. This was the mark that set it apart from the metaphysics of his rationalist predecessors but most notably also set it apart, according to Schelling, from Hegel's.

5.2   The Case for Metaphysical Empiricism

Late in life Schelling began to characterize his philosophy as a case of "metaphysical empiricism," or, alternatively, as rational positivism.[4] "Empiricism" and "positivism" were not to be understood in any vulgar sense. Schelling's philosophy was not a matter of cataloguing facts of experience. It was a matter, rather, of making them intelligible by getting to the ground that made them what they were. And this required the abstractive and therefore negative labor of conceptual representation. While stressing the positivism, even empiricism, of his thought, Schelling also began at that time to insist on the need in science for the moment of negativity. Very likely still mindful of Hegel's early parody of any attempt to produce the Absolute all at once, as if "shot from a pistol,"[5] he reiterated the criticism already directed in earlier lectures at Boehme and Jacobi's intuitionism. He made it clear that he had no principled objection to the schools' metaphysics and their reliance on conceptual reflection. The negativity associated with reflection was necessary to scientific knowledge. He even told his students that they would find no better intellectual discipline than in the schools. The real issue was not negativity as such but how to contain it within the compass of a more fundamental positive thinking. In this, in his opinion, the schools had failed. Their metaphysics remained negative.

But what did Schelling mean by "positive thinking," and how might it degenerate into mere negativity? For an example of what he meant Schelling turned to Aristotle, whose philosophy he began, also late in life, to consider a good, albeit limited, case of genuine "metaphysical empiricism."[6] There was nothing vulgarly empirical about Aristotle's thought, since it approached experience ("moved towards it," was

---

[4] For this, we must return to the *Grounding of Positive Philosophy* already considered in Section 4.4, in connection with the Freedom Essay.

[5] PS § 27; GW 9:24.10.   [6] For Schelling on Aristotle, see GPP 159ff; SSW II.3:99ff.

Schelling's repeated expression) in order to determine *what* made its objects possible, thus rendering their existence intelligible. Aristotle looked for essences. This was a process that required the reflective and therefore abstractive work of conceptual representation. In this, Aristotle's metaphysics had its necessary moment of negativity. However, once it succeeded in determining an essence and thereby delimited one area of possible intelligible experience, it left that area to empirical discovery while itself proceeded to the determination of a higher form of possibility and consequent intelligibility. In each case, the more determinate was the identified possibility, the more individualized were the objects it defined and the less contingent, therefore, was their existence. This process was repeated up to the point at which essence and existence, possibility and actuality, coincided. This was the case of the prime movers of the cosmos. At that point, but at that point alone, thought had to rely for its object on conceptual inference rather than plain empirical discovery. Thus, although the "logical" preceded actual experience throughout, it did not thereby create a gap between the two, not even where the prime movers of the cosmos were at issue. The "logical" was correctly understood as possessing no autonomous determination that would stand opposed to being.[7] This was the crucial point. The "logical" found its realization exclusively in the empirically discovered being whose possibility it brought to light *reflectively*, that is, abstractly and therefore negatively.[8]

Schelling recognized that there were affinities between Aristotle and Kant (the modern Aristotle, in his view).[9] In establishing the essence of a range of objects, Aristotle provided what for Kant would be the *a priori* of an area of experience; moreover, like Kant's *a priori*, Aristotle's essence only defined possibilities of being rather than actual being. However, much time had elapsed between the two, and many historical factors had intervened to reshape Aristotle's original vision – neo-Platonism and Christian beliefs most notable among them. Schelling duly detailed them. Indeed for

---

[7] "According to the subject matter at hand rational philosophy is so little opposed to experience that instead, just as Kant had taught of reason, it does not even extend *beyond* experience, and where experience has its end, reason recognizes its *own* boundary as well, leaving this final concept standing there as something unknowable. According to its subject matter, even rational philosophy is an empiricism, but only an *a priori* empiricism." GPP 161; SSW II.3:102.

[8] "Being is indeed the content of pure thought, but only as potency. But what potency is, according to its nature, is, so to speak, a leaping towards being. Thus, through the nature of its very content thought is drawn outside itself. For what has passed over into being is no longer the content of just thought – it has become the object of a knowledge – empirical knowledge – that exceeds thought." GPP 160; SSW II.3:102.

[9] GPP 163–164, footnote; SSW II.3:106, footnote viii.

both Aristotle and Kant thought could not "extend *beyond* experience."[10] Yet the "beyond" in question did not mean the same thing for both. The difference lay in the new significance that "existence" had assumed in the meantime and "essence" or "possibility" accordingly. For Aristotle, thought began with existents.[11] Explaining them was limited to determining particular possibilities of being that did not, and could not, exceed the actual. Existence was indeed the contingent factor in experience, but in particular; not *in toto*. Or again, actual being encompassed possibilities. Not so by the time of Kant, for in between existence had become an issue, and the question had been raised – "why being and not nothing?" – which for Aristotle would have had no meaning. The possible/actual relation had thus been reversed. Possibility exceeded actual being. Since, however, it lacked a positive content of its own, thought made up for it with its own internal determinations. It thereby made conceptual intelligibility, or the subjective possibility of thinking being, the norm of existence.

Here is where the "logical" acquired a content of its own and the gap was created between the conceptual and the real which, in Schelling's view, made purely negative thinking possible. This was true of Kant's critical philosophy just as much as it was of the metaphysics of the schools that Kant himself had dubbed dogmatic. The only difference was that Kant was aware of the gap, and equally aware of the paradox it generated, namely that the burden of explaining existence was made to rest on thought's subjective resources, a circumstance that, however, made the explaining in principle impossible. The difference was that Kant made the paradox, which otherwise confronted dogmatic philosophy *de facto*, endemic to philosophy as such. In this respect, although critical about itself, Kant's was still, according to Schelling, a case of negative philosophy.

All this explained what negativity meant for Schelling; why, in his view as we have just seen, it was necessary to science; also why it nonetheless had to remain secondary to positive thinking, yet had historically subordinated conditions of actual existence to those of logical possibility. From what transpired from the example of Aristotle's metaphysics, and from occasional direct statements of what he meant by "positive thinking," Schelling had, however, also given some idea of what a truly empirical metaphysics would look like, at least in general.[12] It would be one that moved indeed toward experience from a Prius that explained it. "Prius" was the term Schelling was using in the present context, apparently as the equivalent of

---

[10] GPP 161; SSW II.3:102.   [11] GPP 162; SSW II.3:104.
[12] I am basing the interpretation that follows on GPP 178–181; SSW II.3:126–130.

a priori but without the latter's subjective connotations, for which Kant
was responsible. This Prius, however, had to be a *prius per posterius*, in the
sense that in explaining experience it restored to it an intelligibility immanent to it, one that was abstracted from experience and was represented in
the medium of a concept only for the sake of making it explicit. In other
words, the intelligibility was *recognized* in the experience that the Prius
explained; it was not imposed on it. In this way, the Prius' externality was
overcome at the same time as it was posited in the medium of the concept.

Schelling's own positivism, however, was not of this general kind *tout
court*, for in its case the Prius at issue was God, and God, while immanent
in experience as its ground, nonetheless transcended it absolutely, for it
transcended being as such. In this, Schelling fell squarely within the
tradition that separated Kant from Aristotle. However, that one is aware
of the presence of the Divine in the human being did not seem to pose
a problem for him. Apparently, just as in the earlier Freedom Essay, he
simply assumed that such a presence was a directly ascertainable fact of
experience. The crucial question for him was, rather, how a science of it
was nonetheless possible without falling back upon the subjective resources
of thought alone, that is, without lapsing into the dogmatism of classical
metaphysics or Kant's critical idealizations. And his answer – at least so far
as one can make it out from admittedly cryptic texts – was that the Prius
(God)[13] indeed transcends discursive reason absolutely, and in this sense it
is nonrational ("incomprehensible").[14] Nonetheless, inasmuch as it is
brought under concepts for the sake of reason (as it has to be), it is
represented from the standpoint of the latter; in effect, as appropriated
by it; consequently as *immanent* to it (i.e., to reason as contrasted with
originative experience); and by the same token as transcending experience

---

[13] "For what [positive philosophy] begins with is *a priori* – but *a priori* it is not God, only *a posteriori* is
it God. That is, God is not a *res naturæ*, something that is self-evident, but is a *res facti*, and can
therefore only be proved factually. It is God. It means that this *prius is* God, not according to its
concept [i.e., such as reason brings to the *prius* to make it comprehensible], but according to its
reality." GPP 179; SSW II.3:128.
  "God is not, as many imagine, the transcendent, he is the immanent (that is, what is to become the
content of reason [i.e., by being brought to conceptualization]) made transcendent [i.e., by thus
being conceptualized]. In that this has been overlooked lies the great misunderstanding of our time.
As I have already said, what is *a priori* incomprehensible, because it is conveyed through no anterior
concept [i.e., it transcends conceptual possibility absolutely] will become a comprehensible being in
God, or it arrives at its concept in God. That which infinitely exists, that which reason cannot hide
within itself [for it escapes rationality] becomes immanent for reason [but as transcendent being] in
[the concept of] God." GPP 209; SSW II.3:170. For both texts, the glosses in square brackets are
mine.
[14] In this respect, too, Schelling was like Kant, to whom he explicitly refers. God marks the abyss of
reason. See GPP 204; SSW II.3:163.

negatively. Like negative philosophy, therefore, Schelling's positive philosophy had *to proceed to* experience, as if externally. To this extent, it had its
negative conceptual moment that made it a science. It did not, however,
fall victim to it because it remained animated throughout by the awareness
of the incomprehensible factor in experience, which is the Divine.

Although Schelling did not put it this way, his positive science was thus
dogmatic in form but critical in intent: dogmatic because conceptual, yet
critical because it recognized the incomprehensibility of the object it
conceptualized. But the incomprehensibility was not due to the limitation
of the concept or, for that matter, to the lack on the part of the human
mind of the adequate faculty for it (the lack of "intellectual intuition,"
according to Kant). It was due, rather, to the object itself, which transcended comprehension *tout court* and yet was recognized, and to this
extent known, as transcending it. The consequent ignorance was not,
therefore, of the critical kind, such as could be populated with ersatz
idealizing constructs in lieu of the intended object. It had positive truth
value – not unlike a remembering that knows that it does not have direct
access to the remembered object, yet makes it present just the same, but at
a distance. In the case of the Divine the distance was infinite. *Docta
ignorantia* might perhaps be the right designation for it. But, be that as it
may, the point is again that nothing had substantially changed with
Schelling's turn to metaphysical empiricism since the Freedom Essay.
His science of the Divine, albeit clarified so far as its dogmatic form was
concerned, still remained prophetic when it came to its claim to truth.

There was therefore something disingenuous in Schelling's criticism of
Boehme and Jacobi. Unlike them, he did not produce his knowledge of the
Divine as if "shot from a pistol." Like them, however, he still produced the
evidential base for it out of presumably intuitive conviction. And when it
came to Hegel, who had been the main target of Schelling's attack on
negative philosophy, the misinterpretation of his system verged on parody.
In his view, Hegel's system represented the worst that negative philosophy
had to offer. As he thought, Hegel might at first have recognized the
system's purely logical character but had consequently failed to see that it
was in fact but logic. He had unwittingly hypostasized otherwise purely
logical intentions, and in this he had been guilty of negative philosophy's
supreme error, namely of believing that being can be derived from the
logical. Worse still, he had portrayed this derived "being" as unfolding, *qua*
being, according to the rhythm of conceptual movement.[15] This made of

---

[15] See GPP 150–151; SSW II.3:86–90.

Hegel's system, since it thus represented God as in need of development, a case of theosophy, albeit cast in conceptual rather than imaginary mode.[16] In Schelling's account, it portrayed the divine life as a cycle

> in which God unceasingly descends to the deepest and unconscious being [. . .] where he] is indeed still the Absolute, but yet an impersonal God, that is, a blind and deaf Absolute; [to where, moreover, he] forever climbs downwards only in order to equally unceasingly climb upwards out of it, through ever higher levels until human consciousness is finally reached where he works off and sheds his subjectivity and becomes absolute Spirit, that is, where he first properly becomes God.[17]

In Schelling's view, since this made God in need of development, it also made Hegel an atheist, as he indirectly called him.[18]

By the standards of common piety Hegel might indeed have been an atheist. But Schelling saw him through his own prejudiced eyes. He painted his own system on a cosmogonic canvas, as we said, whereas Hegel, not unlike Aristotle – except when reflecting on religious beliefs or deliberately relying on biblical imagery to make a conceptual point – was peculiarly silent about the physical origin of nature or, for that matter, about the cosmos's relation to a transcendent creator. These were concerns that clearly fell within the scope of classical metaphysics and apparently still were Schelling's. Hegel's single concern was rather the creation of a universe of meaning such as was made possible by the presence in nature of rational activity, in effect of representational reflection. This presence marked a break from nature (a "fall upward," was Hegel's image) because, as made to re-exist in the medium of the concept in the form of social relations, cultures, arts, and sciences, nature was subjected to norms and possibilities that were typically reason's own: as such, they could, and did, do violence to nature's otherwise factual limits. This was the negative moment of rational existence that made reconciliation with its natural past reason's over-arching need. And reconciliation was, as we shall see, the leitmotif of Hegel's philosophy. But the need was satisfied even as it was generated, for it was nature, and none other than nature with all its fragilities, including death, which was transformed into something new by being

---

[16] GPP 177; SSW II.3:124. Schelling was turning the table against his critics.
[17] GPP 163–164, footnote; SSW II.3:106, footnote viii. Of course, Schelling is right: inasmuch that Hegel had said that, he would not have been an Aristotelian. In the footnote, Schelling objects to Hegel being accorded the title of the modern Aristotle.
[18] GPP 145; SSW II.3:80.

invested with meaning. It was transformed precisely in being remembered as reason's organic past.

This explained Schelling and Hegel's common concern with nature and history. But the difference, as it first transpired in the *Phenomenology of Spirit*, was that there was for Hegel nothing *per se* incomprehensible revealed in either nature or history: just reason itself working out its reflective vocation in nature. This, as we said, required a new method of philosophizing.

5.3   Hegel and the Odyssey of Spirit

5.3.1   *How to Read the Phenomenology*

5.3.1.1   *The Phenomenology As "Philosophical Roman"*
Hegel said of the Phenomenology that it was the introduction to the Logic,[19] and as such also the introduction to the whole system of the sciences, yet itself science in its own right and therefore part of the system it introduced.[20] He also thought of the Logic as a self-validating science in no need of prior assumptions. Hence the difficulty that has been the subject of much discussion in the literature and boils down to the issue of the relation of Phenomenology and Logic.[21] If the Logic was as Hegel defined it, it would *prima facie* follow that the Phenomenology only prepared for it subjectively. Like a ladder that can be pushed away once the summit is achieved, it would have been left behind with the coming on the scene of the Logic's absolute idea. In what sense could it also be a science in its own right, itself part of the system?

The difficulty disappears if one reads the Logic as the canonization of reason's reflective awareness of its own rationality – a kind of transcendental logic or, as the scholastic might have called it, a material logic. *Logicität* is Hegel's operative term. The Logic is precisely the methodic exposition of the logicality (*das Logische*) of experience, of the form that makes the latter intelligent. It defines the conditions of intelligibility in general, not unlike the syntax of a language that defines, in an idiom typically its own, the rules

---

[19] I borrow the phrase "Odyssey of Spirit" in the subheading from the title of Volume 2 of Harris (1997).

[20] For an exhaustive study of Hegel's Phenomenology as a demonstration that the logic of abstract thought makes manifest the ways of mutable actual experience, see Collins (2013).

[21] For a review of this discussion in recent anglophone literature, see Collins (2013), pp. 17–21 for the review; pp. 216–222 for the author's position which has much in common with the one presented here.

of order that hold discourse together. And since reason governs experience from the beginning, it should be expected that the logicity at issue (just like the syntax of a language) would find repeated explicit expression in the course of history in a variety of formulations. According to Hegel, however, it was only in his times that the existential conditions were at hand that made possible the strictly scientific exposition of it. On the one hand, the resulting Logic was indeed a self-contained, self-validating science. On the other hand, the process that had historically led to it did not happen haphazardly, for, although weighed by circumstances that might well have been otherwise, it was nonetheless motivated by reason. Unlike the internal course of the Logic, which reflected the process only at a distance (*in abstracto*), the process was affected by contingency. Yet, since reason's norms had still been at play in it, it could still be explained albeit only *ex post facto*, which is exactly what Hegel's Phenomenology did. It, too, was a science, namely the science of historical experience. To be sure, upon coming on the historical scene, the Logic superseded it *but only at the price of being an abstract science.* It was only a shadowing, *Schattierung*, of experience.[22] To forget this, or to presume that with the coming of the Logic the Phenomenology lost objective standing in Hegel's system of the sciences, is not only to forget that the *Logicität* to which the Logic gives voice in the idiom specific to it is that of a universe of meaning; it is also to run the risk of taking the Logic, precisely as Schelling did,[23] as if it were the science not of the *concept* of being (*thought thinking thought*) but of being *tout court*.

Rudolf Haym, in 1857, described the Phenomenology as a "phalanx" of logic, criticism, history, sociology, psychology, and pedagogy, all blended together, certainly the product of a creative and erudite spirit – ultimately, however, no less of a phantasy than Dante's *Divine Comedy*, and without the latter's excuse of being only a poem.[24] Indeed, the Phenomenology is all those things, but with design, since the experience of which it is the science is a complex event at once temporal yet immanently rational. It is *rational*, however, not in the Enlightenment sense of reflecting ready-made eternal truths of an atemporal reason; nor, for that matter, *temporal* in the equally Enlightenment sense of unfolding according to a plot determined

---

[22] Logic 37; GW 21:42.30–43.4.
[23] This is also McTaggart's classical interpretation of Hegel on which Charles Taylor and Frederick Beiser are still nowadays dependent. Cf. McTaggart (1931), pp. 305ff.; McTaggart (1918), p. 1; McTaggart (1910), p. 232; Taylor (1975), pp. 97–98; Beiser (2005), pp. 71ff. For G. R. G. Mure as the first English Hegelian who connected Hegel with both Kant and Aristotle, see Kroner (1953).
[24] Haym (1857), pp. 234–235, 240.

before time.[25] It is rational, rather, because the subjects engaged in it are rational agents. And these, because of ultimately subjective motivations, inject intentions into otherwise merely natural events, with consequences that work themselves out in time objectively. They thus set in motion courses of events which might indeed give the impression *ex post facto* of having been predetermined before time according to eternal truths. There are sciences in Hegel's System that take as their subject matter single aspects of this complex process: the logical, the subjective/psychological, the natural. What is specific to the Phenomenology is that it takes them all precisely as converging into the one phenomenon that we call "historical event"; and, of course, the sense of historical would not be conveyed *in concreto* unless the Phenomenology had itself, as science, explicit historical significance. In a sense, Haym was right. The Phenomenology, like the *La Divina Commedia (Divine Comedy)*, is a work of the imagination. But the difference – the crucial difference – is that, unlike Dante's poem, it has documentable historical significance and convincing explanatory power. The Phenomenology is a philosophical *roman* of historical import. This is how we shall read it.

5.3.1.2   *The* roman*'s Structure*

Why a *roman*? Because the story it relates nowhere, and at no time, happened as recounted; in this respect, the Phenomenology is a product of fiction. Why "philosophical"? Because the plot of the story and the personality of its characters are devised to lead the readers to the truth about the nature of human events, namely that they are the products of reason. The plot, in other words, is conceptually motivated. Why the "historical significance"? Because the events and characters, although fictional, require nonetheless a documentable historical context within which they can be imaginatively placed, as if in real space and time; one, therefore, in which the readers can recognize themselves as personally connected. The story, although fictional in its makeup, is thus no mere fantasy. It bears directly on the readers' present historical situation. These share, but in the historical form specific to them, the same life of reason that the story's characters lived in their times in the forms dependent on their historical circumstances. But to live this life is to be virtually already reflectively aware of the nature of reason. Indeed, the specific form such a life assumes

---

[25] The most obvious late Enlightenment exponent of this view of the universe was Adam Weishaupt, the founder of the *Illuminati*, a secret society within the itself already secret Masonry. See di Giovanni (2005), pp. 44ff.

at any time is precisely a reflection of this awareness. As of 1807, Hegel found himself in this particular situation, namely that his culture had reached such a level of self-consciousness that it was certain that true science was possible but did not yet know how and why. It was Hegel's goal to bring this subjective certainty to objective fruition by making his contemporaries remember how the idea of reason had *ab initio* already objectively worked itself out in the past leading up to their present cultural state. They would thereby also be made subjectively ready for a fully self-aware science of precisely this reason. That was the *Phenomenology's* vocation.

But if the work is to be read in thin vein as a story, who is its putative narrator? Who is its audience? Who are the protagonists? Where is the plot? What is the historical interest?

The question of the narrator is of pivotal significance, for it frames the relation of the reader to the story. The narrator is a historical though anonymous individual who is nonetheless also implicated in the plot of the story he narrates; moreover, in being so implicated, he learns about himself as the historical individual that he is. The narrator is the one who at once generates the story's historical interest, that is, the requirement that it be located in the course of actual events, yet adds to these an extra dimension, the conceptual interest that in turn requires that they be presented with intent in the medium of a fiction. I am referring, of course, to the ubiquitous *we*, first referred to in the introduction and recurring in a variety of forms at crucial points in the rest of the work.[26] This *we* is the philosopher (Hegel himself, in fact)[27] who, as of 1807, finds himself in the world-historical situation just described. There is a culturally widespread belief that true knowledge, or science, is possible – indeed, that it is already with us; yet there is no clarity regarding why this is possible or, for that matter, how we got to the present certainty that it is. One can immediately see how both the historical interest and the need for romanticizing are simultaneously produced. The narrator is a real individual standing at just as real a point in history. His spatio-temporal position is open to documentation. If his interest in how he got to that point is to be satisfied, the required narrative must be one that leads up to it in ways that are equally open to real space/time determinations. This might sound trivial. But it is not. In an Enlightenment universe, for instance, and

---

[26] He first appears in PS § 63; GW 9:58.36ff. In the Logic the role of the *we* is anonymously played by the *Logicität* in general that carries and holds together the conceptual narrative just as the *we* in the Phenomenology carries and holds together the historical side of the latter's narrative.

[27] For this reason, we refer to this *we* as "he."

even more so in a Kantian or Fichtean one, where historical events are by definition only the appearance of a transcendent order of things – mere *Schein*, in other words – history never is in truth what it seems to be. How anyone relates to its course individually, how straight lines are supposedly being drawn despite the asymmetry of one's apparent position, must be, therefore, always a matter of subjective belief, of ideological commitment.

On the other hand, history – I mean, real history – is complicated. Catalogues of events do not necessarily make for meaning. Our narrator must choose such facts as are relevant to his theme of how reason is *with us*, indeed *has been* with us, from the beginning.[28] Moreover, he must craft them imaginatively in order to make the relevance apparent. Here is where the fictional dimension of the narrative that makes Antigone rub shoulders with Martin Luther comes into play, the imaginative plot. It might be said that our narrator is cheating, for, in the very setting up of the theme of his narrative, he is already presupposing the upshot – namely, that there is no history without reason and no reason without history. In this sense, however, all authors are cheats. They know what's to happen from the beginning – or, at least, they seriously have a work at hand only when they know how it ends. And the best of them (like Hegel) know how to intimate the end, without, however, actually revealing it, even with the first line. But the demonstration of the theme is in the story itself, in the plot.

There are several such plots in the Phenomenology, linked together in one narrative by the narrator's engagement in them. We shall get to them momentarily. But first, three points must be made to set up the right framework for the text.

The first is that there is no thesis/antithesis/synthesis procession in the Phenomenology; nor, for that matter, is there one in the Logic. That procession is a myth based on Kant's dialectic of reason (which Hegel, incidentally, considered a conceptual sham) and further propagated by Reinhold, eventually by the so-called Young Hegelians and the later Marxists. Rather, each plot proceeds exactly the way one would expect of a good narrative. There is, first, the detailed account of the factors that go into a given situation – the plot, in other words. Unlike usual stories, in the Phenomenology such plots are conceptual, and the account consists in each case in the analysis of a concept, be this of an object such as "Thing," or a mental state like "Unhappy Consciousness," or a culture, like "Ethical Community." These concepts, to which our narrator dedicates pages analyzing them into the most minute details, are not unlike a Kantian

---

[28] PS § 73, p. 47; GW 9:53.34–35.

a priori. They define the essence of an objective situation: the norm, therefore, of what enters into it meaningfully.

But there are internal discordances in these concepts, like flaws in a plot otherwise intended as internally coherent. If one still cares to speak of "antitheses" in the Phenomenology, here is where they are to be found: in a conflict of determinations internal to the concepts defining the various plots. The story, whether the overall story or each plot, proceeds, however, not by way of thesis to antithesis (this, I repeat, is a myth) but by way of repetition (*Wiederholung*). Once a plot has been defined in principle, Hegel simply repeats it by *realizing* it, to use his usual expression. This means that, whether the context is the search for objective truth, in which case the plots reflect scientific commitments to the nature of reality, or whether it is social in character, in which case the plots reflect original decisions regarding human identity, the story proceeds by portraying the consequences that inevitably befall the individuals existentially caught up in the given context. These individuals are the historical protagonists of the overall story, in the literary personas they assume in the various plots. With their decisions, whether theoretical or practical, they manifest fundamental beliefs regarding their universe and their individual place within it. These beliefs are embedded, as if *a priori*, in the plots they act out. The plots are flawed precisely to the extent that the beliefs motivating them are flawed. The protagonists are not aware of the flaws. But these nonetheless play themselves out in the course of their actions, with consequences that painfully affect them at their most intimate level of existence. And when the pain becomes unbearable, the stage is set for a reformation of the beliefs – for a renewed *a priori* of the human situation, a *Wiederholung*, a new plot for which the previous one stands as its past. This is a forgotten past, just as forgotten as the commitment to the new defining belief regarding human identity that has just led to the new plot. It has gone unconscious behind the back of the protagonists, as Hegel puts it.[29] But the *we*, the narrator, remembers it; he has been instrumental in bringing it about, and this constitutes the unity of the overall narrative.

Here we have an instance of how the narrator would recognize himself as being historically engaged in the story's plot. One should indeed expect logical continuity in the sequence of the concepts defining *a priori* the limits of the narrated actions. Nonetheless, that one set of beliefs would actually follow in the aftermath of the previous, and a renewed humanity thus come into being, carries no existential necessity with it. The internal

---

[29] PS § 87, p. 56; GA 9:61.22.

disruption of one plot provides the existential conditions for its logical reformation, but, so far as the resources of the narrative up to that point go, there is no guarantee that the reformation actually occur. Historical explanation can only be *ex post facto*. For this, a creative leap, a *novum*, is required for which there is no other in the story who would contribute it except the narrator himself inasmuch as he is the historical inheritor of those who made the narrated leaps in real history, and now recognizes the fact. This is the factor that generates at once literary interest in the fictional narrative and the need that although fictional the narrative be framed in real history.

It is in the actions of the protagonists of each plot that, as we said, the limitations of the conceptual framework on which the plot is based manifest themselves. But in the context of the Phenomenology, where the rationality of experience is the main issue, action means, first and foremost, language. This is the second point regarding how plots unfold. Each plot can be defined by the quality of the language spoken in it. There is the opening protagonist's still unreflective, naïvely realist, scattered language of common sense.[30] Then the language of theoretical science, which is no more than sophisticated common sense, the classical metaphysics of the understanding.[31] Then there is the language of mutual recognition, the many forms of which mark the stages in the history of the human spirit. They follow in sequence. There is the symbolic language of the still inarticulate unhappy consciousness (the tinkling of bells and burning of incense).[32] The language of the ethical spirit, which is a language of law and simple command, and also a lamentation about the necessity of Fate.[33] The many languages of alienated culture:[34] fealty,[35] counsel,[36] praise,[37] flattery,[38] base flattery;[39] and those of Enlightenment culture, which culminate in the destructively witty discourse of the

---

[30] This is the language of the "this and that," the "now and then," the "here and there," of sense-certainty that takes itself to be the richest form of knowledge but turns out to be in fact dependent on mere abstractions. PS §§ 90–110; GW 9:63ff.

[31] In sections II, III, and IV, which are based and the still realist language of the "thing," the "thing and its properties," the "thing and its law-governed appearances."

[32] PS § 217; GW 9:25.26–28: "Its thinking as such is no more than the chaotic jingling of bells, or a mist of warn incense, a musical thinking."

[33] PS § 653; GW 9:351.22–24: "The language of the ethical Spirit is law and simple command, and complaint, which is more the shedding of a tear about necessity."

[34] PS § 508; GW 9:276.5: "But this alienation takes place only in *language*."

[35] PS § 503; GW 9:274.16–17: cf. "This consciousness is the heroism of service."

[36] PS § 505; GW 9:275.9–10: "His language [...] would take the form of *counsel*."

[37] PS § 512; GW 9:278.26: "The language of their praise."

[38] PS § 511; GW 9:277.37–278.1: "The heroism of silent service becomes the language of flattery."

[39] PS § 520; GW 9:282.5–6: "The language of flattery, but of base flattery."

philosophes,[40] and finally in the deadly thump of the guillotine.[41] The list can go on: the non-language of moral consciousness;[42] the disappearing one of the beautiful soul;[43] the language of the religious community about itself;[44] finally the discourse of the philosopher, where discursiveness is another word for dialectic.

The Phenomenology also reads like a treatise on language.[45] But the point is that behind a language there is a speaker, and the quality of the speaker's language manifests the speaker's capacity to speak authoritatively; in other words, it manifests the extent to which he or she, in speaking, feels bound to a predetermined script or, on the contrary, knows him- or herself to be responsible for it. By the same token, it manifests the capacity of the speaker's language community to stand by the meaning of its language. Language, as Hegel says, is the existence of Spirit.[46] This is the all-important point. The form of the *we*'s engagement in the narrative depends precisely on the way this *we* can enter into discourse with the narrative's protagonists; and this depends in turn on the degree to which such protagonists have attained sufficient interiorization for supporting the discourse as independent speakers. The development of the self-containedness of their languages proceeds *pari passu* – indeed, it amounts to the same thing – with their development from merely singular characters (*Einzeln*) to self-standing individuals (*Individuum*).

I come to the third point. Schelling's route to the Absolute was through the subject. This, as we said, is the justification, if any, for reading his cosmogony as also an analysis of the subconscious. Hegel's route in the Phenomenology is not to the Absolute, even though some of its protagonists might think that it is. The route is, rather, that of reason to absolute knowledge, where the latter simply means human knowledge which is truly such and not just a semblance of it as it was for all of Hegel's fellow

---

[40] PS § 521, p. 317; GW 9:283.32: "and its language is therefore clever and witty."

[41] PS § 591; GW 9:320.14: "In this flat, commonplace monosyllable is contained the wisdom of the government."

[42] PS § 653; GW 9:351.24: "Moral consciousness [...] is still *dumb*."

[43] PS § 658; GW 9:354.25–26: "But this created world is its speech, which likewise it has immediately heard and only the echo of which returns to it."

[44] PS § 656, p. 398; GW 9:353:34–35: "Religion, which is [...] the utterance [*das Sprechen*] of the community concerning its own Spirit."

[45] Language is present in the Phenomenology at each and every step. For two authors who take this aspect of the Phenomenology seriously, see Hyppolite (1979); McCumber (1993).

[46] PS § 508; GW 9:276.10–12: "For [language] is the *real existence* of the pure self as self; in speech, self-consciousness, *qua independent separate individuality*, comes as such into existence, so that it exists *for others*." PS § 652; GE 9:351.11: "Here again, then, we see language as the existence of Spirit." PS § 716; GE 9:380.31: "[Language] is the soul exiting as soul."

idealists. It is, in other words, a historical journey to the realization of rational life *in concreto*, which for Hegel goes under the name of Spirit. The latter has nothing to do with adding subjectivity to Spinoza's substance. More about this in due course. To the point at the moment is that this route must nonetheless also go through the subject: it coincides with growth in self-consciousness. The *Geist* in *Phänomenologie des Geistes* quite appropriately carries the two meanings in English of "mind" and "Spirit," both at the same time. And this is reflected in the structure of the Phenomenology's narrative. On the one hand, it is divided into sections that correspond to the traditional faculties of the mind: senses, perception, understanding, reason. The narrating *we*, himself a subject, organizes it from the standpoint of what a subject brings to experience. In this the Phenomenology conforms in structure to Kant's critical system. On the other hand, the narrative itself is object-directed. The subject's assumptions, its trains of thought, its decisions, whether theoretical or practical, are all absorbed into the description of the universe which they bring about by re-forming nature in accordance with their intents – the same universe of which the subject instinctively feels to be part. There is nothing in the Phenomenology of the faculty psychology which is still found in Kant's Critique. The faculties are rather, in its context, dimensions of the subject's self-conscious journey across the universe it intentionally weaves over nature. The subject is destined to such a universe the moment reason comes on the scene, and self-consciousness coincidentally with it.

This universe is therefore the virtual object of all the subject's experiences. It informs them from the start of the Phenomenology's narrative, even though its presence in the latter is only progressively articulated explicitly, only as the subject is made to remember it by the narrating *we*. It is this virtual presence that gives the narrative its unity but at the same time also forces it to repeated new starts. Take for instance the naïve protagonist of section I who believes that reality can be described simply with a *this* or *that* – the "Frau Bauer" Hegel mentions in a note in his *Wastebook*.[47] Surely, this Frau Bauer historically enjoyed a more profound feeling for reality in general, including her own, than her language expressed – a still inarticulate feeling, yet no less existentially effective. Only this feeling, the unspoken matrix of all her experiences, could have possibly induced her to believe (falsely) that one need only point at things

---

[47] *Bauersfrau* (Mrs. Peasant). Hegel's *Wastebook*, aphorism 10, in Rosenkranz (1963), p. 539. The epithet is both sexist and elitist, but, we must remember, the narrating *we* belongs to 1807. Moreover, Frau Bauer stands for all of us at our most naïve self.

in order to recognize them for what they are, without first placing them in their proper context. In the subsequent sections this matrix comes in for explicit recognition and analysis at different levels of reflective experience, sequentially, each level more comprehensive than the previous and in fact tacitly presupposed by it as its foundation. There is the theoretical level (sections I–III, V); the communal (sections IV, VI); the religious (section VII); the speculative (section VIII). At each of these sections, a new start is made that leads to a renewed and more existentially complete account of experience. In this respect the Phenomenology is indeed, as just said, a phenomenology of mind. But the further point is that each section also narrates the story of how Frau Bauer (if we let her stand for the human subject in general) learned about herself and the world in which she lives; how she historically came to possess ever more reflectively complex forms of expression, and thereby also became ever more explicitly aware of reason's involvement in the generation of the universe she originally believed to be, like Lessing's ready-made coin, all *there* from the start, simply to be pointed at. In this, the Phenomenology is a phenomenology of Spirit.

In section VII, the one on Religion, Hegel says that up to that point the history of Spirit has been narrated in successive episodes, with each episode a fragment on a continuous line interrupted at nodal points. With religion, however, and the new start it requires, it is time to break up the line at these points, tying the resulting loose fragments together in a single knot at the top. The *we* is ready to retell the whole story from the origin, as indeed he has already repeatedly done in the previous sections; at this point, however, he can do it from the all-comprehensive standpoint of the reason that has been the source of the experiences paraded so far only episodically. Historically, this story has already been told in the medium of Christian mythology. It is the vocation of Hegel's time to comprehend it logically. Accordingly, the idea of absolute knowledge comes on the scene as the Phenomenology concludes in section VIII.

5.3.2   *The Journey and Its Many Starts*

(1)   We can at best only attempt a sketch of Spirit's journey, sketchier in places than in other. Much has been written about the already introduced Frau Bauer, the character who believes she can point at a *this* or *that*, or refer to herself simply as *I*, or capture a moment in time with a simple *now* or *then*, only to find herself forced to admit, upon being challenged by the

we to define exactly what she means by these pointers, that in each case she has missed the intended mark and said more than she intended. She has in fact brought into play a universal (a *this-ness*, a *that-ness*, or an *I-ness*, for instance) of which the intended mark is at best only a disappearing instance and as such inexpressible. Much has indeed been written about this opening move by Hegel, much of it critical. And it must be admitted that Hegel shoulders at least some of the blame for this reaction. His move from the "*this* and *that*," the "*here* and *there*," the "*now* and *then*," to their alleged universal counterparts is indeed highly problematic, for it is part of the meaning of those expressions that they be singular: they are existential designations.[48] Nonetheless, Hegel's intended point is both simple and compelling, and crucial in setting the stage for the rest of the *Phenomenology*. At the level of ordinary experience, there is an existentially irrepressible belief in the presence of big objects like Frau Bauer's barn *over there* or her cow *right here* that naturally also leads to the belief that such a presence poses no problem for experience: it only needs to be pointed at physically or indicated verbally. This is what Hegel calls "sense-certainty," the kind that, as a matter of fact, motivates everybody's ordinary dealings with reality. Only in difficult situations or, as in Frau Bauer's case, when challenged by a philosopher like the *we*, does one recognize that that presence is not as solidly determined as one might have previously believed; in fact, that it appears just as much as it disappears and even appears only in disappearing. This does not make the sense-certainty in question false or the fact that it governs *grosso modo* everybody's ordinary life any less indisputably true. What it demonstrates, rather, and Frau Bauer must learn, is that that certainty is existentially compelling *because*, and not *despite the fact that*, one has already said more about an object than one intends, even when one wants simply to display it directly. For the

---

[48] Hegel defines the spatial universal at the end of the section as a "simple *together* of many *heres*": "[. . .] ein *einfaches Zusammen* vieler *Hier*, das heißt, ein allgemeines." PS § 110 (p. 66); GW 9:70.27. What is not transparent is the meaning of the "together." Is it a universal in the sense that it holds together a number of singulars (such as "*thises*," and "*heres*"), thus constituting a universe of beings? Used in this way, the "together" is more like an idea in Kant's sense, the representation of a totality of individuals, itself an individual. Hegel's "concrete universal" would also apply. This sense carries existential connotations, for only as an individual, however internally complex, can anything exist. Or is it rather the product of an abstraction drawn from many singular *thises* and *heres*, on the basis of which such *thises* and *heres* can, or cannot, be grouped together to constitute a totality? In this sense, the "together" is more like a universal as normally understood, an abstractive essential determination common to a group of individuals. Hegel seems to conflate the two senses, as if a *this*, which would not be such except as radically singular, could be transformed into a universal essential determination (a "thisness," after the manner of "redness") yet retain the sense of a "this" at all.

"pointing at" in fact has the character of a "finding," a matter of locating a "this" within a presupposed context that language holds together discursively. It holds it together by virtue of what Hegel calls "universals," and the more articulated is the context, the greater is the possibility of identifying the intended "this" with precision. Sense certainty is mediated. It is made possible by being mediated. This is the lesson of section I.

In this we see Hegel's originality. At one level, his position was common to all idealists. As given in experience, reality is phenomenal: it inherently points to an "other" before which it tends to disappear and by which, therefore, its presence is mediated. The issue is how to contain this process of disappearing in appearing; in other words, how to determine *in itself* the "other" that appears in the disappearing of the given reality, but in appearing therein equally disappears. For Kant, this "other" was the unknown "thing-in-itself," only ideally determinable, hence the source of the constructivism and consequent formalism that his successors decried. For Fichte and Schelling, in their different ways and differently at different stages of their intellectual journeys, the "other" was the Absolute, or the One, access to which was only by way of intuition.[49] Overcoming the discursiveness of language was for them the *sine qua non* condition for the access. Hegel's position – here his originality – was the very opposite. It is in the language about reality that the latter disappears, but only to reappear in that language's discursive medium as a universe of meaning within which clear and distinct differences can be posited, and therefore significant identities are also established. This might sound like Kant's constructivism. And it can indeed be argued that, of all the idealists, Hegel was the one closest to Kant. But in fact there was no constructivism in Hegel, for Hegel no longer held on to a "thing-in-itself" as the absolute norm of truth, as if the latter were a ready-made coin.[50] Rather, this "itself" lies in the movement of discourse which, reflectively self-contained, sets limits to the dispersive tendency of the reality that is its object, holding it up to norms of true presence. There is no constructiveness involved in this because the discursive movement is itself a form of life, and as such continuous with the phenomenality of the reality given in experience: it is itself a more developed form of precisely this phenomenality. This is the lesson Frau Bauer has to learn step by step in the rest of the Phenomenology, as she and the *we* journey across experience together. Language, which, as Hegel

---

[49] *Mutatis mutandis*, this applies to Kant as well. For him we would need indeed an intellectual intuition for the access, but the fact is that we do not have it. Human reason is discursive.

[50] For the image, which has its origin in Lessing's *Nathan the Wise*, see PS 39; GW 9:30.28.

says, "possesses the divine nature of directly transforming what is merely meant into something else,"[51] is where the "in itself" of reality lies: "The power of Spirit is only as great as its expression, its depth only as deep as it dares to spread out and lose itself in its exposition."[52]

This is the importance of section I of the Phenomenology. It already adumbrates Hegel's foundational metaphysical claim that the Logic makes explicit by positing Becoming as the first complete category of which Being and Nothing are only abstractions. Unlike Fichte's or Schelling's metaphysics, still bound for both to the classical assumption of the primacy of Being over Becoming, Hegel's is explicitly a metaphysics of Becoming. *Being is whatever it is only by becoming it.* What holds this Becoming together into a single universe of meaning is precisely the logicity (*das Logische* already mentioned) of the language expressing it. Spirit – not Substance, or the One, or the Absolute – constitutes for Hegel the truth of experience.

Hegel's critics have repeatedly defended Frau Bauer by claiming that at the end of the day she can refuse to respond to the *we*'s prodding and simply go on relying on her immediate though inarticulate sense of reality. This misses Hegel's point altogether. Of course Frau Bauer has that option. It is her natural option so long as she deals with her barn there or her cow here. But to assume it methodically, deliberately taking it as the starting point of science, is to opt out of history.

(2) The language about "things" comes in for reflection in section II – not that, historically speaking, this language was not already at work in Frau Bauer's attempt at pointing out a *this* or *that* or, for that matter, did not in fact support the attempt from the beginning. Within Hegel's fictional story of self-discovery, however, introducing it at this point is the minimal yet logically compelling move that would resolve the problem posed in the previous section.

Significant about "the thing" is that its meaning is complex, such as cannot be exhausted in a simple grasp. It cannot be simply *taken in* (*capio*), as Frau Bauer thought, but must rather be *taken as such or such* (*per-capio*; or *wahr-nehmen*, or "perceive"). The "thing" is thus a universal, not in any abstractive sense but in Hegel's typical sense of a totality inherently related to a many of particularizing determinations. It is universal in two directly opposite senses. In one, it is universal as a passive medium in which a multitude of determinations inhere, each determining it *in toto*. Each,

[51] PS § 110 (p. 66); GW 9:70.22–23.   [52] PS § 10; GW 9:14.12–14.

however, does not thereby prevent any other from also determining it equally *in toto* – as in the case of sodium chloride, for instance, which is totally salty and totally granular and indifferently both, the two interpenetrating without affecting each other. This is the positive definition of "the thing," also characterized by Hegel as an *Also*. It is itself and *also* its determinations, one of them and *also* any other, indifferently in all cases.

But "the thing" is a universal also in a negative sense. For a thing's determinations would not belong to it in any serious sense if the thing, in being affected by them, did not remain distinct *as thing*, if it did not retain self-identity and to this extent repel them. The same applies to the determinations themselves in their relations to each other and to the thing. Each would not be significant as a determination if, in determining the thing, it did not do so in contrast to other determinations – repelling them; indeed, also repelling the thing in order to retain its identity as determination. *Difference*, such as is produced by an exclusive *One*, is the determining factor. This is the negative aspect of the process of determination, which is just as essential to the concept of "the thing" as the positive. Each aspect (the *Also* and the exclusive *One*) is in fact dependent on the other and intertwined with it, as Hegel demonstrates by the failure of repeated attempts at keeping them apart.

Much of Hegel's analysis in section II is taken up by these attempts and their failures.[53] The analysis is carried out in the persona of the *we* who is always one step ahead of Frau Bauer and makes explicit what has *de facto* been at any moment the lesson of her experience. She now knows that her objects are not simply *there* for her to grasp immediately. She must rather take them *as being there*. But Frau Bauer is still beholden to the naïve realism of sense-certainty. She is also beholden to the belief, which is also at the root of classical metaphysics' monism, that a thing cannot be two opposing or even contradictory things at the same time. She therefore takes her object, *the thing*, alternatively as being just a *One* or just an *Also*, but in each case finds herself shifting to the opposing alternatively precisely in the effort of taking it as she deliberately means.

It is at this juncture, in order to stave off the contradiction into which she seems inevitably led, that Frau Bauer begins to observe herself, just as the *we* has observed her all along. She becomes incipiently critical. She recognizes her subjective involvement in the determination of the object. However, still beholden to her realist assumptions, she presumes one determination to be the truth of the matter and the other to be only her

[53] See the summary, PS § 115; GW 9:73.78–34.

subjective way of stating that truth. But, as things turn out, she finds that she can distinguish in any given case between presumed objective truth and a mere subjective take on it only on the basis of the position she presumed as true in a previous case but has reduced in the present to mere subjective take.[54] The truth of the matter, as Frau Bauer's own behavior attests *de facto*, is that both the *One* and the *Also* go into the objective constitution of the intended "thing." Moreover, as her behavior also attests, the objective interplay of the two determinations reflect the interplay between objective presumption and subjective take that makes up the subjective side of perception. Objective constitution and subjective constituting reflect one another.

In an attempt at avoiding this conclusion, while admitting that the *One* and the *Also* are both objective constituents of the "thing," Frau Bauer seeks to avoid their direct confrontation by parsing them in a relation between two things. She takes the *One* and the *Also* to be objectively attributable to both things, but only depending on whether each is considered alternatively either *in itself* or as standing *in relation to the other*. Here is where the language of the "in so far as," "depending on," "from the standpoint of," or "essential and non-essential" comes into play. For Hegel this is the language typical of common sense, which the latter uses to avoid facing up to the truth, namely that "the object is *in one and the same respect the opposite of itself; it is for itself, so far as it is for another, and it is for another, so far as it is for itself.*"[55] Such a language is a tool of self-deception, for in allowing the speaker (imagine a more educated Frau Bauer) to concentrate on her experience just one aspect at a time, it leads her to believe that what she is saying of that aspect at a given moment is the complete truth of the matter, whereas she has in fact said the opposite only the moment before. In this, she incurs the very contradiction she wants at all costs to avoid.[56]

There is a good reason for Frau Bauer's insistence on taking as the truth of her object only one aspect of it at a time. For she quite rightly expects that the object explain itself; that it be intelligible, as Fichte would put it; and she also rightly presumes that its intelligibility rest on its self-identity, on its self-containedness as being, which, however, she wrongly associates sequentially with each aspect. The irony is that the many locutions she uses

---

[54] "Consciousness alternatively makes itself as well as the *Thing*, into both a pure many-less *One*, and into an *Also* that resolves itself into independent 'matters'. Consciousness thus finds through this comparison that not only does *its* take on the truth contain the distinct *moments of apprehension* and *withdrawal into itself*, the truth itself, the Thing, rather reveals itself in this twofold way." PS § 122 (altered); GW 9:77.3–8.

[55] PS § 128; GW 9:79.4–7.   [56] PS § 130; GW 9:24ff.

for this purpose in fact make the truth of a thing as it is *in itself* depend on conditions external to it; they locate the norm of its truth in something *other than it*. Instead, the lesson to be learned is that the object is whatever it is *in itself* only by being this "in itself" *for another*: it is one only in many and many only in one; universal in singularity and singular in universality. This, as we have just seen, is how Hegel puts it. This is, however, only a first statement of the case, which in isolation might well sound like a warrant for saying anything about anything, just as need be. The point is rather that the truth lies in an identifiable norm internal to an object by virtue of which its many aspects can be held together and the shifting from the one to the other in determining it can be regulated. Frau Bauer's common-sense quest for identity is not being dismissed, only redirected. It should be a quest for a norm of identity.

Aristotle, incidentally, said that much regarding the things of nature. It is by virtue of their form that they become what they are, where this "what" can be different things at different times and in different contexts. At issue in the Phenomenology, however, is experience; more precisely, the unity and self-justificatory power of Frau Bauer's experience of a world which is external to her but of which she knows herself to be a part. Hegel's technical term for the object that would satisfy this experience is that it exists *in-and-for-itself*: it is one regarding which any question of truth can and must be resolved from within it, according to a normal internal to it. This is the object that emerges at the end of section II and becomes the subject matter of section III. The *we*'s story has progressed from perception, where "taking as" (*per-capere*) is the key note, to understanding, where the key note is rather "conceiving" or "comprehending" (*cum-capere*,[57] *be-greifen*). Of course, the concept has been virtually at work in experience from the beginning: it has been the tacit support of both sense-certainty and perception. In the Phenomenology, however, it comes in for explicit consideration only at this juncture. If we want to continue with the trope of Frau Bauer as the carrier of the experience, in order to keep up with the *we* she would have at this point to progress from common sense to the science of nature, and this would indeed require a subjectively creative leap on her part. Of course, in ordinary life she would still rely, as we all do, on common sense, on its language about things and its "pointing at." But she would be enlightened about it.

---

[57] Cf. the *Oxford English Dictionary*, *sub voce*. The imagery associated with *cum-capere* is important. At issue is not just a matter of grasping (*capere*) but of grasping *with* (*cum*), whether along something else or by means of something else, in either case as presupposing a space where the grasping can occur. This space is the intelligible space of the mind.

(3) Section III is long and complicated. Hegel reflects in the persona of the *we* on the language of the sciences of the day. He will continue doing so, but in a broader historical and conceptual context, in section V, as we shall see. Summed up in one sentence, the move in the present section is from an attitude toward the objects of experience still formally bound to common-sense realism (even though already self-critical in practice) to one in which the place and the role of the subject in experience becomes the central concern. This subject will be the concern of section IV.

Despite all complexities and some admittedly obscure passages, the nature of the move is nonetheless clearly discernible. As a start, the "thing" gives way to "force" as the object of consideration. Why force, besides the fact that it was a leading concept in nineteenth-century science? The answer is that in its formal meaning "force" internalizes all the aspects of the "thing" that Frau Bauer distinguished while in practice discoursing about it but that were not part of her original meaning of it. In short, as we have just seen, the thing is both a negative and a positive universal in relation to its particular determinations, a circumstance that finally leads to the conclusion that one needs a whole world of things to determine what any thing is in particular. All this was discovered through Frau Bauer's reflections, which she rightly believed, realist that she is, to be informed by what the "thing" is in itself. With "force" she has an object in which she can read off directly, so to speak, all that she has just attributed to the "thing" reflectively. "Force," as the *we* sees it, was in fact ushered in by her reflection.

All the moves made with regard to the "thing" are thus repeated with regard to "force" but with the crucial difference that they are now motivated by a distinction, the counterpart of negative and positive universal, which defines "force" formally. The distinction is between force considered to be such only virtually and force considered as effective or actualized or, as Hegel also puts it, between force and its expression. It is clear that the two presuppose each other. There is no effectiveness without readiness for it and no serious readiness unless already on the verge of effectively manifesting itself. Equally clear is that some external circumstance is required for this manifestation actually to occur. An only virtual force needs soliciting in order to become effective. A second force is thus brought on the scene, and with it there is set in motion a play of forces reciprocally soliciting themselves for the sake of expression and in counterpart retreating into virtuality for the sake of retaining their identity. This is a play first acted out between two forces which expands into a world of forces soliciting and being solicited, manifesting and hiding at the same time. Unlike the world of "things," this world is not held together by someone's external reflection as parsed out into a number of views of it but by the forces' own self-determining play.

Hegel describes this play in great detail. The next crucial move, however, is precipitated by Frau Bauer's continued reliance on common sense that instinctively makes her look for the play, even though she otherwise conceptually comprehends it, in sense-experiences, these last imagined as a series of disparate events. And since she can obviously not recognize it in them, she projects the play into a world that transcends the experiences but of which these are taken to be but spatio-temporal appearances. Thus there comes on the scene the long-standing distinction in the history of philosophy between appearances and reality, the sensible and the supra-sensible or intelligible. Hegel notes that the distinction is speculatively true, for it accurately reflects the nature of phenomenal reality, namely that it is what it is by manifesting an "other" in which its truth resides. But, as just said, Frau Bauer fails to see this "other" within the appearance of it, a relation of immanence for which she already has a first model in force and its expression. The problem is thereby set for her of connecting the two realms she has imagined, the phenomenal and the real, the sensible and the supra-sensible, despite the fact that the definition of one is already entailed in the definition of the other.

Attention is first directed at the always altering content of the phenomenal realm for which she seeks a norm of appearing, just as she sought a norm for how to determine the "thing." At the present stage, however, she knows what she is doing and even has a name for what she is seeking, namely a principle or law which, as she presumes, lies in the supra-sensible realm of the intelligible. But the realm of phenomena is multifarious, ever-altering in content (as we just said), and to bring it under law in a determinate manner requires a multitude of laws. The intelligible realm, as the source of lawfulness in general, thus morphs into a realm of laws paralleling the phenomenal. Law, as Hegel says, is "the *stable* image of unstable appearances."[58] To the extent, however, that multiplicity is introduced into it and lawfulness is particularized into laws, these also need principles of unity, that is, laws of laws that together yield a whole system of laws. In other words, all the problems that common sense imagines it is resolving by relating the sensible realm to the intelligible are in fact iterated from within the latter. The net result is that, while sense-certainty never ceases to color the realm of the phenomenal, the content of the latter is in

[58] PS § 156; GW 9:96.16.

fact absorbed into the play of conceptualizations that common sense posited on the other side of it in order to explain it. By the same token, however, this other side, the intelligible, is demonstrated to lie nowhere but in its appearances. Its presumed moment of transcendence is not thereby abolished but is only shown to be a moment of phenomenality. Phenomena carry their own explanation.

The salient point in this process is, however, yet to be noted. The determination of "thing" and "force" required that they morphed into two coexisting things and two interactive forces and then each into a whole world of coexisting things and interactive forces respectively. Determination requires mediation, and this is a condition that equally applies to the realm of the intelligible, which is now at issue if it is to be determined as the source of the lawfulness governing the course of phenomena, not just in general but in particular. The intelligible world also needs doubling. But this is a doubling that must occur from within its internal requirements, just as, in the case of "thing" and "force," it did from within the concept of each. The two worlds at issue, in other words, are not the sensible and the supra-sensible, as Frau Bauer might well believe. Her attempt at explaining the one in terms of the other is indeed the occasion for the intelligible world becoming ever more populated with determinate laws, but only historically. Rather, inasmuch as she is already engaged in conceptual activity, in explaining the sensible world, she idealizes: she represents the sensible world in the way it would have to be in order to be capable of being explained, taking her cue from the requirements of lawfulness in general. Or, again, she transfers it into the realm of the intelligible but in a form that makes it the adequate counterpart of the intelligible world originally posited – an adequate counterpart, such as it could not be if still laden with the imaginative content that common sense attributes to it as sensible.

Thus do two worlds emerge. The same spatio-temporal event that counts in one as an act of heroism (i.e., carries positive meaning) counts in the other as a crime (i.e., carries negative meaning); or again, the same event that carries somatic value in one carries psychic value in the other; the water of chemistry in one is the wine of consciousness in the other. The two worlds all the more reflect each other, and logically shift into one another, the more abstraction is made from their sense-content, and the intractable dualities that embarrass Frau Bauer at the level of common sense consequently melt away. Common sense, on which classical science still relies, is totality marginalized, and science comes to the true concept of itself *as science*.

How are these two worlds held together in one universe of meaning? Precisely by the discourse navigating across them, at once overreaching itself yet retaining thematic unity at each step. This is the process of explanation in which Frau Bauer has in fact engaged from the beginning but which now becomes itself an object of reflection. To explain, as transpires from Frau Bauer's action, is to expand on a concept of which one already grasps the sense in principle but for which one needs further clarification/explication in order to be sufficiently satisfied with it. Explaining is a matter of repeatedly returning to an original definition, expanding it in scope – and this might well require theorizing, even much theorizing and much formalizing – but never exceeding its limits. And when does one put an end to this explaining? Precisely when one is satisfied with it.

This is the crucial point that brings the *we*'s narrative back to the very beginning of Frau Bauer's experience and advances it to a new level of self-awareness. There is a reason why she would be from the beginning invincibly certain about reality being *there*, its determinations presumably ready to be read off on inspection; or why, as in actual experience this proves not be the case, she would simply reformulate the nature of that reality's presence without ever faltering in her lived realism. The fact is that her certainty regarding reality is at the same time a certainty regarding herself as the existentially unsurpassable point of access to it – the point at which she orients herself in the discovery of it. From a third person's view, that point might well be taken as just one physical position in a series of like positions, and so Frau Bauer herself might take it to be in her role as reflective observer. But in lived experience it is the *here* around which reality organizes itself – where the "whence" and "whereto" first assume meaning; at which, therefore, reality acquires the value of being *for her*. Any doubt about this reality would thus redound on Frau Bauer's self-certainty, and this, of course, is existentially inadmissible.

There has been a subtext, in other words, to the *we*'s narrative, which comes to the fore only with Frau Bauer's self-aware engagement in explanation.[59] That the *we* has had leverage over her so far, effectively prodding her to come up with the right determination of the "*this* and *that*," is because there is more at issue in that determination than what reality is *in itself*. At root, the issue is how Frau Bauer herself stands with respect to it: her capacity to let it be manifest for what it truly is. This is an

---

[59] Hegel's own image for the revelation of this subtext is of Frau Bauer finally reaching behind the veil of phenomena and discovering herself as subject therein. PS § 165; GW 9:102.16–17.

issue that affects her personally, which in fact motivates all her experiences and for this reason also makes her responsive to the *we*'s questioning. Experience is from the start a process of explanation, of laying out the right space for truth to emerge. And this is a task for which Frau Bauer must rely on her own inner resources. To put it in historical terms, Hegel, as impersonated by the *we*, has learned Fichte's lesson, already present in Kant's *Critique*, that sense and sensibilia are by no means the most fundamental dimension of experience. There is a subjective dimension to it that shapes it at a more comprehensive level and provides the motivating factor for the objectifying activities that originate in sensation. "Feeling" is the most primitive, albeit already complete form, of precisely this dimension. As Fichte said, feeling is the concrete self. Now that, in deliberately engaging in the work of explaining, Frau Bauer has become reflectively aware of her own subjective contribution to the constitution of objects, or at least should have become so aware, the stage is therefore set in the *we*'s narrative for starting all over. It is a matter of reflecting on experience precisely as a process of self-constitution.[60]

(4) Section IV is perhaps the best known of the whole Phenomenology – certainly the most influential in the shaping of the Hegel tradition. Here we find the "battle of prestige" and the "master/slave dialectic" made famous by Marx and Kojève; also the iconic figures of the Stoic and the Sceptic, each with its special kind of subjectivity; finally, the portrayal of the "unhappy consciousness" that Kierkegaard made his own. Nonetheless, most note-worthy at the very outset is that, while the conclusion of section III clearly

---

[60] Sections IV, V, and VI make up the bulk of Hegel's work. Together they constitute (like I, II, and III) a conceptual totality, of which sections VII and VIII finally make explicit the unifying principle. We said earlier that the *we* proceeds at each stage by first defining the *a priori* governing a certain field of experience; then by observing this *a priori* as it is realized historically; finally by coming up with a renewed *a priori* that incorporates in its form the results of the observed realization. This renewed *a priori* presumably resolves the difficulties *de facto* encountered in the course of the realization. This schema also applies, but quite in general, to the relation of section IV to the two following sections. At the stage of section IV, the *we* is in possession of a maximally abstract, yet in principle already complete, concept of subjectivity. It is in the position, therefore, of recognizing the existential problems that being a subject necessarily brings in train, as well as of identifying the judgments that a subject must make about its identity in the effort at coping with precisely the said problems. All this is done in principle in section IV. The resulting experiential schemas are then historically realized in the subsequent two sections; first, within the universe of meaning which the physico/social sciences generate (section V); second, within the universe of communal existence (section VI). These two universes reflect each other, not unlike the two worlds of laws in the realization of the concept in section III. The experiential matrix that holds them together at root is however made manifest only in the concluding sections VII and VIII that deal, respectively, with Religion and Philosophy. These two provide the ultimate *a priori*, the motivating factors, of all experience.

shows that Hegel had learned Fichte's lesson, the opening of section IV shows just as clearly that he was not a Fichtean *tout court*. In a patently non-Fichtean move, which is just as much anti-Cartesian, Hegel opens the section by dwelling upon the concept of life. The body is where the pre-history of the human subject lies. The form-relation that defined the "thing" was between substance and properties; for "force," it was between potency and effectiveness; for "law," between rule and actual governance. In the context of life, it is now one between living organism and environment. The earlier relations are reiterated in the form of a process by which a living individual actively transforms what would otherwise be just a presence external to it into means of self-determination. It transforms water into drink, grass into fodder. It creates a new, organically indexed world within which it is at home.

Frau Bauer now holds quite a different relation to the experience that is the object of her reflection and the subject of the *we*'s narrative. She previously supported the objects she observed in the medium of her representations. She was the one holding their aspects together, the same aspects that the objects themselves only displayed *seriatim*, without comprehending them. Frau Bauer indeed comprehended them but only externally: hence the formalism of her knowledge or, for that matter, the formalism of the theoretical standpoint in general. In the present context the objects she observes comprehend themselves instead, and this is another way of saying that, in comprehending them, Frau Bauer is in fact reflecting on herself. The *we*'s narrative thus becomes one about her in person. Her body is quite in general the object at issue, desire being its basic determination. In principle this body is a subject even at the level of sheer animality. As Hegel says,

> Even the animals are not shut out from [the] wisdom [of the Eleusinian Mysteries of Ceres and Bacchus] but, on the contrary, show themselves to be most profoundly initiated into it; for they do not just stand idly in front of sensuous things as if these possessed intrinsic being, but, despairing of their reality, and completely assured of their nothingness, they fall to without ceremony and eat them up.[61]

But how does one move from merely organic existence to typically human existence? While Hegel is clearly not a Fichtean *tout court*, as we just said, he would not have learned Fichte's lesson if he did not do justice to Fichte's insight into the autonomy of the self.[62] In effect, how does one move from

---

[61] PS § 109 (p. 65); GW 9:26–30.   [62] Which is also the insight behind Kant's "I think."

such violence as one should expect to break out in nature because of conflicting desires to the battle of prestige with which Hegel iconically figures the origin of human history? Kojève's Marx-inspired reading of the text is unfortunately misleading. Kojève bases his reading on the capacity of abstractive reflection to absolve desires of their naturally appointed limits, thereby rendering them infinite. From "infinite desires" he imperceptibly shifts to "desire of desire," whence to "desire of prestige" and to "personality." But natural desire, even when infinitized by abstractive reflection, might indeed give rise – mechanically, as it were – to unfettered systems of power relations. We know from history that it does. Fichte, as we saw in Chapter 1, also knew that. This might be sufficient for a Spinoza or a Marx, or anyone committed to a purely naturalistic interpretation of human conduct. But not for Hegel. Take the warrior battling before the walls of Troy, the mytho-poetic background of Hegel's battle of prestige. He is still innocent of abstractive reflection but knows with his body (*feels*, in other words) that he would not deserve the name he carries were he not ready to stand by it. In satisfying his otherwise natural desires (abducting Helen, for instance), what counts most is not the physical satisfaction but the *right* to it. But this amounts to communal recognition, despite the fact that the satisfaction at stake is eminently singular (nature guarantees that much) and that to extort it and thus to invest singularity with universal significance inevitably leads to conflictual claims of rights. Thus our hero must stand by his claim to universal recognition at his most singular, courting death for its sake.

Prestige is a matter of feeling, not just desire; and feeling, to cite Fichte again, is where the concrete self is first realized. We saw this already in Chapter 1 when defining the realism of German Idealism as typified by Fichte, specifically by Fichte's early attempt at deriving genetically the feeling of respect for the law that Kant had only presumed. Moral feeling was Fichte's concern in that particular instance, but his analysis easily extends to feeling in general and first finds its place in Hegel's Phenomenology precisely at this point. The problem with Kojève's interpretation of the text is that it misses its Fichtean moment. It misses what Hegel called in one of his aphorisms "the *Fichtes Verdienst*: Fichte's contribution."[63] Kojève's power relations, as well as the violence and the risk of death that come with them, are still a product of nature, albeit

---

[63] For the "eloquent testimony that Hegel left [in this aphorism], midway through his Jena years, to his change of heart about the importance of Fichte in the evolution of German Idealism," see Harris (1995), p. 79. For the history of the aphorism, its loss and recovery, see also Harris (1995), pp. 79–80. This is the aphorism (trans. p. 80): "Only after the history of consciousness does *one know, what one*

intelligent nature. However brutal in their physicality, such relations are still perfectly consistent with the Adamic pre-fall paradise. Not so with the emergence of Hegel's Spirit – for it is none other than Spirit that in the battle of prestige makes its first appearance. Rather, the battle requires the fall from the innocence of precisely that paradise. This fall (which for Hegel was an "upward" one) is the *novum*, the existential creative leap which, as we said, occurs at every turn of Hegel's phenomenology and at the present turn marks the shift in the *we*'s narrative from substance to subject. It consists in the emergence of a new conceptual space (call it "moral," but in a very broad sense), which is itself the product of reason but qualitatively different from any already encountered because it is totalizing in its effect: it transcends nature as a whole, embracing it. The characters who now begin to populate the *we*'s narrative all tread their way within the compass of this space. They are all new versions of Frau Bauer. What makes them new, however, is that their being beholden to particular objects of desire, even the fact that they desire at all, has become a problem for them. They need to justify the fact, whether by owning or disowning it, in either case by taking a stand with respect to nature which is not determined by nature itself but in which, in taking it, they feel bound by a norm that rather transcends it absolutely. Their vocation in nature as human beings thus becomes for them the overriding concern.

What exactly is this vocation? Here we must retrace our steps. We said that there is a concept at the head of every section of the Phenomenology that serves as the norm or *a priori* for the exposition of the typical experience that follows. In effect, this exposition consists in translating the concept into concretely determinate phenomena, a process which for Hegel amounts to realizing it. We also said that the motive force behind this realization is a complexity in the original concept that can be the source of confusions. In the case of Frau Bauer, the confusions were so far of a theoretical nature. Now that the subject has come on the scene, and the leading concept is precisely that of subjectivity, they would have to be of a more existential nature, a matter of lifestyle. The complexity at issue is of course Hegel's dual claim: on the one hand, that organic nature is where the subject originates; on the other hand, that the subject comes on the scene only inasmuch as its presence asserts itself as transcending the nature on which it still depends for its pre-history. Realizing the concept consists in reconciling these two claims. As we have seen from Frau Bauer's

in these abstractions has through the Concept: Fichte's credit." Harris has "earning" instead of "merit" or "contribution."

experience, the realization requires parsing the concept's complexity in a relation between two terms (in doubling the concept, as Hegel puts it). In her experience, the terns were external views of the intended object; in the present, where subjectivity is at issue, the terms are instead living individuals who work out in their mutual relations the difficulties that coming to terms with nature brings with it. The realization is essentially a social affair, and so are the failures and achievements that go with it and actually propel it forward.

But to return to the question just posed, the defining mark of this process of realization is precisely *reconciliation*, and this is the mark that equally defines for Hegel the vocation of humankind. It is the positive moment of Hegel's exposition of subjectivity which, while seriously incorporating Fichte's negative moment of transcendence, does not let it have the last word. Reconciliation (*Versöhnung*) with nature – or returning to it after the "upward fall," but with a difference – is the leitmotif of Hegel's idealism; not emancipation (*Freilassung*) from it, a typically Enlightenment note that resonates, rather, in Fichte's idealism.

The stages through which this process of reconciliation comes to explicit awareness of its own truth are many and complex. Section IV presents them in essence, and they are returned to in section VI where Hegel enlarges on them with recognizably historical material. But the essence is already at hand in the battle of prestige. Violence is for Hegel the factor coeval with the emergence of subjectivity and the consequent beginning of history. Phenomenally, the violence is acted out in a principled battle between individual contestants. But it must be stressed that in directing the violence to one another, the contestants direct it first and foremost to themselves individually. They direct it at their organic nature whose limits they would transcend in order to assert their autonomy, thereby, however, also endangering their existential basis. This, as we said, is the Fichtean negative moment of the experience. The positive moment is the effort at containing the violence – *containing*, not abolishing, which would be impossible short of relapsing into immediate nature and putting an end to history. It would mean transforming it (sublimating it, if you will) into the works of reason and Spirit – above all, recognizing it for what it is and acting accordingly.

This is essentially done in the master–slave relation that follows the battle of prestige. The battle is institutionalized in the form of a social contract that averts the immediate threat of death. It transforms doing violence to nature into creatively working at it. The moments of this social arrangement, together with the feeling-tones that they elicit, are subsequently acted out in the medium of intellectual reflection, parsed out between the figures of the Stoic and the Skeptic. But they are fully comprehended only in the religious figure of the Unhappy Consciousness that follows.

This unhappy individual is the inheritor of the slave, one who has undergone the intellectual discipline of Stoicism and Skepticism and has objectified, in the figure of a transcendent God, the norm, the command to autonomy, that since time immemorial had induced him to battle for prestige. It also occasioned his fall into slavery because of the fear of death that made him incapable of standing by it. He now knows that the master's authority was actually not just the master's in particular but was derived from something greater, common to both. He also knows that the dissatisfaction he felt in his relation to the master was in fact only a reflection of the dissatisfaction typical of the human situation. Namely, the more one tries to purify oneself of nature in order to rise up to God, the more one thereby merges with him; the more, however, one also forgoes self-identity and therefore also the right even to admit that one suffers evil when in fact one actually does. This is indeed the case in the world of the Stoic or, for that matter, the universe of Spinoza. But if, on the contrary, one brought God to the level of nature, infecting him with finitude, one would lose him in the comings and goings of human vicissitudes, making him disappear as anything divine – like the Skeptic who, in his frantic search for truth, in fact dissolves it.

The source of the unhappy individual's dissatisfaction lies, in other words, in his relation to God, just as it lay for the slave in his relation to the master. However, its resolution already lay in principle in that relation. The slave's work was actually the master's, in the sense that the master was the one who reaped its fruits. But the master was able to enjoy the fruits' natural content only because the slave had prepared it *for him*, working on nature, at once fearing it (in this he took it seriously) yet measuring it in accordance with the master's authoritative demands. He only needed to recognize that the source of the master's authority transcended the master no less than it transcended himself also to recognize that he, the slave, was the effective master, the one who humanized nature. He was the one who effectively injected into it the distinction between right and wrong measure. He spiritualized it. All that he needed for personal satisfaction was, therefore, a conversion, a change in attitude, such as neither Stoicism nor Skepticism, however, afforded him but religion did. And a conversion is also what the unhappy believer needs. He must learn that all the work he does to bridge the gap between God and nature is in fact God's work, for in that work alone does God make his effective appearance in history, in the form of Spirit. As Hegel puts it in a different context, "The principle by which God is defined for human beings is also the principle for how humanity defines itself inwardly, or for humanity in its own spirit."[64] There is no dissatisfaction as such in human experience. There are dissatisfactions, rather, due to effective yet always only particularized evils.[65] Some of these are irredeemable. Spirit nonetheless prevails, since only by virtue of its presence are the evils recognized for what they are, and the distinction between right and wrong is maintained. And there is satisfaction in that. This is the historical lesson that the believer must learn, and also the subject of the rest of the *we*'s narrative.

(5) To understand the place of section V in the narrative, and in particular its relation to section VI, one must go back to the conclusion of section III, where Frau Bauer finally recognizes how much she is subjectively implicated in the objective determination of a *this* or *that*. She has become explicitly aware that her conceptual activities – "reason," in a word – are the factors making possible the presentation of an object as what it is in itself. She is also aware that there is personal satisfaction in the achievement of such an objective presentation; even that the quest for the satisfaction motivated her experiences from the beginning. The *we* therefore proceeded in section IV to a reflection on the existential conditions that make for subjectivity. Feeling, as it transpires in that section, is this subjectivity *in concreto*, the matrix of all experiences. Frau Bauer cannot, however, be expected to abandon her realism, and not just because of her common sense attitude that at all times stays with her. The deeper reason is that a subject, while aware of itself, cannot say what it itself is, even to itself, without painting itself on an external world. Feeling is an existential attitude, not a determination of content. The theoretical moment, though not the fundamental one to experience, is nonetheless essential to it. It makes sense, therefore, that Frau Bauer would instinctively treat herself like a thing in nature among other things, but with distinctive traits. There is nothing wrong in this; it is even necessary, as just said. But it is wrong to believe that one is thereby capturing a subject precisely as subject. This is the mistake of which the *we* must disembarrass Frau Bauer in section V before being able to resume in section VI the narrative of section IV,

---

[64] Hegel (2006), p. 203; *Vorlesungen*, Vol. 4a, p. 413.
[65] This is totally different in Fichte and Schelling. For Schelling, evil is a cosmic reality; for Fichte, only a phenomenal semblance.

subsuming the language of theory to the language of social decisions and ethical/moral commitments.

This explains the content of section V and its division into three parts. The motivating factor throughout is the certainty that reason is to be found everywhere in nature, above all at its most singular where it counts most existentially. In the first part, this certainly plays itself out in Frau Bauer's belief that she (now a sophisticated scientist) can actually observe reason in nature: in effect, discover the latter as governed by universal laws even in the most particular details. "Observation" is the keyword. It is relatively easy work to arrive at a taxonomy of nature which objectively reflects the universal/particular/singular relation that otherwise governs discourse reflecting its rationality. It is a matter of finding it, first, with regard to nature in general, externally parsed over space and time, and, in a second stage, internally parsed within the lifecycle of living things. Only too naturally, therefore, interest shifts in observation from the laws regulating nature to the process by which such laws are discovered, that is, finally, to the laws governing the process that are internal to the observer.

Logic and its laws thus become the object of observation, but logic understood as itself a natural phenomenon, its laws as simply a further extension of natural laws in general.[66] It is understood that there is no opposition in thought-processes between form and content, in contrast with the processes observed so far. The simplicity of form issues into a multiplicity of content and this multiplicity directly flows back into simplicity, the whole movement a self-contained totality, a *being-for-its-own-self*. This is the form of the rationality that observation has been seeking in reality all along and which has in fact sustained all its efforts. It is finally found, but affected precisely by "the character of something *found*, something that is *given*, i.e., a content that merely *is*."[67] It is naturalized, in other words, or turned into the hybrid of thought-intentions and natural determinations which is the object of observational psychology.

On the one hand, there is (but thus naturalized) the moment of self-contained individuality of this *being-for-its-own-self* – the self as such. The observer identifies with it and claims to have intuitive access to it,[68] but in fact only naturalizes the self-awareness that goes with thought in general. On the other hand, there is the moment of being, equally naturalized in the

[66] For this, see PS § 300; GW 9:167.33–168.23. In what follows Hegel gives his own version of Kant's critique of rational psychology.
[67] PS § 300; GW 9:167.34–35.   [68] PS § 301; GW 9:168.3324–32.

form of a world external to the self. Both the individual self and its external world have a content that the psychologist derives from observation, inwardly directed in one case, outwardly directed in the other. This content is in fact a hybrid of thought-intentions and natural determinations ("a contingent medley of heterogeneous beings")[69] which the observer nonetheless seeks to bring under a system of laws. There emerge two such systems, depending on whether the content is represented as inner or outer, the two in fact paralleling each other. The consequent task of psychology is to relate the one system to the other, a task that revolves around the question of whether the activities of the self are the ones responsible for shaping the content of the outer world or, on the contrary, the external world shapes such activities. The problem is that, as it turns out, it is just as consequentially possible to take one position as the other. There is no constraining principle for the choice in question, which choice therefore devolves on the freedom of the individual observer. But laws are nothing unless they carry necessity, and, since this freedom preempts it, observational psychology proves to be no science at all.[70]

A further result, however, is that interest in observation shifts again, this time to the individuals that populate the world. The duality of universalizing being and individualizing self is supposedly effaced in them, since the self is taken at its bodily surface where it is already singularly determined yet also affected by universalizing features.[71] Ethnicity is an example.[72] These features replace the external world as the presumed source of the necessity that makes an individual's behavior predictable and therefore a suitable subject of science. But again, contingency breaks out. It ultimately remains indeterminate whether the posited necessity is due to one given feature or to some other factor. This line of inquiry also fails.

The long disquisition on physiognomy and phrenology that concludes Hegel's reflection on "observing reason" (the first segment of section III) might appear strange. Yet it makes perfect sense in context. These two pseudo-sciences represented for Hegel a most extreme, even desperate, attempt at grounding a science of human behavior by pinning the latter's predictability on such radically singularizing features as the shape of a nose or the surface of a skull. For Hegel, however, these attempts only exposed once and for all the limitation of any science based on direct observation

---

[69] PS § 303; GW 9:169.20–21.   [70] PS § 308; GW 9:171.9–17.

[71] PS § 310; GW 9:171.30–172.8. One must remember that the goal of observation is to recognize reason in the details of nature. Conceptualizing the *this* or *that* is still the issue.

[72] "We have here a general human shape, or at least the general character of a climate, a continent, a people, just as before we had the same general customs and cultures." PS § 311; GW 9:172.10–12.

alone.[73] It is of course appropriate to search for reason in reality, even at the singular level of existence: in the *this* and *that* of Frau Bauer. There is no vestige of Cartesianism in Hegel. But it is wrong ("silly," Hegel suggests in one passage)[74] to expect the internal structure of the concept, where rationality is generated, to be displayed at the surface level of nature, as if rationally constituted objects were things and their individuality rested on the peculiarity of such bits of matter as a nose or a skull. Truly reason-based individuality is an achievement – a social one at that. The point has already been made in section IV, to which Hegel now alludes. But it is bound to escape one whose interests, like those of the observational scientist, are narrowly theoretical. Hegel's disquisition on physiognomy and phrenology, both of which he quietly derides, is in fact a *reductio* of the attitude motivating observation when not properly criticized and limited. As Hegel says in conclusion, "Thus it is that this final stage of Reason in its observational role is its worst; and that is why its reversal becomes a necessity."[75]

The nature of this reversal requires close consideration. The protagonists who now come on the scene have a clearly discernible historical pedigree. Although fictional, and as such elevated to the status of universal human types, they are concrete individuals. There is no longer the need of a Frau Bauer to carry the *we*'s narrative. The new protagonists do it. Retrospectively, they presuppose the subjectivity already achieved by the end of section IV. They have been touched by the Christian experience and are subconsciously motivated by the belief that God is "with us."[76] Proleptically, they therefore point to section VI; in particular, to the Enlightenment period which is also the *we*'s most recent past. They are his senior contemporaries. But they do not belong there, because, although subjects, they do not act *as subjects*. They maintain a theoretical attitude with respect to their own selves. They indeed transcend nature, just as the scientist does when observing it. But, while transcending it, they nonetheless think of themselves in categories only suited to the things of nature, asserting their independence before it only by the device of manipulating it to their advantage, maximizing otherwise nature-appointed desires. Here, in this part of the *we*'s narrative, is where the typically Spinozistic category of desire has its place. The portrayed individuals are those whose subjectivity has been informed by the Christian experience, yet see themselves in

---

[73] Physiognomy and phrenology were culturally influential in Hegel's time, and Hegel would have been remiss not to reflect on them.

[74] "*albern*": PS § 346; GW 9:192.10.   [75] PS § 340 (p. 206); GW 9:189.8–9.

[76] So is also the observational scientist in seeking reason in nature.

a universe which is in fact Spinoza's. Natural satisfaction and the power that goes with it are the keywords. Where the observing scientist seeks to see in nature a self-contained system of universal laws, these individuals rather seek the satisfaction possible within it by dint of right desires and rationally orchestrated plans of action.[77] They seek a well-contained and self-sustaining system of desires and satisfactions. But any such system is just as unattainable for desire as it is for observation. And, just as in the latter the quest for reason leads to foolishness, in the other, the quest for satisfaction in nature leads to suffering at its hand. As Jacobi had predicted of Goethe's *Mensch*, when nature is made to satisfy Spirit, it takes its revenge in the shape of Fate.

The gallery of individuals in the second and third part of the section all attest to this result.[78] There is the individual who deliberately dedicates himself to a life of sense-pleasures, seeking satisfaction therein, and testing the limits of power in seduction,[79] only to discover that he thereby gives himself over to forces that overreach him. Nature awaits him, like a fate, precipitating his destruction. Then there is the individual who takes the law of his heart as the overarching law of existence, and, in a frenzy of self-conceit, believes that he can work for the welfare of all humanity on the basis of that law. But in fact he only orchestrates his destruction. Or, again, there is the individual who takes the methodic cultivation of personal virtue as the way to bring order to the world at large but only discovers that the world has ways of its own that constantly come in the way of virtue. The next move is for the same individual to place himself right within that world, as one whose very concrete individuality, complete with talents that make him a sort of perfect spiritual animal, sets the norm of what counts as rational behavior. But what counts as objective norm for one is unavoidably interpreted as subjective interest by some other who equally takes his individuality as objective norm. There thus arises a contest of conflicting normative claims that leads to the testing of behavioral laws and hence, in a final effort at justifying one system of such laws over another, to a process of explanation. But, as already transpires by the end of section III, explanation turns upon itself, unable on its own to reach the intended objective result.

---

[77] A contemporary counterpart of such individuals is one who believes that one can plan one's life and find satisfaction by following the prescription of rational choice theory. This was in fact the formula of the Enlightenment humanism as Spalding defined it. See di Giovanni (2005), pp. 8–10.

[78] We are simply sketching an otherwise very complicated narrative, replete of historical references to the Enlightenment world.

[79] This is Goethe's Faust.

The problem so far, whether in observation by way of explanation or in praxis by choice of lifestyle, is that satisfaction is sought in the wrong place – materially, in the content of experience, where finality is in fact impossible. It is impossible, not because nature, which is the material object of experience, is complicated (physically, of course, it is) but because reason, with its requirements of reflective completeness, with its demand for self-containedness (*an-und-für-sich-sein*), makes it impossible. In a word, it is impossible because experience is *a priori*. The Enlightenment sought reason materially, in a supposed complete system of experiences, and this is what made its rationalism superficial – its reason abstract, to use Hegel's terminology. The individuals just portrayed in the *we*'s narrative, the observer included, belong to the Enlightenment, as we said. For this reason, although their discontent is no doubt real and their fate painful, it is nonetheless existentially superficial. They do not know themselves. They lack interiority.[80] They have not reflectively awakened to the deeper spiritual malady that actually affects them, adding to their discontent an edge of true unhappiness which for them only colors it unaware. This is the unhappiness of the believer at the end of section IV, to which the *we*'s narrative returns. It is an unhappiness caused by reason itself, whose vocation, which is also humankind's vocation, is to contain the conflict between transcendence and singularity which it itself creates. It is a vocation that reason must absolve out of its own resources. This is the origin of the anguish that makes the believer's unhappiness more than just a matter of discontent.

The return to this unhappiness is signaled at the conclusion of this section V by the introduction of one more individual, but of a totally different character than the previous. This is Antigone.[81] Her figure takes the narrative back to the heroic culture of warriors battling for prestige before the walls of Troy. Her story is well known. Antigone is born in a community where reason's authority is lived as a fact of daily existence, embodied in a nature enchanted with gods and in the community's historical governance. Her witness to its effectiveness lies in the fear and respect she feels for the customs and social arrangements which she assumes the gods have appointed in nature from time immemorial; also in the obedience she feels that she owes to the king. His commands, though dependent in content on historical circumstances, nonetheless bind

---

[80] Marx famously said of the proletariat that they suffered but did not know that they did. This is also a case in point.

[81] PS § 437; GW 9:236.8.

absolutely. She unreservedly accepts as sacred both the particular role she discharges in her family as daughter and the authority the king exercises over her without regard for person. But, as it happens, a conflict occurs between a family obligation to which she feels bound by the gods – that she bury the body of her dead brother – and a command from the king that would prevent her from discharging it. She opts to obey the gods. The key word is "opts." Indeed, Antigone acts in character, abiding by her divinely appointed vocation as daughter. But it is significant that she does it deliberately, fully cognizant that she is contravening the king's command, and in full expectation that she will be justly punished for it. The action has become for her a personal issue, a matter of conscience. Neither the sacredness of nature nor the historical authority of the king, both of which she nonetheless still respects, motivate her. What motivates her is, rather, the internal authority of reason – the idea of Law, as Kant would put it. The idea has been with her all along, and the authority of nature as well as the king's have in fact been parasitical on it. Only now, however, in the medium of the highly singularized voice of conscience, does it become self-conscious. Nature is disenchanted and royalty demythologized. It remains to be seen how the universalizing authority of reason and conscience's individualizing yet absolute claims are to be reconciled. This is the theme of section VI.

(6) Much of section VI has already been anticipated. In this section especially, the Phenomenology takes on the guise of a treatise on language. The first segment, "The Ethical Order," depicts the cultural world in which Antigone feels at home but of which she precipitates the end. This is not to say that the conflict has not in fact been working itself out all along in the existence of her community, below the surface of its apparent natural harmony, or, for that matter, that it has not already exacted its price in the tragic fate of individuals. Nor is this to say that reconciliation is not also already at hand. Both conflict and reconciliation are the product of Spirit, the substance of the human vocation. But the point is that in the world of that community, of which the defining voice is the impersonal one of the oracle, the two are indeed acted out and experienced – not, however, *as such*. The community's deeds are perceived as blending with the course of the world order. That is the flaw for which it is fated to destruction.[82]

---

[82] In Hegel's interpretation of Greek tragedy, the flaw consists in taking as natural, i.e., as divinely appointed, social arrangements that are in fact the products of pre-reflective creative decisions. This prevents the social agents from actively taking at hand the disruptive consequences of these

The difference in the world that follows the ethical order is that the conflict is institutionalized as an opposition between a ruling authority on the one side and individual subjects of legal obligations on the other. Each side is explicitly aware of its independent standing with respect to the other: the ruling authority as norm-setting; the individual subjects as the ones who demonstrate the effectiveness of the authority by realizing its norm at the level of actual existence. By the same token, each side equally demonstrates its dependence on the other: the authority because without being recognized and acknowledged as such, a norm is mere *flatus vocis*; the individuals because, without their feeling bound to the norm, without exhibiting it (so to speak) in their particularized body,[83] they would not personally perceive themselves as belonging to the community created by the norm-setting authority. In other words, each side needs the recognition of the other in order to occupy its social space effectively. And here is the problem. For, at this primordial stage, the norm (the promulgated law) is much too abstract. It can indeed bind the individuals to which it is addressed, but without regard for their singular differentiations. These individual subjects, for their part, can in turn only respond to it in kind, that is, recognizing (but only formally) their dependence on the law for their status as norm-bearing individuals, but without thereby deriving from it the satisfaction they would expect as individuals concretely invested with universal value.

Bridging the gap between these two sides of a society, or, in other words, reconciling its two opposing yet interdependent interests, thus becomes the society's defining task. Essentially, the reconciliation consists in overcoming the formalism of an already explicitly rational yet still inchoate social arrangement. In the course of the *we*'s narrative, political power becomes ever more interiorized. Authority, rather than being only

arrangements – disruptive because not recognized for what they truly are. The agents suffer these consequences as if the victims of an anonymous fate. Oedipus suffers the power that the unconscious exercises over reason precisely because it is unconscious. At Thebes (another of Hegel's examples) the social order is disrupted when the first born, naturally taken as the rightful heir to the throne, happens to be twins. Or again, the divinely appointed role that the sister unreflectively plays in the family is itself a source of communal disruption ("the irony of woman," as Hegel calls it) for she at once prepares the brother for public life yet flatters him because of his sensuous beauty, thus making him prone to sensuous temptations. Antigone's case is special because exceptionally creative. She acts in character (as divinely appointed) by burying her brother yet is at the same aware that she is committing a crime by disobeying the human law: she feels guilty about it. She does not simply ignore the human law as if it were beyond her ken but feels its force even while acting in character. She thereby undermines the human/divine divide on which her culture is based. Human, i.e., rational, law has power even in the realm of the gods.

[83] The Apostle Paul was decapitated, instead of crucified, because he was a Roman citizen.

accidentally connected with the individuals historically wielding it, is seen as invested in them because of the effect its exercise has in promoting the welfare of a society. Whatever the historical circumstances that brought the rulers to power, their vocation is to promote precisely this welfare. This is the warrant for their authority – which authority therefore more directly addresses itself to the subjects under its rule *as individuals*. The distant Roman emperor progressively morphs into the more familial figure of the King. The subjects, for their part, even as consciously engaged in promoting their interests as members of particular families or interest groups, come to recognize that in these activities, while advancing their particular good, they at the same time contribute to the welfare of the whole. Their particularity progressively assumes public relevance.

The distance between universal authority and personalized obligation is thus progressively bridged from both sides. The two sides actually collude in the process. It is a matter of the two retrieving and repossessing, but under the explicit rule of reason, all the customs and beliefs that populated Antigone's world but were held together in quasi-natural order. They were set free upon the advent of explicit reason, no longer anchored to the historical sanction of community life. In Hegel's image, borrowed from the physics of the day, they became like spiritual masses ("spiritual" because originally the products of creative decisions) roaming in the new social space created by formal reason, assembling and reassembling according to historical circumstances. They thereby exercised their influence over the life of individuals and communities, but they did so without internal guiding principles. Reconciling formal rule of reason and particularity of individual existence lies precisely in providing such principles – in effect, in recreating Antigone's organic world, but as the explicit product of reason.[84] *Bildung*, "education," "the creation of culture," are apt words for describing the process. The *we*'s narrative follows its progress through the Roman period, early Christianity, the Middles Ages, all the way down to the *we*'s modern world, in each case identifying the implicit judgment – the creative cultural commitment – on which the life of a given social arrangement depends. And in each case, as one would expect, since language is for Hegel the existence of Spirit, the judgment is enshrined in a particular type of language.

The irruption of Christianity in the Roman world impressed upon the process a historically particular determination that shaped its progress

---

[84] This process is still ongoing nowadays, where even "gender" is no longer taken as a simple given, let alone as a differentiating mark on which social existence is organized.

thereafter. Christian beliefs and Christian practices figure prominently in the *we*'s narrative. It is nonetheless important to note that the alienation which is the factor motivating the process's progress, although *de facto* playing itself out in this Christian medium, has its origin, according to the narrative, in the legal formalism of the Roman world.[85] At the source of the feeling of alienation that inspired the Christian belief in a transcendent yet incarnate God there stands the anonymous figure of the Roman Emperor. He is the one who disrupted the natural order of things of the earlier social world and caused the peoples to roam in pilgrimage across the land in search of God's presence. In their pilgrimages they also worked at the land and thereby created new worlds of culture. This was an object-directed work. Long before the Roman Emperor, however, Antigone had already elicited with her discovery of the voice of conscience the subjective moment implicit in that work, which, in Hegel's time, had become the preponderant cultural force. In the *we*'s narrative, the line of reason coming explicitly to its own thus runs from Antigone's antiquity, through to Roman Empire, directly to Hegel's own modern world.[86]

It is only appropriate, therefore, that section VI concludes with a return, but at a highly interiorized level of experience, to the primordial battle of prestige with which section IV begins, and that reconciliation is again sought through mutual recognition. At the end of section VI the contest is no longer between warriors battling before the walls of Troy but between consciences, and the time is Hegel's own. The iconic figure is the beautiful soul who comes on the scene in response to Kant-inspired morality.[87]

This character is a contemporary of our narrator/author, who at this stage of the Phenomenology has himself become a protagonist of the narrative. This is Hegel coming to terms with the post-Enlightenment Romanticism of his age, precisely raising the issue of what reason is all about. The two *personas*, the heroic warrior and the beautiful soul, thus stand like end-pieces to sections IV/VI of the narrative. Both are engaged

---

[85] This is quite a departure from the Hegel of the early theological writings, who attributed the formalism and concomitant sense of alienation which he believed had affected the whole history of the Christian West to its Judaic heritage, still a reflection of Abraham's relation to his transcendent God. This heritage had presumably obscured Jesus's message of love. There is nothing of this in the Phenomenology. See di Giovanni (2010).

[86] Christian culture is thus itself a product of the classical world, according to Hegel. Its Judaic heritage, which no doubt shaped it in many ways, is for it, nonetheless, only a historical accident. In the early Hegel, Abraham is the one iconically depicted as the first rational man, since he disrupted humankind's relation to nature. In the Phenomenology, Antigone is, instead, this first man.

[87] "This self of conscience, Spirit that is directly aware of itself as absolute truth and being, is the third self." PS § 633; GW 9:341.17–18.

in a battle of prestige, the one at the risk of physical death, the other, the beautiful soul, who is clearly a Christian product, now battling for the supremacy of individual conscience, in his case at the risk of spiritual death. Hegel himself hints at the connection between these two battles.[88] In both – important to note – the protagonist has from the start of the experience already resolved the problem of reconciling universality of norm and singularity of nature; has done so essentially by spiritualizing nature without the compromises of the characters in between, but for different reasons. The heroic warrior because, standing at the origin of history, reflection is for him only inchoate. Normativity, communal recognition, death, valor, all blend together in the one *feel* for prestige. Quite different is the situation of the beautiful soul, at the end of history. The heroism is of a different kind. This is the character who has undergone the alienating experience of culture, who more recently has submitted to the discipline of the guillotine, itself a spiritual creation that brought heaven to earth,[89] and who has also heard the transcendent voice of Kant's "ought," at whose command he stood before nature in fear and trembling. And now, in a heroic effort at redeeming his singularity, he attributes to the voice of his conscience, dependent as this voice is on the highly particularized historical circumstances under which it is formed, the kind of universal authority that only God would have. It is a matter of wanting to be like God. So it is that a battle of conflicting witnesses to universal truth, all based on the singular voice of conscience, inevitably emerges: all are equally witnesses to universal truth; all, therefore, are implicitly violent. And the risk incurred in the battle – a risk to which every contestant has in fact already fallen victim from the very start – is to be exposed as a liar.

Whether at the beginning or at the end of history – or, for that matter, as the Phenomenology's narrative shows, in between – conflict, even violence, whether physical or spiritual, normally both at once, is essential to the human situation: it is the medium in which the synthesis of universal and singular, reason and nature, is consummated. We are violent *because* we are rational. This is the all-important point at which Hegel sheds any vestige of Platonism. This is what it means to bring the eternal within the temporal. The story, however, does not end there. Before the walls of Troy,

---

[88] In the sense that, in both cases, the validation of a judgment does not lie in its individual content but in its being recognized as *one's own judgment*. Recognition is simply for the sake of recognition. "The action is thus only the translation of its individual content into the *objective* element, in which it is universal and recognized, and it is just the fact that it is recognized that makes the deed a reality." PS § 640; GW 9:345.6–8.
[89] "The two worlds are reconciled, and heaven is transplanted to earth below." PS § 581; GW 9:316.7–8.

after Achilles had wreaked his vengeance over the body of Hector, Priam came to him to reclaim his son's body for honorable burial. And Achilles and the Gods agreed that that was the right thing to do. Where violence shall be, the community intervenes, not to do away with it, which would be impossible indeed, but to contain it and redeem it. The community is itself a product of reason. In the Phenomenology, the *we*'s narrative portrays the series of social arrangements which, at least in the West, have institution-alized violence and by the same token have also contained it. At the end, when the beautiful souls are existentially forced to recognize that the source of the violence lies in the attempt to be like God, they also understand that they are not perpetrating violence just *de facto* but that they must do it if their natural singularity is to be invested with universal significance. We are evil because we are rational. Therefore the beautiful souls learn the lan-guage of confession and forgiveness.[90] The community of those who know how, not indeed to abolish, but to contain and redeem evil, is thus created.

This is the religious community. The *we* also learns. He learns that religion, which, as he recognizes, has so far appeared in the narrative only on the sidelines, is in fact the matrix within which all the narrated forms of human conduct have in fact unfolded. He therefore starts retelling his story from the start, in section VII, as a story about religion. It is in the medium of religious beliefs and liturgical practices that individual identity is first created. Such beliefs and practices are essentially rational. We are religious because we are rational.[91]

5.4 History and Mythology of Reason

We shall have to say more regarding religion and philosophy in Hegel or, more precisely, regarding the reconciliation that is possible in each.[92] At the moment, however, we must return to Schelling's confrontation with Hegel.

---

[90] The significant text is at the conclusion of section VI, starting at PS § 665; GW 9: 358 ("Das Urtheil ist aber . . . etc"), to the end.

[91] This is how Edward Caird, perhaps the most insightful nineteenth-century interpreter of Hegel, summed up the latter's attitude toward Christianity: "But the real difference between [Hegel] and Schleiermacher is that he regards Christianity as itself an essential product of reason, and indeed as that form in which reason first, so to speak, defined to itself its own nature, or brought that nature to self-consciousness. Accepting, therefore, in the literal sense, the *anima naturaliter Christiana* of Tertullian, he could admit that Christianity should take its place with other religions in the natural process of development without claiming for it any exceptional position of *Urbildlichkeitl* [primor-dial culture], while, on the other hand, he had the confidence that no change of form, produced by the free application to it of the idea of development, could be fatal to its essential truth." Caird (1891), p. 407.

[92] Chapter 6.

Now we should be able to see why Schelling could not understand Hegel or, for that matter, why he would miss the nature of the new method of philosophizing that Hegel was working out in the Phenomenology. Schelling painted the course of experience as if its events acted out in time a play of forces already accomplished in God's inner life before all time. They derived their reality precisely in mirroring this life. Nature's unconscious was the place where this life first manifested itself and where reason, itself a temporal phenomenon, found its point of incomprehensibility. For Hegel, on the contrary, the truth of experience was to be found nowhere but in the course of its events. Their motive force – to make the point as abstractly as possible – was the nothingness that made their being essentially always an achievement, the always particular end-point of a process of becoming. And the most effective of this nothingness was the reflective negativity that reason brought to experience, thereby opening for it ever new creative possibilities of being.

This difference was reflected in the two philosophers' phenomenologies. Schelling was just as scrupulously concerned with the archeological details of different cultures and different languages as Hegel, perhaps even more scrupulous. Yet the narrative he drew out of such details was necessarily mythological in quality, as Schelling's *Ages of the World* clearly demonstrated. It had to be mythological, for it was circular in intent: it was the account of the fall from, and the return to, an original natural/divine state in which alone temporal events have their truth. All that happened in time was already all *there*, in God's self-manifestation *in illo tempore*, not unlike Spinoza's modes, which never exhibited in their unfolding anything truly new. For this reason, while insisting on the positive reality of evil, Schelling in fact denied the individual freedom that alone made it possible. There was freedom on a cosmic scale, at the moment of creation. And there would be freedom at the moment of consummation, in the act by which God brings all things back to him. In between, however, where from a human point of view freedom counts most, only determination reigns.

Quite different was Hegel's case. His Phenomenology is in many ways, no doubt, a work of fiction, but never a mythology, for it is rooted in lineal time. It was possible for Hegel to explain how and why human events unfold as they do and to attribute responsibility for them. It was possible because of the rational intentions running across them, on the basis of which one can always narrate a story that makes sense on its own merits. Or if it does not make sense, *that* it does not is itself a significant circumstance worthy inquiring about. In either case, there is no need to go beyond the events to discover the true story, one which in visible history would presumably be displayed only in symbols. For Hegel, *the visible story is all that there is.* In either case, moreover, the explanation can only be *ex post facto*, because of the creative negativity of reason, the same which is responsible for the intentions that run across the events and make their explanation possible. The narration, in other words, has to be open-ended, never simply the repetition in time of an already accomplished story *in illo tempore.* The events' truth is simply what they are. In this, namely in the intent to make sense of events, Hegel was like all historians.[93] History is always narrated with intent.[94] In Hegel's case, the intent was to make manifest the process by which reason becomes aware of its own rationality in the course of playing its determining role in human affairs. The narration spanned from Antigone's Troy to Hegel's Jena. Moreover, in typical nineteenth-century Eurocentrism, it assumed that the history of the West epitomizes human history as such. This is what makes it for us not just fictional as it was in Hegel's own time but dated as well. Nonetheless, even at its most fictional or (for us) dated, it was essential to the fabric of Hegel's Phenomenology that it at least shadowed recordable events.

We have already remarked on Fichte's attitude toward history and have also noted how it mirrored Schelling's, still playing out with the latter the ambiguity inherent in the monism the two philosophers shared. It was the same ambiguity that had made it impossible for them to communicate on the subject of "nature." We also said that, while Schelling had no language for the individual caught up in the vicissitudes of God's march across history, Fichte, ever the existentialist, did. We must now revisit this claim, before resuming the Phenomenology's narrative from where we have just left it, with religion making its official appearance on the scene. Fichte's language for the individual is religious in nature, just as it was for Kant and also is for Hegel. Ultimately, the difference between Hegel's Idealism and that of Fichte and Kant – or, for that matter, the difference that marked Hegel's return to Kant, however qualified this return was – is an issue that comes to a head precisely in religion. Or more precisely, it revolves on whether, and why, an irreducible distinction can be maintained between religion and philosophy.

---

[93] There is quite a broad range of possibilities separating "chronicle" and "history."

[94] A recent instructive example is Margaret MacMillan's *The War that Ended Peace: The Road to 1914* (2013). See also the conclusion of Mann (1996), and Milan Kundera, as cited in *Harper's* magazine, March 2, 2007, pp. 12–13: "By definition, what a narrator recounts is a thing that has happened. But each little event, as it becomes the past, loses its concrete nature and turns into an outline. Narration is recollection, therefore a summary, a simplification, an abstraction. The true fact of life, of the present prose of life, is found only in the present moment. But how to recount past events and give them back the presentness they have lost? The art of the novel found a solution, the past in *scenes*."

CHAPTER 6

Of Things Divine and Logical

"Even as the content, God, determines itself, so on the other side the subjective human spirit that has this knowledge determines itself too. The principle by which God is defined for human beings is also the principle for how humanity defines itself inwardly."

Hegel[1]

"Metaphysics falls entirely within logic. Here I can cite Kant as my precedent and authority. His critique reduces metaphysics as it has existed until now to a consideration of the understanding and reason."

Hegel[2]

"Here again, then, we see language as the existence of Spirit. Language is self-consciousness existing *for others*, self-consciousness which as such is immediately *present*, and as *this* self-consciousness is universal. It is the self that separates itself from itself, which as pure 'I' = 'I' becomes objective to itself, which in this objectivity equally preserves itself as *this* self, just as it coalesces directly with other selves and is *their* self-consciousness. It perceives itself just as it is perceived by others, and the perceiving is just *existence which has become a self.*"

Hegel[3]

6.1   Religion and Feeling

Religion brings us back to the phenomenology of feeling that we borrowed from Fichte in Chapter 1. We are back to it because feeling, as Fichte said, is the concrete self, and religion is the dimension of a subject's existence in which the subject is manifested precisely as such: where, as a self, the

---

[1] Lectures on the Philosophy of Religion of 1827. Hegel (2006), p. 203; Hegel (1985), p. 413.
[2] Letter to Niethammer, October 23, 1812. Hegel (1985), p. 277.   [3] PS § 652; GW 9:351.11–28.

subject achieves objective existence. We said that feeling in Idealism is like a primordial judgment about one's identity. It is an existential judgment, for it has to do with *who* one is. It is made by confronting an other, namely nature, which the one making the judgment necessarily presupposes historically. And it is reflected in the significance (the felt determination) that this "other" assumes because of the judgment. *Who* one is, *is* how one feels about that other. Nonetheless, the judgment is about oneself, and it is achieved by virtue of a principle internal to the one performing it. Reason, or better, the force of its logicality, is for Hegel the principle at issue. This is what Hegel essentially means by the "cunning of reason" (*die List der Vernunft*).[4] Whether, in its attitude toward nature, the self assumes the attitude of mere observer, taking nature as if it were all already *there*, or whether it approaches it as something to be appropriated through work, thus transforming it into social and political realities – moreover, whatever the language in the medium of which the attitude is expressed (for language is the existence of Spirit) – in all cases the self's underlying preoccupation, the one that effectively colors all its experiences, is its identity precisely as self-validating individual. This is a reason-generated preoccupation that works behind the scenes, so to speak, but makes its manifest appearance in religion, in the various forms the latter has historically assumed.[5] These forms were in fact the matrix of all the experiences previously exhibited in the Phenomenology.[6] They reflected a culture's fundamental decision regarding what it means to be rational.[7]

Accordingly, in section VII of the Phenomenology, Hegel retells his story from the beginning but as a story about religious practices and religious languages. And, since religion is essentially realized in every form it historically assumes, the only difference lying in the degree to which it is reflectively aware of itself in each,[8] the story, just as it has been for all the experiences previously considered, is at once the recollection of humankind's past and a further clarification of the mind regarding itself.

---

[4] Cf. PS § 56; GW 9.40.4–7, where Hegel speaks of the cunning of the activity of knowledge in the context of his idea of science.

[5] Hence Hegel can say that "the history of religion coincides with the world-history." Hegel (1971), Addition to § 562, p. 296.

[6] "Religion is the consummation [*Vollendung*] of Spirit into which its individual moments – consciousness, self-consciousness, Reason, and Spirit – return and have returned as into their ground." PS § 680 (translation slightly altered); GW 9.366.9–11.

[7] PS § 680; GW 9.9–34, for the crucial text.

[8] Miller translates the segment in section VII entitled "*offenbare Religion*" as "Revealed Religion," obviously with reference to biblical religion. But this is not accurate. A more accurate translation would instead be "manifest religion," i.e., a religion which is just *that*, and shows it.

We shall get to the story, but not before touching base, so to speak, with Fichte and Schelling again – with Schelling only incidentally, for all that might be said about him and religion has substantially already been said. We have to return to them because it is in the contrast of their idea of religion with Hegel's that the difference between Hegel and his idealist contemporaries is at its clearest. It is a difference that ultimately comes down to one in the relation of religion to knowledge.

6.2   Fichte on Religion

In the 1810–1813 versions of the *Wissenschaftslehre* the idea of God is introduced as a principle of Science. These versions of Fichte's Science are much more phenomenological in character than the 1804 lectures we earlier considered at length.[9] In the latter, it is the Light, or intelligibility in general, that is the source of evidence and the foundation of all knowledge. "God" appears only indirectly, mostly in polemical excursions decrying the habit of conceiving God as a substance, the existence of which could be demonstrated in the way one demonstrates the existence of things. There is no indication of a philosophical theology. In 1810–1813, on the contrary, Fichte provided at least the idea for a theology which, however, he never produced – just as he never produced a science of nature even though he had the idea for one.[10] Fichte was simply not interested in the details of such possible sciences. As for religion, it made an appearance in the 1804 lectures, but only as one of the canonical five modes of experience,[11] which in the lectures remained at best only sketched.

Religion must nonetheless have been prominently present in Fichte's mind in 1804, as is apparent from two other series of lectures which he subsequently offered to the public, and, unlike those of 1804 actually published, both in 1806. These were, namely, *Characteristics of the Present*

---

[9] God is the principle in these versions of the *Wissenschaftslehre*, not in any dogmatic sense but inasmuch as the idea of God is the objectification of the appearing in experience of appearance. Here are two instructive texts, both as cited by Schmid (1995) on pp. 22 and 28 respectively (my translation): "Appearance does not *come to be* [*wird* nicht], but is from [*aus*] God; is as God himself is in himself. Becoming lies only in appearance's self-understanding; but it is there absolutely, and therefore not [with reference to] something else. This absolute becoming is exactly none other than this self-appearing. It might be difficult for the human dogmatic propensity to come to think this genetic form simply and solely as form of appearance: nonetheless, the right understanding of transcendental idealism rests on this insight, and nobody comes to it to whom this has not become clear." "A disposition which is possessed by this appearance [namely, of the idea of God as the ground of the supra-sensible world] and is driven to act by it is called religious, and this whole phenomenon [*Erscheinung*] is called religion."

[10] Schmid (1995), p. 27.   [11] Fichte's *Fünffachkheit*: "five-foldness" or "quintitude."

Age (*Grundzüge*)[12] and *The Way towards the Blessed Life* (*Anweisung*).[13] Both have to do with religion, considered from the standpoint of the understanding in the first and from the standpoint of reason in the other. Both take their starting point from the conclusion of the 1804 lectures. The three series constitute a triad that must be treated together. As Fichte stresses in the 1806 texts, his fundamental science of knowledge (such as he had expounded for his auditors in 1804) would not have been possible without presupposing, on the part of his audience, at least a faint inkling of the presence of the divine in them. This inkling is to be assumed in everyone. As such, it requires reflective exposition. Fichte's doctrine of religion was precisely this exposition. It constituted the existential counterpart – duly presented in 1806 in a popular style more suited to its content – of the preceding expounded, but unpublished, science of knowledge.

We shall see in due course the difference between religion considered from the standpoint of the understanding and from that of reason. We are only concerned at the moment with how religion, as a typical human mode of existence, fits with the 1804 lectures. These, as we have seen, methodically deconstruct all the fixed representations of the imagination and the understanding with which common sense and dogmatic metaphysics routinely determine reality in order to render it intelligible – in fact, however, only succeeding in obscuring the true source of its intelligibility. Fichte had replaced them with other categories of thought that have the merit of representing reality as nothing fixed in itself, nothing substantial, but as a disappearing presence which in its disappearing nonetheless makes manifest the One Light which is in fact the source of its intelligibility. This Light itself remains invisible. At the same time, however, it makes all things visible but precisely as its manifestations. It was as if, under Fichte's guidance, the auditors of his lectures saw their customary world disappear before their eyes but only to be given back to them, unchanged in content and yet totally different.[14] The difference lay on *their* side, in their attitude toward it, or in their *feel* for it, for they had now transposed themselves onto the side of the Light – onto God's side, in the language of religion, and saw only God in them as their truth: "But herein does Religion consist, that man in his own person and not in that of another, with his own

---

[12] *Die Grundzüge des gegenwärtigen Zeitaltere* (1806). English translation in Fichte (2008). Cited with page number from the English translation and reference to the GA.
[13] *Die Anweisung zum seligen Leben* (1806). English translation in Fichte (1977). Cited with page number from the English translation and reference to the GA.
[14] *Anweisung*, 365–366; GA I.9:103.16–23.

spiritual eyes and not through that of another, should immediately behold, have, and possess God."[15]

One cannot help being reminded of Kierkegaard's Abraham who, in making ready to sacrifice Isaac, even in actually sacrificing him according to Kierkegaard's adaptation of the biblical story, remains steadfast in the certainty that his beloved and only son would nonetheless be given back to him and that God would be true to his promise that he (Abraham) would be the father of many nations. But Abraham's certainty is achieved by virtue of the absurd, in a leap of faith subjectively consummated in fear and trembling, before a God who remains hidden. Not so in the case of Fichte's auditors: no need for faith; no place for the absurd. By submitting to Fichte's apophatic discipline, things were given back to them in the full vision of their truth, as manifestations of God. In their eyes, they were absorbed into a self-manifesting God. Theirs was therefore a new life lived with a new intensity, in a state of *bliss*. No fear or trembling for them; no dread; just bliss. But this, according to Fichte, was a feeling that they had harbored all along, albeit unbeknown to them. Fichte had only helped them to become aware of it. It was a feeling in fact enjoyed by mortals even when they believe they are suffering. There was for Fichte no room in experience for the original state of sin or the guilt traditionally preached in Christian doctrine, no room for any original state of misery. This explained his dislike, even hatred, for Paul the Apostle, whom he considered the perpetrator of the doctrine of the fall and of the subsequent need for sacrifice and redemption. Fichte thought of these doctrines as unchristian. It was rather the task of a true doctrine of religion to make people aware of the blessed life they in fact lived, and thereby to bring its bliss to full fruition of enjoyment. Religion was this blessed life.

But for this, a method of exposition was needed that was radically different from that of Science proper. "Popular," not to be understood as either "imprecise" or "non-deliberate," was Fichte's term for it. In his words, "The scientific discourse eliminates truth from among the errors which surround it and oppose it on all sides and in every form; and [. . .] shows the truth as that which alone remains after their exclusion. [. . .] By this method truth emerges before our eyes out of a world full of error."[16] But to see truth before one's eyes requires the right eyes, precisely the subjective capacity to see "with [one's] spiritual eyes and not through that of another" which is religion. The relation between the scientific discourse of the 1804 lectures and the popular discourse of the two subsequent series

---

[15] *Anweisung*, 316; GA I.9:69.8–11.   [16] *Anweisung*, 319; GA I.9:71.28–72.1.

was thus circular. On the one hand, only by virtue of the insight attained through the negativity of scientific reflection could Fichte's auditors come to clearly comprehend the blessedness of their existence. But this presupposed that they already lived in this blessedness and that, in principle, they were therefore capable of submitting to the discipline of the scientific method, that is, it presupposed the right religious attitudes, the right feelings. Popular discourse dealt precisely with these attitudes/feelings. Historically one entered into the circle through religion, in effect by making the historical individual aware of where he or she stood in the world, of what that world meant for him or her at the moment, and of what it could mean in the future if he or she would just live his or her life with the greater intensity that science alone makes possible.

The love of God (where the "of" is to be understood at once as subjective and objective) was thus for Fichte the subject matter of a philosophy of religion.[17] It was, quite explicitly, the subject matter of the *Anweisung* lectures. But *amor Dei* is only the existential counterpart of vision *sub specie æterni*. The *Anweisung* had, therefore, to already be science, but in a style that directly elicited the right *feel* for truth, as its method indicated. It was the inverse of the one followed in the 1804 lectures. Where in these Fichte was intent on deconstructing images and abstractive concepts, the method in the *Anweisung* was constructive. The intent was to provide the auditors with the right imagery, the kind that, just like the language of John the Evangelist, would speak to the heart while engaging the mind. The lectures were like a meditation on the gospel of John, a philosophical play on the gospel's two themes of *logos* and *agapé*.

6.2.1 The Anweisung: The Word As God's Manifestation (logos)

Fichte begins with what is avowedly only a simile for the relation of finite human beings to God.[18] We all know what it means to know. Knowledge is *of* being, an "other" which is distinct from the knower. However, knowledge would not be possible except by virtue of a medium, the concept, which makes this "other" present to the knower. And, inasmuch as the

---

[17] Cf. "The intellectual love of the mind towards God is that very love of God whereby God loves himself, not in so far as he is infinite, but in so far as he can be explained through the essence of the human mind regarded under the form of eternity; in other words, the intellectual love of the mind towards God is part of the infinite love wherewith God loves himself." Spinoza, *Ethics*, part V, proposition 35.

[18] There also is a silent commentary on Schelling throughout the work. According to Gueroult (1974), Fichte is trying to assume a middle position between him and Jacobi.

concept realizes this presence, that is, precisely *as concept*, it cannot be anything in itself. In itself, it is a nothing that adds absolutely *not a thing* to the being it makes present. It indeed renders it manifest *as being*. "Manifestness," however, is not a state that affects the latter internally – it is not a positive determination in any way limiting it. This is the crucial claim. Nonetheless, it must also be admitted that there is a distinction between being and its manifestation. But the distinction is one that must fall squarely on the side of the concept. The latter would not be true to itself if it did not disappear before the being it makes present: in this, and only in this, it distinguishes itself from it. Distinction is a function of its nothingness.

But *to whom* is the manifestation? The simple answer is that it is God who manifests himself to himself – in a self-manifestation, however, which is realized only on the side of the manifestation itself, namely inasmuch as the latter manifests itself to itself as being God's self-manifestation. In no way does this self-manifestation add to God himself. This, as just said, is the simple (though certainly not transparent) answer. The difficulty lies in further imagining how in this manifestation God would appear in a multiplicity of determinations, whereas he is himself one and simple.

Here is where the simile requires that one adhere strictly to the concept of "knowing" as such, resisting common sense's inclination to stray outside its definition. The knower, *as knower*, is totally absorbed into what he knows. *That* alone, that is, *what he knows*, is his reality. However, inasmuch as he nonetheless distinguishes himself from it (as he must, for otherwise he would not know that he knows), the knower must reflectively make himself an object of knowledge distinct from that reality. He has to determine himself in opposition to it. But this requires that he conceptualize himself, in effect that he represent himself to himself as an "other of himself," which "other," however, would thereby fall on the side of the very reality from which he wants to distance himself. Not that he does not distance himself from it. On the contrary, he does, ever farther upon each of the reflections to which he is subsequently led as he inevitably fails in all cases to determine himself. This is a process that initiates *ab infinito* and extends *ad infinitum*, since reflection has no internal limits. One historically finds oneself always already within it. But the significant point is that the reality from which the knower tries to distance himself is phenomenal, only a disappearing appearance of being (it is God's manifestation, his *e-sistence*[19] or standing-out). In the process,

---

[19] For the use of e- and ex- in Latin, see the Lewis and Short, *A Latin Dictionary* (Oxford: Clarendon, 1969), *sub voce* "*ex.*"

therefore, it is this phenomenality of reality that is parsed out into infinitely many but only transiently fixed particular appearances. These are the knower's takes on phenomenal reality as the knower repeatedly flounders in his attempts at self-determination, only letting the intended determination fall by the side. This is how manyness comes to be, or better, appears to be. It is strictly a function of the inherent nothingness of phenomenal existence, of the repeated doubling of its nothingness in reflection which refracts God's existence into a multitude of aspects or modes.[20]

This is no doubt a difficult image to digest, but it was Fichte's popularizing attempt at coping with the inherently intractable paradox of the One and the Many that crops up on any monistic view of reality. It was the same paradox he had dealt with analytically in 1804. One can nonetheless appreciate the intuition motivating him; it is the same that, roughly one century later, must have motivated Jean-Paul Sartre as well. In experience a subject is aware of herself as distinct from the world which she experiences; she even feels as if she presides over it untouched by it. Yet the moment she would want to determine herself as distinct from it (or again, the moment she would want to say *what* she herself is) she has no choice but to draw the required being-determinations from the very world she *feels* distinct from. As a *self* with a history of her own, she is in fact reduced to a determinate path traversed across the world she would preside over. Moreover, even that the path is *her* path is only an idealizing construct, since the path's course is demonstrably determined by the world it traverses. It is as if the whole of intentional existence, the life of consciousness, were but a play at being real that forgets it is a play.

Of course, on the strength of this intuition alone, Fichte's simile could just as well be taken as a manifesto of atheist naturalism. In this, Sartre's resemblance to Fichte would be striking indeed.[21] But the crucial differences is that Fichte was addressing himself to an audience of believers who felt themselves to be nothing except in God; indeed, to be God's self-revelation. That was Fichte's presupposition, the *sine qua non* of his whole science. And, on that presupposition, the being over which an individual subject traces the course of his life's peregrination is itself revelatory. It has

20 "Our Being is ever *in itself* the Being of Being; [...] that which *we ourselves*, and *for ourselves*, are, have, and possess, – *i.e.* in the Form of ourselves, of the Ego, of Reflexion in Consciousness, – this is never Being *in itself*, but only Being in *our Form*, as essence or Nature." *Anweisung*, 465; GA I.9:166.13–17. The "Being of Being" consists of the reflective takes on the infinite reflection of being. The latter is being-initself or God. For this, see lectures 3 and 4. For the division between the infinitude of reflection as such and the quintitude, cf. *Anweisung*, 367; GA I.9:104–105.
21 For Sartre and Fichte, cf. Gardener (2005).

none of the solidity of Sartre's being; its existence is itself phenomenal. On that presupposition it also follows that, despite reflection being in itself "absolutely free and independent,"[22] the internal unfolding of the worlds it creates in consciousness, or, for that matter, the historical sequence of such worlds, is subject to universal and immutable laws to which reflection itself is bound. The necessity of these laws is factical, ascertainable only *ex post facto*, binding the phenomena that the laws govern only externally. But this is for directly the opposite reason as for Sartre. For the latter, it is because being is in itself intractable to explanation: the illusion is to believe that it is tractable. For Fichte, it is because explanation is already *all there*. Existence is God's Word, and the illusion is rather to think that one can add to it substantially. The point is ultimately not to explain existence but to recognize it for what it is, that is, as God's *e-sistence* as it *de facto* appears in its many reflective manifestations.[23]

6.2.2   The Grundzüge: The Ages of the World

As a matter of fact, these manifestations aggregate in configurations that are all essentially equal, in the sense that they all equally manifest God, yet differ in the quality of the consciousness which is realized in each.[24] Such configurations fall into two sequences. One, which we shall consider now while reserving the other for later,[25] extends in time – time itself being the basic form of God's existence. We also know these configurations as historical epochs or ages of the world. At issue in each is precisely the extent to which this existence is explicitly recognized in it. And since reason is the faculty by which the recognition is realized, the difference between them depends on the degree of their rationality.

---

[22] *Anweisung*, 359; GA I.9:99.10.

[23] Fichte is commenting on John: "In the beginning *was* the Word, and through him all things made that are made." John 1.1. Cf. *Anweisung*, 386; GA I.9:118.24ff. He goes on after further citations: "This proposition is wholly equivalent to that which we propounded: – that the World and all things exist only in Consciousness, – according to John, in the Word – and only as objects of conception and Consciousness as God's spontaneous expression of himself; – and that Consciousness, or the Word, is the only Creator of the World, [...] and of the manifold and infinite variety of things in the World." 387; GA I.9:119.27–32. He has just said: "'Away with that perplexing phantasm!' – might the Evangelist have said [...] 'away with that phantasm of a creation out of God of something that is not himself, and had not been eternally and necessarily in himself'." 387; GA I.9:119.14–15.

[24] Or, as Fichte puts it, it is the same energy, the same life, at work in each. The difference lies in the subjective consciousness of this energy that differs from epoch to epoch. Cf. *Grundzüge*, 45; GA I.8:236.32–237.29–238.2.

[25] In Section 6.2.3.

There are five such epochs, according to Fichte, each representing a particular achieved kind of humanity, a particular way of living on earth which *in concreto* constitutes a "race." Fichte describes the epochs in the *Grundzüge*. "There are, according to this view," Fichte says, "*Five Principal Epochs of Earthly Life*, each of which, although taking its rise in the life of the individual, must yet, in order to become an Epoch in the Life of the [human] Race, gradually lay hold of and interpenetrate all Men."[26] And he continues, summarizing their characteristics:

> 1st, The Epoch of the unlimited dominion of Reason as Instinct: – *the Stage of Innocence of the Human Race.* 2nd, The Epoch in which Reason as Instinct is changed into an external ruling Authority; – the Age of positive Systems of life and Doctrine [that have] no power to convince but on the contrary [...] demand blind faith and unconditioned obedience; – *the State of* progressive Sin. 3rd, The Epoch of Liberation, – *directly* from the external ruling Authority – *indirectly* from the power of Reason as Instinct, and *generally* from Reason in any form: – the Age of absolute indifference towards all truth, and of entire and unrestrained licentiousness: – *the State of complete Sinfulness.* 4th, The Epoch of Reason as *knowledge* [...]: – the State of Progressive Justification. 5th, The Epoch of Reason as Art; – the Age in which Humanity with more sure and unerring hand builds itself into a fitting image and representative of Reason: – the State of completed Justification and Sanctification.[27]

The third Age, which was also Fichte's Age, is the one that takes up most of the *Grundzüge*. Fichte is intent on showing how, in the state of total dissolution of long-standing beliefs and rules of behavior created by a new self-awareness on the part of reason, the foundations are also being laid for the subsequent "Epoch of Reason as *knowledge*" which his own Science heralds. Fichte has no doubt regarding his historical role in the unfolding of human history, or reticence in declaring it. Clearly he saw himself as the new John the Evangelist, again proclaiming the latter's gospel of God's presence on earth but in the medium of the rational concept. As for the final Age, "the State of completed Justification and Sanctification," which in the third stage is only being announced and foreshadowed, it would eventually mark a return to the first. Reason would then pervade all aspects of human life with the same naturalness and innocence as it did in the first, except that this naturalness and innocence would no longer be just a *given* but would be an achievement of art, the product of humankind's effort at

---

[26] *Grundzüge*, 7; GA I.8:201.2–5.   [27] *Grundzüge*, 7; GA I.8:201.7–23.

remaking nature after the image of reason – as it was indeed even at the beginning, but only at the end would become fully conscious of the fact.[28]

This is Fichte's philosophy of history. History unfolds according to a plan which Fichte, as he claimed, can lay out *a priori* by virtue of an idea of humanity which is, however, presupposed as already established in the science of being. The story of the human race is in fact the story of God's *e-sistence* in time; it is the story of the progression of reason which is itself but the progression of God's own knowledge of himself. It follows that the unfolding of history follows with inexorable necessity. Or it might be even more accurate to say that for Fichte it does not unfold at all, except in the admittedly epiphenomenal view of one immersed in it and not yet fully aware of his or her own nothingness – a nothingness, however, by virtue of which he or she rejoins the one absolute reality that "all voices call by the name of God."[29] In Fichte's words:

> *Whatever actually exists, exists of absolute necessity; and necessarily exists in the precise form in which it does exist; it is impossible that it should not exist, or exist otherwise than as it does.* Hence, to whatever possesses real existence we cannot attribute any beginning, any mutability, or any arbitrary cause. [. . .] The Existence of God is not the mere foundation, cause, or anything else of knowledge, so that the two could be separated from each other; but it is absolutely Knowledge itself. [. . .] But further: a World has no Existence but in Knowledge, and Knowledge itself is the World, and thus the World, by means of knowledge, is the Divine Existence in its mediate or indirect manifestation; while knowledge itself is the same Divine Existence in its direct or immediate manifestation. If therefore any one should say that the World might also not exist; that at one time it actually did not exist; that at another time it arose out of nothing; that it came into existence by an arbitrary act of God [. . .]; it is just the same as he should say, that God might also not exist.[30]

This explains Fichte's passionate attacks on the biblical story of God entering into covenants with a chosen people, as if God could act arbitrarily, choosing one object or one course of action rather than another.[31] This was a story consistent with the other story of humankind's fall, which was behind the Pauline doctrine of sin and redemptive sacrifice and which Fichte rejected because it obfuscated the figure of Jesus as the first self-conscious manifestation of God's *e-sistence*.[32] It also explains why Fichte

---

[28] *Grundzüge*, 7–8; GA I.8:201.23–202.10.   [29] *Grundzüge*, 104; GA I.8:296.20–21.
[30] *Grundzüge*, 104–105; GA I.8:296.15–34.   [31] *Grundzüge*, 82ff.; GA I.8:274ff.
[32] For Jesus as a special manifestation of God, see, among other places, *Anweisung*, 390; GA I.9:122.21–24. For one of Fichte's attacks on Paul, cf. *Anweisung*, 382; GA I.9:116.1–6.

thought that one should dispense with any myth of creation or, for that matter, of a beginning of the world in general or the human race in particular.[33] The fact is that the world and humankind *are*, and that we, as individuals, find ourselves always already in them; or, more precisely, the fact is that we find ourselves already existing and therefore already engaged in the world that our existence (which is God's knowledge) generates. To want to find any absolute beginning is tantamount to wanting to place oneself outside temporal experience; that is, on the side of God, separating God from his own self-knowledge and thereby falsifying both his nature (inasmuch as one can speak of a nature of God at all)[34] and that of phenomenal existence.

This last point is especially important. It explains Fichte's attitude toward history and the philosophy of history. On the surface it might appear that the *Grundzüge* and Hegel's Phenomenology are engaged in parallel historiographical projects. Both claim to document the stages of reason's progress in self-awareness. Both dedicate much attention to the "present time" – in effect, to the dawning and the eventual dissolution of the Enlightenment. In their respective accounts of this present time, moreover, many of the details dovetail. The main thread of the story is the same. Yet the two projects differ radically, reflecting the two philosophers' just as radically different metaphysical positions. Hegel's history is avowedly fictionalized as a story of reason as such. Nonetheless, it must still have truly historical resonance. The author, in effect Hegel himself, must be able to recognize in it his own temporal past. This is so because the reason whose progression in time is being narrated is *ab origine* continuous with a physical nature that exists in itself, and, even though reason disconnects itself from it as it emerges, thereby reducing it to a past, this past remains nonetheless *reason*'s past, irreducibly still present even as past. It persists as the test of reason's effectiveness in creating its own typically rational world. Quite different is the situation with Fichte, for whom reason has no past and nature is itself only an idea. In the context of his metaphysical assumptions, reason's self-knowledge is ultimately nobody's self-knowledge in particular but only God's knowledge. Fichte can indeed dispense with the biblical myth of humankind's origin, but that is because on his account the whole of history is, and must be, only myth-making.

---

[33] As Fichte will forcefully argue in the 1805 version of the *Wissenschaftslehre*, "nothing comes from nothing": "God is the creator of the world: Not at all. For there is no world, and there can be none, for only the absolute *is*, and the absolute cannot however really and truly proceed outside itself. [. . .] Nothing comes from nothing; nothing eternally remains nothing." GA II 9:288.16–31.

[34] Fichte does it only reluctantly. Cf. *Anweisung*, 464–465; GA I.9:166.1–34.

This is reflected in the way Fichte poses the task of a philosophy of history at the beginning of the *Grundzüge*. The issue is not one of retrieving a past in order to better make it one's *own* past but to construct a story about humankind in general and its present situation that is consistent with the presupposition that reason's past or future are after all already present. Fichte feels free to dispense with empirical inputs but relies instead for the convincing power of his story on the resonance that it has with his auditors' inner life. As he says:

> [The philosopher confines] himself strictly within the limits which [his being a philosopher] imposes on him, paying no respect whatever to experience [...]. It is an entirely different question whether the *present time* be actually characterized by the phenomena that are deduced from the principle which he may lay down, and thus whether the Age so pictured by the speaker be really the Present Age [...]. [For that] every man must consult for himself the experience of his life, and compare it with the history of the Past, as well as with his anticipations of the Future.[35]

But, of course, to recognize one's life in Fichte's picture of the Age, or, for that matter, in Fichte's idea of history in general, one must already live that life with Fichte's intensity.

How does one achieve such an intensity? The stages through which an individual's life must go in order to achieve it and in the process give rise to the Ages just depicted make up the second of the two sequences of configurations of phenomenal existence introduced earlier. For this we must return to the *Anweisung*.

6.2.3   *The* Anweisung: *Love As God's Affect (*agapé*)*

Since history is for Fichte an account of God's *e-sistence*, his philosophy of history is also a philosophy of religion. It is the philosophy of religion according to the understanding to which we have already alluded. The *Anweisung* is rather, on Fichte's statement of the case, philosophy of religion according to reason. Fichte distinguished the two in the concluding lecture of the *Anweisung*,[36] declaring that this last series of lectures only brought to conclusion the previous series of the *Grundzüge*. Just why the philosophy of religion should be assigned to the understanding, as presented in the *Grundzüge*, but not to reason as presented in the *Anweisung*, is not obvious. Very likely it is because the *Anweisung*, much more than the *Grundzüge*, which was based on the immediate experience of external facts,

---

[35] *Grundzüge*, 2; GA I.8:196.25–197.2.   [36] *Anweisung*, 490; GA I.9:182.32–35.

required the kind of self-awareness on the part of his audience that is typical of reason.

Just as human history progresses through five Epochs, so does the life of the individuals coursing across them progress in five stages. This is the "quintitude" or "fivefoldness" of individual phenomenal existence. Fichte describes the stages in Lecture 5, first, however, discounting the life of incontinence – the kind, presumably, that would be found at any stage. At issue is rather the degree to which reason's reflection is effective in each – it being understood that the progression in a subject's views of the world on which the stages depend, just as the progression of historical epochs, does not have its origin in time.

> Understand me thus: – those higher views of the World [as they progressively occur] have not their origin in Time, nor so that they are first engendered and made possible by views wholly opposed to them; but they subsist from all Eternity in the unity of the Divine Existence, as necessary determinations of the One Consciousness, even although no man should comprehend them, and no one who does comprehend them can invent them, or produce them by mere thought, but he can only perceive them.[37]

It so happens that, at any stage of humankind's progression, "some favored and inspired men [such as Jesus and Fichte, of course] find themselves, as it were by miracle, without their own knowledge and through mere birth and instinct, placed at once on a higher standpoint from which to survey the World."[38] These men are necessarily misunderstood, even persecuted. Yet they are the ones who are instrumental in raising humanity to a higher intensity of life, thus pressing history forward.

We can dispense with describing these levels of intensity. Their characteristics correspond to the historical ages to which they respectively give rise and which Fichte has described in the *Grundzüge*. Of special significance for the *Anweisung* is that the interiorization of the law that makes possible the Third Age (Fichte's Age) coincides with the emergence of the "self." The latter consists in a new reflective awareness of the particularizing reflection which is responsible for parceling out into a variety of life forms the otherwise infinite reflection of phenomenal existence. This is the particularizing reflection which, as we said earlier,[39] is at the origin of the Many. It is as if, in this Third Age, the particularizing reflection reflectively took hold of itself and thereby gave rise to what we call "subjectivity," a feeling that betokens self-containedness of existence.

---

[37] *Anweisung*, 369; GA I.9:106.5–11. [38] *Anweisung*, 369; GA I.9:106.13–15. [39] In Section 6.2.1.

The feeling defines the Third Age, and it is also the reason for the latter's creative ambiguity. For, on the one hand, the feeling can easily give rise to the illusion that the "self" has an individual reality of its own distinct from, even opposed to, that of universal being. This is the reason why the Age displays a hitherto unknown antagonism to religion. It takes the age-old instinctive belief that all things are immersed in God which is at the root of religion as a betrayal of human individuality. But, on the other hand, the same feeling, because of the new life-intensity it betokens, can also be (at least at the hands of Fichte) the occasion for a new, but this time no longer just instinctive, realization that all things are simply the Divine.

The feeling can also, therefore, be the occasion for a new and more intense form of religiosity. For religion is the blissful life, as Fichte said at the very opening of the *Anweisung*; it is the life lived in the certainty of being blessed. But blessedness entails satisfaction, and satisfaction requires at one and the same time that one be confronted by an "other," yet that in this "other" one nonetheless find oneself realized, fulfilled. But this is the definition of love. Subjectivity thus provides precisely the factor that brings to explicit awareness the motive behind God's manifesting himself in the "other" of phenomenal existence: it is because in this "other" God recognizes himself and, in this recognition, finds satisfaction. Fichte insisted that one should not ask the *how* of God's self-manifestation but be rather satisfied with the *that* of it. One can nonetheless ask for the *why*. And the answer is clear: God manifests himself so that he may love *himself*.[40]

However, we must remember that we are still operating within the framework of a simile. That God manifests himself so that he love *himself* is a way of speaking about God in order to signal the nature of true *human* love. God's affect is the *true* human affect. To love oneself truly is to find one's realization, and therefore one's satisfaction and bliss, in a transcendent "other" of which one's singularity is only a passing manifestation, itself in truth only a nothing. To love oneself is thus to be absorbed into the other's love for itself, whether this "other" be humanity in general or ultimately the energy of life as such (call it God) which one's singularity always presupposes.[41] This love, according to its intensity, such as is made possible by love's self-awareness of its nature, is the motivating

---

[40] *Anweisung*, 464–465; GA I.9:167.15–168.3. The whole of book X is significant.

[41] "Thus, in so far as man is Love, – and this he is always in the root of his life and can be nothing but this, although it may be that he is but the Love of himself, – but especially in so far as he is the Love of God, he remains eternally and for ever one, true, and unchangeable as God himself, and is in reality God himself; and it is not merely a bold metaphor, but a literal truth, that John utters when he

force behind the various levels of moral life that Fichte describes, ultimately the higher form of morality at which the prophets of divine love (Fichte being the latest) make their appearance. The conditions are then at hand for religious existence and the bliss that goes with it. This existence, on Fichte's premises, would be eminently private – not, of course, in the sense that it is inexpressible because singular but, on the contrary, because it transcends singularity and therefore cannot be captured in words. It is just felt. It colors all aspects of one's existence without determining any *per se*. It is only in action, in the quality of the latter, that it is indirectly manifested,[42] given witness to.

6.2.4 Wissenschaftslehre *and Religion*

In the 1786 essay, *What Does It Mean to Orient Oneself in Thinking?*,[43] Kant speaks of an "immeasurable space" which is a projection of reason's desire to know, and to this extent is itself a creation of reason. Yet this space is obscure. Reason finds itself in it as in a "dark night" where it falls victim, as if naturally, to the illusion of being able to achieve knowledge of objects that transcend experience, whereas these are in fact only projections of its theoretical interests. But fortunately critique intervenes to disabuse reason of such an illusion. There are other interests than the theoretical, equally rational. These are moral, motivated by moral action. These provide reason with the warrant for accepting as true at least some of its otherwise merely illusionary objects. But this is an acceptance made on subjective grounds alone, without yielding speculative satisfaction.

Apart from being the source, I suspect, of the image of "space of reason" that Wilfrid Sellars introduced in the literature, this text is important because it shows that Kant never abandoned the supremacy of speculative reason in the context of his system; he only critically clipped its wings, to use his well-known image. He never relinquished as a goal, even if only as an unrealizable ideal, the knowledge that classical metaphysics claimed to

says: – 'He who dwelleth in Love, dwelleth in God, and God in him'. It is only his Reflexion that first separates him from this Love which is his own proper Being and not any foreign Being; – and that strives, throughout a whole manifold infinity, to lay hold of that which he himself is and remains, now, everywhere, and for ever. Hence it is not his inward Essential Nature, – that which is his own, which belongs to himself and to no other, – that is subject to continual change; but it is only the Appearance or Manifestation of this Nature, which in itself is withdrawn from outward Appearance, that suffers this continual change. [...] The eye of man conceals God from him, only because he himself is concealed from himself by it, and because his vision never reaches his own true Being." *Anweisung*, 469; GA I.9:169.4–20.
[42] Cf. *Anweisung*, 470; GA I.9:169.29–170.11.   [43] Kant (1996).

deliver. For this reason he retained the "thing-in-itself," albeit as an unknown. Also for this reason, he had to maintain that nature as experienced by us is a mere phenomenon; as such, however, its existence is necessarily heteronomous and therefore frustrates any desire to see any morally intended course of action actually realized. It was the need to relieve this frustration that gave the warrant for accepting, but only on the strength of subjective faith, a view of the universe which was in fact still that of Enlightenment metaphysics. Kant, as we said earlier,[44] never left classical metaphysics behind.

But Fichte did. This is what makes Kant's 1786 essay even more significant. The essay allows us to measure the distance that Fichte had indeed traveled away from Kant. He had not just clipped metaphysics' speculative wings; he had completely done away with it in any recognizably classical sense. This was already the case in the Jena *Wissenschaftslehre*, where the "I" is no longer a logical function (as for Kant) but instead expresses a supposed original actuosity. But it only found consistent articulation in 1804, when the "I," as we have seen, is replaced by a space that no longer has subjective connotations. This is more like the space in Kant's essay, except that it is no longer the product of reason. And it is not dark. Fichte had filled it with light, but a very peculiar light, for instead of bringing out the contours of things as light normally does, it dissolves them, for they are in truth the mere products of reflection.

In this Fichte was the first postmodern philosopher, or, if we read Spinoza as Fichte interpreted him, second only to Spinoza. *That* we exist is the fundamental fact of experience. As such, the fact stands within the latter neither as a principle of explanation, whether transcendent or transcendental, nor as anything self-explanatory. Rather, it makes the whole issue of explanation moot. The whole point is to live the fact, and to live it intensely. Reflection, the processes of explanation that it sets in motion, equally any appeal to intuition, are just part and parcel of the texture of such a life. But that they should be such is itself not subject to explanation. They can indeed be *genetically* deduced, but this only means that they can be displayed as modes of living a life which is in fact already lived in full from the beginning, as one would recognize if one were sufficiently attentive to it.

For this reason Fichte could say that being, understood as the principle of a ratiocinative metaphysics, is only the product of a reflection that distracts from the pervasiveness of Divine Life. For this reason he took nature as being nothing *in itself* but only an idea. He therefore repeatedly

---

[44] Cf. Section 1.2.

inveighed against any doctrine of creation,[45] and disparaged the apostle Paul because of his doctrine of fall and redemption. There is no sin, according to Fichte, no radical evil to atone for. There are only people who are "bad" only in the sense that there is "no good" in them, for they still feel that they have a *self* that sets them aside from the whole of existence.[46] Everything that occurs, occurs necessarily and for the best; and should anyone notice misery surrounding them, then that misery is the best that could be in the world.[47] All this might sound like a repetition of Enlightenment metaphysics, another version of Leibniz's Theodicy. Yet everything is said in a totally different, even opposite spirit – not as claims supported by reasoned arguments, which, according to both Fichte and Kant would only yield sophistic conclusions; not, in other words, as arguments based on abstract possibilities that throw light on the present. It is said, rather, precisely in order to keep all such arguments and possibilities at bay. It is said in order to restrict one's view to just the present. This present is *all* that there is, and to divagate into speculations about what might be, or would be, is to fail to live *energisch*.[48]

For this reason, finally, bliss is, for Fichte, humankind's typical feeling – a special kind of feeling indeed, more of an affect than a feeling, for it does not conform to Fichte's early analysis when Kant's guilt was the issue. Guilt presupposes the opposition of universalizing moral law and singularizing natural desire, precisely the kind of opposition that calls for the Pauline doctrine of sin, punishment, and redemption that Fichte abhorred. But Fichte has reduced both nature and the moral law to mere appearances, such as have no validity except from a finite viewpoint. He has run God's Word and God's Love, which are also humankind's word and humankind's love, into each other, with no effective residual distinction that would make for particularization and opposition. His *amor Dei*, no less than Spinoza's, is just intellectual; his *logos Dei*, again no less than Spinoza's, nothing ratiocinative, it rather devolves into vision. The love is a love in general, with no particular object in view. It is the disporting of vision with itself, and bliss is its fruition.[49] There is love in general, and

[45] *Anweisung*, 387; GA I.9:119.12–18.   [46] *Anweisung*, 397; GA I.9:126.28–31.
[47] *Anweisung*, 460461; GA I.9:164.9–17. As if there were no room for despair in the human situation. Here is where the inhumanity of Fichte's humanism, and of the whole classical metaphysics tradition, comes clearly to the fore.
[48] Inasmuch as the idea of God enters religion, it has for Fichte only pragmatic, not speculative, value. Cf. Schmid (1995), p. 28.
[49] Hegel silently criticizes this attitude in the preface to the Phenomenology. Cf. GW 9.18.29–33. Miller § 19. There is a biblical echo of Proverbs 8:30–31. Fichte had not been true to his own principle of negativity.

bliss, indeed; for the rest, there are particular desires and particular power relations, exactly as for Spinoza, all of them real only for a finite viewpoint.

How does the *Wissenschaftslehre* relate to religion? The answer is clear. *Wissenschaftslehre* is itself religion, and its practice is the only true *opus Dei*.

6.3   On Faith, Religion, and Knowledge

In 1804, two years before the *Anweisung*, Schelling published a tract by the title of *Philosophy and Religion*,[50] in response to C. A. Eschenmayer, a noted scientist of the day, who had just published a book, *Philosophy in Its Transition to Non-Philosophy*,[51] in which, while agreeing with Schelling's views on nature and its relation to God, he held that, upon arriving at the pinnacle of science with the speculative idea of the Absolute, one needs the further factor of faith.[52] His point was that profane reason and the intuition on which its idealizations are based are world-directed; such idealizations are only a representation (*Nachbild*) of God from a human standpoint. Eschenmayer posited, therefore, a cognition which was neither subjective nor objective; one which did not draw God into man but was, rather, oblivious of itself as cognition, a sort of revelatory intellectual sentiment. This is what Eschenmayer called faith. Only in faith would one know that the *Nachbild* of speculative knowledge was in fact true to its original.

Schelling responded with what amounted to a rendition of Spinoza in idealistic idiom. In retrospect, the tract provided the conceptual framework for the Theogony he shortly later laid out in the Freedom Essay. Reflection is the key to the response. Schelling maps out God's relation to finite reality over the idea of an idea reflectively representing itself as idea. On the one hand, the originary idea would not truly represent itself unless in the reflecting representation it gave itself *in toto*. And, since the idea is self-contained, that is, it is *for itself* (*per se*), this has to be the case for its representation as well, that is, the latter too must have being *per se* precisely as representation. On the other hand, such a representation would not attain the required independence unless it clearly distanced itself from the originary idea that it represents – in effect, by recognizing that, as the

[50] *Philosophie und Religion*, in SSW 6:11–70. English translation in Schelling (2010).
[51] There is a French translation. Eschenmayer (2005).
[52] In the course of 1804 and 1805 Schelling and Eschenmayer were in correspondence. Excerpts of the correspondence are included in the English translation of *Religion and Philosophy*. These excerpts are the source of my account of Eschenmayer's position. Cf. Letters of July 24, 1804 (to Schelling), pp. 63–65; July 23 and 30, 1805 (to Schelling), pp. 67 and 69. For another publication of Eschenmayer on the Divine, see Eschenmayer (1806).

counterpart of that idea, its own "being" is a matter of being, *per se,* just a nothingness. Indeed, *that it is* at all can only be imagined as originating in a fall from the originary idea, in a leap (*Sprung*) from it which cannot, however, be attributed to the originary idea *per se* (for that would require an outward reference qualifying it) but which must be rather represented as an act of sheer freedom on its part. This freedom is reflected in the representation by the facticity of its being. This facticity is what keeps represented and representing idea apart, and also, inasmuch as this relation symbolizes God's relation to finite reality, the factor that preempts any attempt at deriving the latter from God, whether the derivation be all at once (creation) or incremental (emanation). The separation of the two is absolute. Yet the two are One. God or the Absolute is One. This is the relation which is articulated in reason's idealizations. However, it is first apprehended, all at once, in intellectual intuition. Schelling posits such an intuition at the beginning of his exposition, with the admonition that it must be presupposed throughout.[53]

This is only a sketch of Schelling's otherwise intricate disquisition,[54] which is replete with references to historical precedents and Schelling's criticisms of them. In essence, his response to Eschenmayer was that there is no need for faith. Faith adds nothing to what intellectual intuition already provides. The implication, of course, was that for Schelling philosophy *was* religion and religion *was* philosophy. In this Schelling was at one with Fichte. However, the ambiguity endemic to monism, which we have already repeatedly noted still made its appearance, this time in the quality of the specifically religious expression they each associated with their philosophy. For Fichte, this expression was the sermon, the popular exposition of the *Wissenschaftslehre* intended to raise people at large to its level of comprehension. The *Anweisung* was a protracted sermon. For Schelling, as we would expect, the expression was rather aesthetic. As he said: "Religion, if it seeks to preserve itself in unscathed pure ideality, can therefore never exist [...] other than esoterically in the form of *mystery cults.* [Exoterically, however,] one presents religion to a nation through poetry and its arts[, in its mythology]. Mindful of its ideal character,

---

[53] "We presuppose only that without which everything that follows remains uncomprehended: intellectual intuition. We posit this with certainty because there can be no discontinuity or manifoldness inside it. Anyone who had to describe what he perceived in it could only describe it as *pure absoluteness*, without any *further determination*. We ask that the presence of this pure absoluteness without other determination be preserved forever and is never again lost sight of." PhRe 18; SSW 6:29.

[54] See especially PhRe 22–24; SSW 6:33–36.

however, proper religion relinquishes the public and withdraws itself into the secret darkness of secrecy."[55] The expression, whether esoteric or exoteric, had to be sensate. Nonetheless, even for him, no less than for Fichte, religion was ultimately consummated in the eminently private intuition of the Divine.

This is quite different from Hegel, for whom the language of religion was essentially communal. Nonetheless, on one score Hegel agreed with Fichte and Schelling, namely on denying that historical faith is of the essence of religion. To be sure, Hegel had a more sympathetic attitude toward faith than Fichte who, in the spirit of the Enlightenment, rather considered its positive content the purview of obscurantists and power brokers. More in tune with Schelling, faith was for Hegel a knowledge still unaware of what it in fact knows, a still immediate knowledge uncritical of itself yet not without speculative validity.[56] When it came to religion, however, only a religion that did not know itself as religion required faith. Truly self-transparent religion did not.[57]

Yet, this being said, it must immediately be added that for Hegel religion was not philosophy, and philosophy not religion. The distinction was essential. Indeed, it ultimately marked the distance that separated Hegel from his idealist contemporaries, for it brought into play, as we shall explain further, precisely the nature of his metaphysical commitments, the status of his Logic as metaphysics.

With this, we can resume the Phenomenology's narrative from where we left it at the coming on the scene of religion. At issue is subjective identity, or "the self."

---

[55] Schelling deals with the subject in an appendix to *Philosophy and Religion*. The quote is on p. 51 (SSW 6:65–66), but, regarding mythology, see also pp. 54–55 (SSW 6:68–71). The subject is broached by Schelling (p. 51) in connection with the State's relation to religion which can be at most only indirect.

[56] At issue here is not moral faith, toward which Hegel was not at all sympathetic. For Kant and faith, cf. Section 1.3. Also: di Giovanni (2003). On faith and knowledge in Hegel, cf. the Encyclopaedia Logic, §§ 63 and 554.

[57] In connection with the world of culture, Hegel refers back to the religion of the ethical world. In this world the religious practices associated with the cult of the departed are not a matter of *faith* (*Glaube*), for the presence of the departed is of the substance of familial life. The practices are not directed at a world beyond, alienated from the present, which is the purview of faith. Alienation from the actual present belongs to the world of culture and also, therefore, to its religion. Nonetheless, even in the ethical world there is, albeit not at the surface as in culture, a disconnect between the ways it represents itself in its laws and practices, and its actuality. Also its religion, therefore, although not an insubstantial product of consciousness as it is in culture, is in essence *only* faith, *nur Glaube*. Cf. PS § 528; GW 9:287.27–288.1. I suspect that the English "belief" would be *Glaube* in this broader sense.

6.4 Hegel on Religion: Reconciliation

6.4.1 Religion and the Self

Hegel had already left Spinoza, and by implication Fichte and Schelling, in the preface to the Phenomenology. He did so when declaring that the True has to be grasped and expressed not as *substance* but as *subject*;[58] or again, that "substance is essentially subject."[59] This was not to say that substance is a mere product of thought or, for that matter, that the subject is a pure activity of thinking. Rather, it meant that substance cannot be anything *a se* and *per se* as was the Absolute of classic metaphysic. Substance is nothing divine. It has meaning only to the extent that a subject, beholden to reason, writes on it – as if by a magic which is in fact the cunning of reason – its own story of someone achieving self-identity in this very writing. The subject, in other words, is a concrete self engaged in history, and religion is the concrete expression of this engagement.

In section VI of the Phenomenology, at the point in the narrative where the beautiful soul comes on the scene, Hegel reviews the forms of "self" that have appeared so far.[60] As he broaches religion in section VII, he returns to them, associating with each the form of religion most typical of it.[61] The first self is the legal persona that historically was the product of the Roman Empire. The second is that of culture, which culminates with the abstract self of the Enlightenment and the self-disrupted self of morality. The third, and the only truly concrete self, is that of conscience, which comes on the scene with the beautiful soul.

To be sure, selfhood is every self's motive force. It is a matter of asserting the universal validity of one's individuality despite the historical singularity that affects it, such as only comes from nature. But, prior to the beautiful

---

[58] Cf. GW9.19.3ff.; PS §17. The current translations of the passage are misleading. Miller's reads: "Everything turns on grasping and expressing the True, not only as *Substance*, but equally as *Subject*." Pinkard's amounts to the same: "[. . .] not just as substance but just as much as *subject*." Hegel (2018), p. 12. But Hegel says: "Es kömmt nach meiner Einsicht [. . .] alles darauf an, das Wahre nicht als *Substanz*, sondern eben so sehr als *Subject* aufzufassen und auszudrücken." There is no "not only" in the passage (Miller), nor "not just" (Pinkard), only *nicht*. One needs to expand Hegel's otherwise elliptic statement to bring out its meaning clearly: "In my view [. . .], all depends on grasping and expressing the True, not as *substance*, but [on grasping and expressing it] rather as *subject* just as much [as not as *substance*]." The "so sehr" has the meaning of "as strongly," as when one says, "es regnet sehr," "it rains hard." The point is that one must grasp and express the True as subject exactly as much as one must grasp and express it as *not* substance. The rest of the paragraph confirms this reading. To grasp the two sides equally is Schelling's move, not Hegel's.

[59] "That Substance is *essentially Subject* is expressed in the representation of the Absolute as *Spirit*" (stresses added) PS § 23; GW9:22.3–4.

[60] PS § 633; GW 9:341.17–342.3.   [61] PS §§ 673–677; GW 9:363.9–364.32.

soul, the self has done this by engaging with nature only in principle, abstractly – in fact, as Hegel puts it, letting it go free. The self of the Enlightenment, the product of the idea of rights in general, made only a *pro forma* reference to the nature where such rights were to be exercised. The result was that natural interests could run their course alongside declared beliefs in things divine, in fact unfettered from them, free of them, and effectively motivated only by the natural desires. Utility (*Nützlichkeit*), Hegel says, was the *de facto* religion of the Enlightenment.[62] As for Kant's moral self, it came complete with the idea of a nature as it ought to be. It created its own moral world. But the idealized nature this world required was existentially incompatible with the historical nature which was the *de facto* context of the self's actions. The self was therefore forced to undeclared compromises, to dissembling intentions that courted hypocrisy if not outright lying.[63] The merit of the beautiful soul, as we remember it from where we left off the Phenomenology's narrative, was that it accepted no such compromises. It openly acknowledged that conscience commands with absolute authority yet in a voice which is patently conditioned historically. As particular and finite, the beautiful soul nonetheless openly claimed for itself divine authority. In this it sinned. It introduced evil into the universe. It had to do so, however, precisely in order to be a self-validating individual. Its vocation, which was also the vocation of human-kind in general, was thus one of redemption, in effect, a matter of reconciling the natural and the divine.

This vocation informs all the dimensions of human existence narrated in the Phenomenology. Religion is a special case because the object of its representations and practices is precisely this vocation; it is where the vocation is objectified *per se*. In the dramas of conflicts and reconciliation that religion plays out on its imaginary stages, projected in either a "world above" or a "world below," and acted out by protagonists with whom humans spontaneously identify, these same humans see their present existential situation displayed before their eyes. But just because it is acted out on stages which are not visibly their own, for they are the

[62] PS § 675; cf. also § 579. GW 9:364.1–9; cf. also 513:32–514.7. This has nothing to do, of course, with nineteenth-century Utilitarianism.
[63] PS § 676; GW 9:364.11–16. This text is to be read in connection with Hegel's extensive critique of the typically moral conduct (where "moral" is to be understood in a Kantian sense) in section VI, subsection C.b, of the Phenomenology, under the title of *Verstellung* (Dissemblance). Hegel exposes the duplicity of any form of behavior governed by Kant's moral view of reality. He finds any such behavior internally contradictory. PS §§ 616ff.; GW 9:332ff. Hegel calls the moral view "a 'whole nest' of thoughtless contradictions," with explicit reference to Kant's KrV B637. PS § 617; GW 9:332.25–28.

products of the imagination, they do not recognize that they, the visible humans, are the ones setting the stages. In those dramas they therefore live their vocation only in faith. In truth, however, reason is the true stage on which the human situation is being played out. Reason sets its terms originally. And as the historical humans, by virtue of the discipline of actual experience, progressively recognize themselves in their religious imagery – recognize that only in their visible present is their vocation to be realized, and the hitherto rational meaning of the imagery is thereby made explicit for them – so does faith progressively yield place to knowledge. Religious faith's path to self-enlightenment proceeds *pari passu* with reason also progressively coming on the stage explicitly *as reason*. This does not mean that religion therefore disappears before reason. Reconciling is not the same as comprehending reconciliation. It means, rather, that only in a culture where religion manifests itself in its beliefs and practices for what it truly is are the conditions also at hand for the concept of reason and rationality – the absolute idea, as Hegel calls it – also to appear on the scene. In section VII of the Phenomenology, Hegel traces the progression of religion in self-comprehension; in VIII, that of reason. But it is in the Logic that he explicates the idea of reason in all its determinations.

6.4.2 *Religion in the Form of Art*

When it comes to religion, Hegel's narrative is especially dense, for obvious reasons. Reconciliation is the object of religion in all its various historical forms, and religion achieves this perfectly in each, but only consistent with the degree of self-awareness humanity has achieved at the historically given time and place associated with it.[64] Each form, therefore, necessarily reflects in its imagery the same degree of self-awareness as is also achieved in more particularized forms of experience, whether sensitive, perceptive, conceptual, social – in brief, the same experiences Hegel has already subjected to reflective analysis earlier in his narrative. He now retrieves them all, included in his religious narrative. Moreover, since each stage of religion only repeats the previous but at a higher degree of reflectivity, the imaginary figurations of the previous are still present in it, demoted in significance yet still interfering with its transparency. Add to this the

---

[64] H. S. Harris rightly points out that it is wrong in a Hegelian context to speak of a more or less perfect religion. One can speak of a more or less rationally self-aware religion, but the point of religion, ultimately, is that it *satisfy* – not that it *explain*. In this, all religions are perfect. Harris (1991), pp. 518–519.

constant, albeit normally only tacit, references to chronicled human events, and the result is indeed a densely textured text.

Nonetheless, the overall pattern of development is clear. To repeat, we have the historical individual engaged in reconciling norms of reason with limitations of nature. The crucial point, however, is that the desired reconciliation is in principle already achieved even as the need for it arises – witness the feeling of awe which this individual experiences before nature at the dawn of humankind, the fear of its uncanniness, the sense of culpability when the victim of its power. The feeling's witness is to the power that reason has already exercised over nature by enchanting it, endowing it with powers it would not otherwise have; doing so, moreover, without thereby encroaching on its otherness – on the contrary, even rendering it all the more conspicuous because of the new powers given to it. The fact is that Spirit is with the individual from the beginning: the individual's problem is only one of recognizing the fact, in effect of growing in self-knowledge. For this, the feelings originally experienced before nature have to be liberated from the immediacy masking their true essence. They need expression, objectification. Religion intervenes to provide the needed objectification with its cults and imaginary figurations.

Above all, however, religion provides feelings with language. For language is the great mediator. It is, as Hegel says, "an outer reality that is immediately self-conscious existence."[65] Essentially, it is the manifest mediation of nature and reason, or "the soul existing as soul."[66] Language figures in section VII, therefore, just as prominently in Hegel's treatment of religion as in his treatment of the birth of the political state in section VI, that, too, a product of Spirit. And, just as in that case he assigns a special language to each social arrangement, one consistent with the specific political personality achieved by it, so does he also assign a signal language to each form of religion according to the manifestation of Spirit achieved in it.

But we are getting ahead of ourselves. We want to catch Hegel's narrative on religion first at the point where he returns in VII to the culture of the warriors battling before the walls of Troy in VI – where he returns to the Ethical Order, in other words, for it is there that the gods, hitherto the still mute personifications of the forces of nature or the antagonistic "animal spirits" that animate peoples still unconscious of their universality,[67] begin to have a voice. Regarding the very beginning of religion – the "night of

---

[65] PS § 709; GE 9:380.27–28.   [66] PS § 709; GW 9:380.31.
[67] PS § 689; GW 9:372.21–25. I take it that Hegel has tribal gods in mind.

[Spirit's] essence,"[68] as Hegel calls it – we need only note that this beginning is no "golden age" for Hegel, whether understood as an imaginative construct devised for moral purposes in Fichte's sense or, in Schelling's, as the first human stage of a theogonic process. It is just the beginning of humankind, a presumably recordable event to which one cannot, nor would want to, ever return. The immediacy of the feelings for nature that characterize it holds the secret of Spirit's origin. The point is to reveal it.

The emergence of the community defined by the Ethical Order marks a qualitative leap in the revealing process because its members are already essentially free, in the sense that they are certain of themselves, satisfied with themselves *as individuals*. Nonetheless, this certainty, this satisfaction, is still only a lived one, only experienced in the adherence to hallowed customs or the fulfilment of socially imposed obligations, without deliberate reflective awareness. In an image which Hegel repeatedly uses in parallel contexts, their self-awareness is like a light that illumines outwardly without, however, shining back on the source that illuminates it. "The soul [. . .] is still not the self that has descended into its depths and knows itself as evil."[69] Or, as one might say, the individuals act personally but not as persons. The religion of the Ethical Order is accordingly still one of the underworld, rooted in the unconscious. It is animated, on the one hand, by reverence for the spirits of the departed whose once lived personality has in death been transformed into a force of nature; on the other hand, by fear of Fate, as nature appears to the living, an unknown quantity possibly intent on thwarting their lives. The function of religion is to allow the light of the living's self-awareness (which is really the light of reason) to shine back onto their unconscious so that they recognize that it was the actions of the departed, while still alive, which in fact causes nature to appear as Fate. The pathos of nature, as Hegel puts it, is to be transformed into a pathos of Mnemosyne.[70]

Art is the medium in which religion first accomplishes this transformation. The artist is creatively inspired in his or her work. He instinctively knows that his work derives its value as object of admiration and adoration from what he has put into it. But the artist is so absorbed in his work as to forget the inspiration which is at the source of it; inasmuch as he is subjectively affected by it, in the affection he fails to go past the feeling for the sacred in general. Hegel has two forms of art in mind. One is

---

[68] PS § 685; GW 9:370.23.   [69] PS § 715; GW 9:383.7–8. The reference is to the beautiful soul.
[70] PS § 729; GW 9:389.28–390.8. It is the memory of a community's past heroic deeds that binds the community together.

sculpture. The sculptor knows, while working on raw material, how to distinguish between what is essential to a beautiful figure and what would, rather, be merely contingent to it. The god within him tells him that but the sculptor does not know it. The product, the god-sculpture, while reflecting the inspired artificer, does not speak to him, or, inasmuch as it speaks, it does in oracles – utterances that need deciphering since they come from nowhere definable. The other art form is the sacred song, a language effusion in which the artist's inspiration indeed finds subjective expression, but, since the expression lacks objectification, it conveys nothing definable. Devotion is the subjective attitude typical of this form of religion – "devotion," the German *Andacht*, the etymological root of which (*Denken*, "thought") more clearly conveys Hegel's meaning. It is a thinking that is satisfied with itself, even full of itself, but only in general, not knowing why. In this, the satisfaction is a perturbed one.[71]

Cult intervenes to mediate the static form of the god-statue and the fluid effusion of the sacred song.[72] It animates the former while giving objective shape to the latter. Hegel says of cult that it is "only a *secret* fulfilment."[73] The fulfilment is of the promise that religion holds from the beginning that God is with the community. It is a *fulfilment* of this because cult is ritualized activity, a set of performances which, as such, engage the performers at their most singularized level of existence, raising it to self-awareness as reflected in the gods for which the performances are enacted. Action, one must remember, is for Hegel an existential achievement and therefore necessarily individual. The fulfilment is nonetheless only *secret* because, as Hegel goes on to say, it is achieved "only in imagination." The self being realized is still not one "that has descended into its depths and knows itself as evil [as the Beautiful Soul does, the product of Christianity], but it is something that only *immediately* is [*ein seyendes*], a soul that cleanses its exterior by washing it [. . .] while its inward being traverses the imaginatively conceived path of works [. . .] ridding it of its particularity, as a result of which it reaches the dwelling and the community of the blest."[74]

This community is still in the future since it requires the full disclosure of Spirit. In the Ethical Order the community is still a people (*Volk*)

---

[71] I.e., the satisfaction is typical of the Unhappy Consciousness in IV.

[72] "The movement of the two sides constitutes the Cult: a movement in which the divine shape *in motion* in the pure feeling element of self-consciousness, and the divine shape *at rest* in the element of thinghood, mutually surrender their distinctive characters, and the unity which is the Concept of their essence achieves existence." PS § 714 (translation modified); GW 9:382.28–33.

[73] PS § 716; GW 9:383.13–14.   [74] PS § 715; GW 9:383.6–12.

substantially held together by ties of birth rather than a society of self-aware individuals.[75] Nonetheless, the cult of the Ethical Order already marks a milestone on the way to the future community, and Hegel goes into great detail explaining how the cult works its magic. There is, for instance, the ritual associated with interpreting the oracle. While the oracle itself presumably sets the norm of interpretation, for it is *its* meaning that must be brought to light, nonetheless, since its wording is at best ambiguous, at worse cryptic, in order to achieve that goal the interpreters must bring to it their own preoccupations, their current interests. The result is that, while the god is the one who has spoken, his meaning is understood only in the medium of the interpreters' language, which is thereby *de facto* validated as the truly effective conveyor of meaning. Something parallel occurs in the case of sacrifice, which is a people's paramount cultic act. In sacrifice a people offers the gods something which is of vital importance to it, such as an animal on whose flesh its members would otherwise feed. As a token of the seriousness of the gift, the animal is burnt, but not all of it.[76] A portion is retained, which the gods themselves presumably give back to the celebrants to feast on. It is given back to them as a sign of the gods' acceptance of their sacrifice, and, since it is a something which is the gods' own – for it has been gifted to them – in feasting on it the celebrants thereby commune with the gods, even consume them as part of their sacral meal. In this, however, while still beholden to the gods' authority, the celebrants demonstrate that they are on a par with them.

Cult thus transforms devotion into celebration, the perturbed internal contentment of the former into the open enjoyment of the latter. However, it achieves its consummate form only in the festival, a people's celebration of its gods which in fact devolves into a celebration of the people itself. The festival has a universalizing effect on the people's perception of itself. In songs and dances; by adorning its dwellings which, like temples, thereby acquire sacral significance; by admiring the athletes as they perform in the festival's games, and in celebrating their beauty,[77] a people's preoccupations with the gods of the festival recede to the background (*untergehen*). These gods are the factors that still bind the

[75] Miller translate *Volk* as "nation." This is a perfect translation – and Hegel, too, refers to *Volk* as *Nation* in this context (GW 9:389.3) –, but only if one keeps in mind the etymological root of "nation" – *nascor/natus*: "to be born," "begotten." However, the translation, might be misleading nowadays, since "nation" is inevitably associated with the post-French Revolution "nation state."
[76] Hegel notes one exception: when the sacrifice is to the gods of the underworld with whom one would not want to commune. PS § 718; GW 9:384.19–20.
[77] *Fechter* is more appropriately translated in context as "athlete" instead of "warrior," as it is by Miller. Miller's translation of GW 9.388.19–27 (PS § 725, p. 439) is not transparent.

people's Spirit to nature. What comes forth is instead a new awareness of the human form as such, of human things *as human*. Beauty is no longer celebrated just in a statue, frozen in a given natural material, but as living, as manifesting itself in movement and thus creating its own sacred space. The people's gods shed their otherwise all too particularizing original natural traits accordingly. In this they reflect a new universalizing self-awareness on the people's part. They cease being just this people's gods and become the gods of other peoples as well, while the gods of other peoples equally become this people's own.

A new Spirit has emerged which calls for a new religion, albeit still as art. Its medium is language which, as Hegel says, is the true habitation of the gods.[78]

> In both representations that have just come before us there is present the unity of self-consciousness and spiritual essence [i.e., the inwardness of the single celebrants and nature as spiritualized by their actions, objectified in the figures of the gods[79]]; but they are still not equally balanced against each other. [. . .] The perfect element in which inwardness is just as external and externality is inward is once again speech, but it is neither the speech of the Oracle, wholly contingent and individual as regards its content, nor the emotional hymn sung in praise of the individual god, nor again is it the meaningless stammer of Bacchic frenzy. On the contrary, it has gained a lucid and universal content; a content that is *lucid*, because the artist has worked his way out of the initial enthusiasm, originating wholly from substance, into a [definite] shape.[80]

This artist is the Minstrel. His inspiration is no longer from below, only a first reflective but still indefinite stirring of nature. It now comes definitely from above, from a Muse to whom the Minstrel openly addresses himself. In his work the Minstrel does not just display the spiritualizing of nature unconsciously. He narrates it; he recollects it as achieved through the actions of individuals who no longer attain their objects only ritually but do so in results portrayed as historically visible. In the epic, as Hegel says (for the epic is the novel manifestation of religion),[81] the extreme of universality is linked with the individuality of the Minstrel through the particularity of the heroes of a people. Nature, already spiritualized as the object of reflection, is particularized by being figured as a world of gods. The heroes, for their part, although individuals like the Minstrel, since they

---

[78] PS § 727; GW 9.388.32–389.1.   [79] My gloss.   [80] PS §726; GW 9:388.3–16.
[81] Hegel's treatment of these forms of religion is, on the face of it, diachronic but need not be so. The forms can just as well be taken as contemporaneous, together giving witness to the complexity, the surface unevenness, of a *Volk*'s self-awareness at any moment of its history.

are imaginatively represented (*vorgestellt*), like the gods assume universal significance.[82]

Here, in the Minstrel's "universal song," the pathos of nature is transformed into a pathos of Mnemosyne.[83] Surrender to the uncanny sway of the unconscious gives way to trust in creative memory. The recollected story is one of gods and humans acting together. This is indeed already a union of the divine and the human but as an accidental mingling of figurations of both. And Hegel has an easy time demonstrating how in the narrative the gods have the worse of it. Humans defer to their power, yet the gods' intentions are in fact realized only because of the deeds of humans. In the narrative of these deeds, the gods' presence turns out to be redundant. Moreover, since the gods interact with humans and take sides in their affairs, they themselves begin to act like humans, in relation both to humans and to each other. As gods, they appear empty and at times even comic figures.

It is an easy step from epic narrative to liturgical drama. The epic is doomed because, while its narrative has a hold on its audience by satisfying the latter's unconscious need to see the human and the divine united, it trivializes the union and, consequently, the need redounds on it as an internal destructive force. The epic self-destructs, as indeed all imaginative thinking eventually must if it lacks self-understanding.[84] In this case, tragedy is the inheritor.

The society of the Ethical Order is still the one in play, and religion is still this society's celebration of itself as it celebrates its heroes and its gods. The difference is that, whereas in the epic the heroes' *gesta* are narrated, in tragedy the heroes speak in their own voice. They are the ones narrating the *gesta*, and it is the human situation which is being celebrated on the stage where the *gesta* are being enacted.

> The language [in tragedy] ceases to be narrative, just as the content ceases to be one that is imaginatively presented. The hero is himself the speaker, and the performance displays to the audience – who are also spectators – *self-conscious* human beings who *know* their rights and purposes, the power and the will of their respective nature and know how to *assert* them.[85]

The spectators are ordinary people, the same who would also sacrifice to the gods and revel in festivals. In the theater, however, which is the new cultic space, they are given an objective view of the consequences of living

---

[82] PS § 729; GW 9:389.28–390.8.   [83] PS § 729; GE 9:389.35–390.8.
[84] PS § 731; GW 9:391.7–33.   [85] PS § 733; GE 9:39.16–21.

in the world presupposed by the cult associated with their gods. These consequences are presented as actually suffered and from the standpoint of the ones suffering them. The spectators' attention, otherwise absorbed in their customary ways, is thus redirected by way of the stage back to themselves, like a light shining back on their unconscious. As spectators, they have no voice of their own – or better, their voice is that of the chorus. It is a generalized voice, coming from no one in particular, as contrasted with the voice of the actors on stage. It is directed to the gods, in songs sung in praise of them. Indeed, the gods still hover in the background; they are part of the furniture of ordinary people's life. The chorus's voice is still the voice of traditional wisdom. But the point is that the gods are not on stage. They have become redundant, as in fact they already were in the epic. Inasmuch as they do have a presence on stage, it is felt like a force that redounds on the actors to their destruction but only because they, the actors, have empowered nature with it.

This is the problem – one which has already repeatedly made its appearance in different contexts but deserves being restated as it brings the Ethical Order to its demise. The ethical individuals have in principle already rationalized nature. They have already brought it within the space of their rationally induced interests. Or again, they have transformed it into a spiritual substance (*Wesen*), in the medium of which they actualize themselves as the rational individuals they are. And here lies the problem. For, as individuals, they must be *recognizably* so; this means being marked out by a singularity for which they are dependent on their natural pre-history, on the where, when, and how they happen to be born. Yet, as rational, this same singularity must somehow claim for itself universal validity. The problem is that the ethical agents have not yet clearly sorted out the two requirements; hence, they have yet to reconcile them. They have populated their objective spiritual essence with gods of the nether-world (Nature) and gods of the heavens (Reason) – mindful, of course, that these two sets of gods would impose conflicting obligations on them, yet also self-consciously ignorant of how and why the ensuing conflicts would play themselves out in their lives. These, as a result, are lived in trepidation before an ever threatening fate (hence the need for ritual sacrifice).

In essence the problem is that the ethical individuals have yet to remember how their ethical world came to be in the first place and how they were responsible for it. They simply take it as given. Above all, they take as given that the singular position they occupy in their society because of birth or past-history, whether as sister, brother, king, or warrior, has been appointed for them by nature. It is in this appointed position that their

singularity finds validation and they accordingly act in accordance with the
obligations associated with it by sacred tradition. While subjectively feeling
as agents, they objectively see themselves as characters plying their vocation
on a cosmic stage. For this reason the actors in tragedy wear a mask. The
mask is their public *character*. But there is a tension between the mask and
the individual behind it. The mask tends to slip off until it falls altogether
and a renewed order, with its particular liturgy, comes on the scene.

The tension is due to the conflicts in which the individual actors find
themselves unknowingly entangled precisely because they act in character
and, in knowingly following a course of action dictated by either the nether
or the upper world, in either case unknowingly transgress the dictates of
the other. Hegel repeats the play of the known and unknown that he has
already detailed at the beginning of section VI. But the essential point is
that parceling out the one objective substance (*Wesen*) into two different
powers on a cosmic panorama is only to universalize Spirit, whereas Spirit
is effective only in action, and the latter is necessarily individualized.[86] In
the dramas enacted on stage, it is Spirit that is therefore being actualized. It
is actualized in the actors who thereby become aware of being the ones
responsible for the conflicts in which they have found themselves entangled. They are the ones responsible for the fate that, accordingly, befalls on
them. Their subjective feelings as agents acquire objectification. In Hegel's
words, Spirit is actualized "in self-conscious *individualities* – heroes, who
place their consciousness into one of these powers [of *Wesen*], find in it
determinateness of character and constitute the effective activity and
actuality of these powers. This universal individuation [of the powers]
descends again [. . .] to the immediate reality of existence."[87] It is the
human situation as *human* which is manifestly being celebrated on stage.
It is as if the actors stepped into the audience and the audience ascended on
stage. "The self-consciousness of the hero must step forth from his mask
and present itself as knowing itself to be the fate both of the gods of the
chorus and of the absolute powers themselves, and as being no longer
separated from the chorus, from the universal consciousness."[88]

A new self-awareness is born. The previous reconciliation with oneself
and one's world that is made possible, however tragically, by Greek religious drama is no longer existentially sustainable. Tragedy yields to
Comedy where the dramatic interest lies exclusively in individuals and
their day-to-day affairs. But for this a new mind-set is required than that of

[86] Cf. PS § 734; GW 9:392.35–393. [87] PS § 735; GW 9:393. 26–31.
[88] PS § 743; GW 9:397.24–27.

the Ethical Order, a new social structure and a new religion celebrating its innermost commitments to reality. The Roman Empire provides the social structure; Christianity, the religion which is openly concerned with the individual as such.[89]

6.4.3 Manifest Religion

6.4.3.1 The Concept of Manifest Religion

We are at a crucial juncture in Hegel's narrative, and following Hegel we must take stock of how we arrived at it, recapitulating the journey from the standpoint of Spirit which, with religion in general but most explicitly so far with the religion of art, has come on the scene in person. "Spirit," Hegel says, "is the knowledge of oneself in the externalization of oneself; the being that is the movement of retaining identity in its otherness."[90] Spirit stands for the identity that individuals otherwise born of nature achieve inasmuch as, by virtue of their actions, however particularized and dispersed these are because directed at nature, nonetheless transform the latter so that they can recognize themselves in it. They transform it into essence, or intelligible substance. This transformation is the underlying interest that motivates all individual actions, despite their particularized and historically conditioned content. Spirit, however, is an achievement, indeed an achievement of reason, for the self-recognition, the self-awareness, or self-containedness of existence that it entails requires resolving in action the tension created by transforming nature in thought while at the same time being born of it. Spirit has a history.[91]

The universe of Spirit constituted by the Ethical Order to which Hegel returns is a case in point. Its characteristic is that the two moments of substance, as the unconscious origin of rational agency and at the same time its conscious product, are experienced and lived *in toto*. But they are so experienced immediately, without the two being explicitly sorted out, whether as affecting the structure of a community or the lives of its

---

[89] Hegel does not mention either the Roman Empire or Christianity by name, but the historical references are patent. Kojève stresses the Christian and consequently Hegelian centrality in experience of individuality: "Christianity finds the solution to pagan tragedy. For this reason, after the advent of the Christ, there no longer is any room for credible tragedy, i.e., for conflict which is inevitable and without resolution. The problem henceforth is the *realization* of the Christian idea of individuality. And the history of the Christian world is none other than the history of this realization." (My translation) Kojève (1947), p. 192.

[90] PS § 759, p. 459; GW 9:405.18.

[91] "Time [. . . is] the destiny and necessity of spirit" so long as spirit has not achieved sufficient certainty of itself and needs, therefore, to enrich itself from experience. Cf. PS § 801 (p. 487); GW 9:429.13–19.

individual members. This immediacy makes for the beauty, but also the fragility and the pathos, of the universe thus constituted. With the advent of a new sense of individual identity on the part of those involved in it, the universe is fated to break down. The two aspects of spiritual substance fall apart, on the one hand, into a self which is certain of itself as transcending nature, but only in abstract, by way of claim, without effective contact with it; and on the other hand, into a dispersed array of all the spiritual components of the previous order, now let loose because of the lack of an effective principle ordering them. Nether and upper worlds, the gods who are their respective denizens, are all jumbled together, still exercising their power, but arbitrarily, with no internal coherence. A new universe of Spirit comes on the scene, one that is born of the need of reassembling this dispersion. It is a matter of overcoming the abstractness of the self which, by right, should be the informing principle of order.

Legal Status is the name of this new universe abstractly defined according to its concept. We have already met it in section VI of Hegel's narrative. However, for the subjective feeling animating it – I mean, for what it would mean personally for someone to live in such a universe – Hegel retrieves the figures of the Stoic and the Unhappy Consciousness of section IV. These are the defining figures of the new universe that has thus emerged. The Stoic knows that in thought she is in possession of the spiritual substance which is, after all, a product of her reason. In this she finds satisfaction, not, however, without a comic moment, for she also knows that, as possessed in thought, substance is also divested[92] of all its otherwise rich spiritual content, the same that in an earlier age of innocence she enjoyed immediately. The content is now dispersed unrecognizable.[93] She equally experiences this emptying of spiritual substance as a loss of it, and because of this she grieves, with "the grief that expresses itself in the hard saying that 'God is dead.'"[94] In this, she is the Unhappy Consciousness which, as Hegel says, "constitutes the counterpart and completion of the comic consciousness [of the Stoic]."[95] The Unhappy Consciousness stands for the "tragic fate of the certainty of [the Stoic] self that aims to be absolute. [It is] the consciousness of the loss of all *essential* being in *this certainty of itself,* and of the loss even of the knowledge about itself."[96] In a way it is she, the Stoic, who has killed God, for, in abstracting

---

[92] The word that Hegel uses in this context is "*Entäußerung,*" self-divesting, self-relinquishing. Miller's translation, "alienation," though not necessarily wrong, has narrower connotations. *Entäußerung* is not the same as *Entfremdung.*

[93] Cf. PS § 753; GW 9:401–402.   [94] Ibid.

[95] PS § 752 (the whole paragraph is relevant); GW 9:401–402.   [96] Ibid.

him in the form of an absolute of reason out of spiritual substance, she has precipitated the content of the latter into the dispersed leftover in which God can no longer be experienced as a living presence. The spiritual substance is still there, nature is still spiritualized, but now in a negative sense. The world of the here and now is felt as evil: God is dead. This is how the Unhappy Consciousness experiences the world.[97] The product of the Legal Status, it marks at the same time the emergence of a new spiritual landscape. This is the world of culture. The catalyst for it is the suffering to which the Stoic is subjected as a singular individual immersed in day-to-day existence even when reflectively denying it. Individual suffering precipitated the demise of the ethical order; it also precipitates the downfall of the Legal Status. When that suffering turns into a resolve to mend the otherwise disrupted spiritual substance in the hope of redeeming the evil of the world, the work of culture is underway. This resolve is a new creative leap. Historically, Christianity is the religion associated with it. In the narrative that follows, it is the religion whose faith eventually comes into conflict with the reason of the Enlightenment which is culture's final product. In conflict with this reason, however, faith also comes to realize how much it shares with it. And, since in the world of culture faith pervades all aspects of human existence positively, in its medium reason, for its part, is finally poised to achieve an explicit and positive conception of itself, the same that Hegel believed motivated his own age.[98] Hegel, accordingly, sees the Christian sacred story as at the same time a story of humanity becoming aware of its rationality. Christianity is the "manifest" religion; also "absolute," as Hegel occasionally refers to it, for in it Spirit finally emerges manifestly *as Spirit*.

6.4.3.2 The Sacred Story

The story is that of the Incarnation, the defining dogma of Christian faith. It is as if the master in Hegel's master/slave dialectic were to take pity upon the slave; as if in an effusion of love he were to descend to his level and, as a new man whose substance is the union of both the human and the divine nature (a union of slave and master),[99] he undertook with the slave the work of culture. The sacred story is about the nature of this work, a knowing telling of

---

[97] Cf. PS § 752; GW 9:401.24ff.

[98] This is quite in contrast to the Enlightenment's abstract reason which – because of its negative attitude toward the content of culture as typified by the *philosophes* – produced the terror of the French Revolution, by bringing the heaven of faith down to philosophical earth. That was a dead end, a pseudo reconciliation.

[99] "[D]ie göttliche Natur ist dasselbe, was die menschliche ist ... " "Divine nature is the same as human nature." PS § 460; GW 9:406.8–10. Lest the impression be given that Hegel is a Thomas Aquinas redivivus, it should be noted that Hegel's statement is radically heterodox. The Council of

it which, however, does not know to be such except in inspiration. As knowledge it is, like culture itself, self-alienated. As Hegel puts it, the believer thinks (*denkt*); his beliefs are no mere phantasy but intelligent and compelling.[100] Yet he does not know why they are so. Imaging thoughts rather than pure concepts are the representational medium in which the beliefs are expressed,[101] and devotion (*Andacht*) is the typical feeling in which they are interiorized.[102] Both, imaging thoughts and devotional feelings, are indeterminate by nature, and for this reason, precisely because of their indeterminateness, turn out to be vulnerable to the *philosophes'* destructive language of wit.

Unlike the *philosophes*, however, Hegel is interested in the speculative value of the sacred story, the intelligence motivating it. The descent of God is not a case of gods mingling with humans, acting like them and thus exposing themselves to comedy. In the descent, God maintains his distance. Even as interiorized by the slave the master retains preeminence. He has become the Stoic's Absolute, or the *a priori* of reason by virtue of which the slave, now the unhappy individual of culture intent on working at nature, is in the position of explicitly raising the latter to spiritual substance.[103] The union of the divine and human nature achieved in God's descent is thus asymmetrical. The divine nature embraces the human; the new man is God.[104] Or again, the same unhappy individual is for Hegel an idealist but certainly not of Schelling's type. There is in God no duality of thought and extension, the two paralleling each other; nor are there two processes, one from nature to subject and the other from subject to nature, each retracing the other (Schelling of 1800). Nor again is there an original entity held together by an internal gravitational pull yet at the same time wanting to break free of it

---

Chalcedon is clear on the subject. The divine nature in Christ is not the same as the human. The union is of two distinct natures in one trinitarian indexed substance.

[100] Beliefs in the gods of the Ethical Order were not a case of faith thus understood, because of the lack of subjective interiority characteristic of that type of humanity.

[101] Hegel refers to these thoughts as *Vorstellungen*, the literal translation of which is simply "representation." But *Vorstellung* is a generic term that Hegel must be using in the present context in a specialized sense which is perhaps best rendered as "imaging thought." Miller has "picture thought."

[102] The consummate religious community "does not [conceptually] grasp the fact that this depth of the pure Self [for "substance has here succeeded in becoming absolute self-consciousness,"] is the violence (*Gewalt*) by which the *abstract* divine Being is drawn from its abstraction and is raised to a self by the power of this pure devotion." PS § 787 (translation modified); GW 9:420.26–28; also: lines 21–22.

[103] I say "explicitly," because nature has already been raised to spiritual substance the moment intelligence sets in.

[104] In this Hegel is literally in accordance with the Chalcedon creed. As an individual, the Christ is not God *and a* man: he is just God (or, to be precise, the second person of a Trinitarian God).

and gain consciousness (Schelling of 1809). There is no derivation of subjectivity from an original cosmic substance. The slave's master, abstracted
out of the ethical substance, reveals itself as the self-conscious subject it was
from the beginning. This subject is unqualifiedly first, just as for the
Christian believer God is first. The Absolute that Hegel sets out to discover
at the beginning of the Phenomenology is none other than absolute knowledge, or knowledge knowing itself as truly such.[105]

Moreover, as Hegel says, the "consciousness [of the Christian] does not start
from *its* inner life, from thought, and unites *within itself* the thought of God
with existence; on the contrary, it starts from existence that is immediately
present and recognizes God therein. The moment of *immediate being* is present
in the content of the concept."[106] To which he adds, "The believer is immediately certain of Spirit, *sees*, *feels*, and *hears* the divinity."[107] The figure of the
Christ might indeed be the work of the imagination. But Hegel's point is that
the figure is nonetheless felt by the Christian as historical, precisely the point
that made Christian dogma superstition for Fichte but already speculatively
valid for Hegel. Positivity is sacred for Hegel just as it is for the Christian.[108]
There is nothing Cartesian about Christian consciousness. It is not
a consciousness shut up within itself but, on the contrary, one for which the
where and *when* of the divine man it represents in imaging thought is a pressing
issue that needs resolving on historical grounds, in real space/time. Of course,
this is impossible, and that it should be attempted is a sign for Hegel of the
believer having already been corrupted by Enlightenment reason.[109] But that it
should have been a concern at all, however misguided, is the operative factor.
There is no such concern when the pagan gods of the epic narrative are at stake,
even though they are represented as interjecting themselves into the affairs of
humans. The drama of the new man is played out in Christian consciousness
on the stage of history, not the imaginary one of the theatre. This is the reason
why, with the advent of Christianity, art could no longer be religion.[110]

Fichte had no patience with the Christian sacred story, let alone with
pagan myths. This cannot be said of Schelling, for whom all myths, but in
particular the Christian belief in the incarnation, were manifestations of
God. But Schelling retold the sacred story from the standpoint of God, as

---

[105] "God is attainable in pure speculative knowledge alone and *is* only in that knowledge, and is only
    that knowledge itself, for He is Spirit; and this speculative knowledge is the knowledge of the
    manifest religion." PS § 761 (I have replaced Miller's "revealed" with "manifest"); GW 9: 407.1–4.
[106] PS § 758 (translation slightly modified); GW 9:405.1–4.   [107] Ibid. GW 9:404.36–37.
[108] This was Hegel's discovery in the pre-Jean years. For this, cf. di Giovanni (2010).
[109] Cf. PS § 766; GW 9:409.1–4. The reference to Higher Criticism is only implicit.
[110] But it remains art, of course. In fact, it is liberated *as just art*.

a realization of God rather than the actualization of human beings. He placed the story on an imaginary cosmic stage, part of a cosmogonic process within which the human individual ultimately does not count *as individual*. Therefore he ended up only paying lip service to the irreducible reality of evil, as we saw. Hegel's retelling of the story is instead from the human standpoint; evil is therefore necessarily at the center of it. As Hegel says in a different yet relevant context, "The principle by which God is defined for human beings is also the principle for how humanity defines itself inwardly."[111] Reason's transcendence over nature that transforms the latter into an enemy to reconcile, an evil to redeem,[112] is the drama which is played out in God's incarnation: his being born, dying and being resurrected. The drama, exactly as it has been in the Phenomenology from the beginning, is one of reconciliation – of humanity with itself.

Hegel imagines all the forms of consciousness hitherto brought on the scene, together with the gods of the religions associated with them, as standing in a circle around a manger.[113] These are the spiritual elements that the emergence of explicit reason dispersed and both the Roman Emperor and the Stoic consciousness rendered ineffective by simply warehousing them, so to speak – the Emperor in the physical space of the Pantheon, the Stoic in the intelligible of the universal, in either case unanchored from the lived social contexts in which they were born. They now stand awaiting a renewed birth of Spirit which would mean a rebirth for them also, but transformed, given new shape in a new universe of meaning. A more descriptive image, however, one more in keeping with the sacred story, would have been to have them stand around the cross on which God is crucified for taking on upon himself the sins of humankind, and because of this he dies but is then resurrected victorious over sin. This is the Pauline doctrine of death and sin, resurrection and redemption, which Fichte found especially abhorrent but which for Hegel was the sacred story at its most speculative value. For the story is in truth that of the slave, the remote precursor of culture, who in fear of death overcomes it by working on nature. It is equally that of the beautiful soul, the final product of culture, who in confessing its sin also finds redemption for it.[114]

[111] Lectures on the Philosophy of Religion of 1827. Hegel (2006), p. 203; Hegel (1985), p. 413.
[112] Cf. § 777; GW 9:413.37–414.8. Hegel is showing how the drama of good and evil, which is essential to human existence, is portrayed in religious imaging thought.
[113] PS § 754; GW 9:403.8–16.
[114] For a different reading of Hegel on religion, see, among a vast literature on the subject, Hodgson (2005) and Williams (2017). For my review of this last, see di Giovanni (2018). For the influence on Hegel of the mystics and the heterodox tradition, see O'Reagan (1994). For an instructive contextualization of the pre-1800 Hegel in terms of Hegel's Old-Württemberg religious and

This needs expanding but only by retrieving what has already been said. The sacred story is one of death and resurrection because, without the fear of death, the self-assurance of a subject to be a world unto itself that marks in human experience the moment of transcendence over nature would not be serious. Nor would be God's taking on human nature be felt by unhappy humanity to be serious if the new man were not seen as actually dying. But death ceases thereby to be just a biological event. It is interiorized into the life of Spirit, the witness to its effectiveness in transcending nature. This is a theme which, as we have seen, Hegel has pursued in his narrative from the beginning at different levels of reflection. Without the fear of death, there would be no prestige-motivated battle of heroes; none of the creative work of the slave or the consequent work of the world of culture; no society predicated on the cult of death as in the reign of terror that was the Enlightenment's final product; nor one based on hypocrisy as in the moral world. The fear of death is at the same time the coming to be of a new life, namely a life of reason, in each case embodied in the life of a community. All forms of religion celebrate the birth of this life. The sacred story narrates it according to its conceptual truth, albeit in iconic form. It raises death to the very definition of spiritual existence. As Hegel says,

> The *death* of the divine Man, *as death*, is *abstract* negativity, the immediate result of the movement which ends only in *natural* universality. Death loses this natural meaning in spiritual self-consciousness, i.e., it comes to be its [. . .] concept; death becomes transfigured from its immediate meaning, viz., the non-being of this *particular* individual, into the *universality* of the Spirit who dwells in His community, dies in it every day, and is daily resurrected.[115]

Interiorizing death means looking for self-validating life, one which is truly to be had only as partakers of the life of the community of those who labor in the field of the Spirit – in effect, who labor at coming to terms with one's place in history.

Looking back at the Fichte/Schelling controversy regarding the nature of nature in the early years of the 1800s,[116] we can now understand why the two were shadow-boxing, with no common ground on which to meet. They missed the one point in lived experience which, on the one hand, gave immediate evidence of the effectiveness of the "I think" over nature and, on the other, rendered biological nature speculatively relevant for it – the one point, in other words, where the two might have met. As things stood, for Fichte nature was only an idea; the truth of any science based on it consequently dependent on moral commitment. As for Schelling, nature was indeed spiritualized from the beginning (it was God), but, when it came to its moment of subjectivity, Schelling had to fall back either on Fichte's "I," which on his own reckoning was only an abstraction, or on myth-making. The bliss that comes with love in general, with no determinate object, was Fichte's commanding feeling; Schelling's was either the admiration of beauty or a generalized feeling of sadness that hovers over nature because of its fragility.[117] None of these did the work of Hegel's fear of death.

But there is more to the sacred story. It is also one of sin and redemption. For the unhappy individual laboring at spiritualizing nature *labors*, that is, is an agent whose actions would not be effective unless singularly determined. But at the same time the action would not be rational unless it were self-validating and as such also universalizing in intention. But this amounts to wanting to be like God, to be determinedly absolute.[118] And in this there is sin, the spiritual evil which is the inevitable consequence of spiritualizing nature, the source also of the feeling of guilt, which is the moment of pathos affecting all human action. The whole of Hegel's

---

[117] This is Schelling's comment on plagues: "Universal disease never exists without the hidden forces of the ground having broken out [*sich auftun*]: it emerges when the irritable principle, which is supposed to rule as the innermost bond of forces in the quiet of the depths, activates [*aktuiert*] itself; or when aroused Archaeus leaves his peaceful dwelling in the centrum and steps into his surroundings." EHF 34; SSW I.7:336. Regarding Schelling's feeling of cosmic sadness, I am not saying that in proper contexts it is not a valid aesthetic experience, or that it has not been given objective expression in art. See, for instance, the theme in painting of *"et in arcadia ego"* as documented by Erwin Panofsky: https://fdocuments.in/document/erwin-panofsky-et-in-arcadia-ego.html. The point is that the experience is *only* aesthetic.

[118] I am abbreviating Hegel in an effort at presenting his position more intuitively, just as I have done in Chapter 5 in connection with the beautiful soul. The fuller (but by no means full) statement is that the beautiful soul originally extricates itself from the internal contradictions created by Kant's moral standpoint by withdrawing in spirit within itself, accepting its own subjective voice of conscience as the truth. In this withdrawing within itself, it does not simply let nature lose on its own, indifferent to moral values (as it is the case in Kant). It makes nature evil, outside the pale. That it be evil is a spiritual product, just as that death be a scandal is a spiritual product. It is a product which, however, redounds on it. For the beautiful soul becomes inevitably entangled with nature the moment it wants to communicate effectively with others, for the sake of gaining self-validation. Hegel's crucial point is that the beautiful soul's situation is typically human. Reconciling with it requires first acknowledging it. Cf. "Evil is nothing other than the self-centeredness of the natural existence of Spirit." PS § 777; GW 9:413.37–414.1. What complicates the reading of this group of paragraphs, which specifically deal with the incarnation and evil, is that Hegel is repeatedly aligning the moments of religious belief with the moments of the concept, clearly in order to show that religion and philosophy have the same content. Cf., especially, PS § 771; GW 9:410.29–411.17.

narrative – of which we have given only the nodal points, mostly in order to document how profoundly it differs in content and inspiration from anything Fichte or Schelling have to say on human history – is an account of how the human individual, in acting, becomes progressively aware of precisely this truth. And in the process, the more this awareness forces itself upon the acting individual, the more deliberate and sophisticated, even cynical in the case of Kant (whose morality in Hegel's view issues in hypocrisy), are the attempts at staving off the conclusion that every spiritual achievement is violent just because it is rational. It inevitably brings its evil in train.

The achievement of the beautiful soul, the figure that comes at the resolution of the process, is that it knows this: it knows not just that it is guilty but that it cannot be otherwise if it is to be effectively spiritual. For this, it confesses. But the beautiful soul also knows that the God before whom it confesses its guilt cannot effectively pass the judgment condemning it without doing so determinedly (exactly what Kant's imperative cannot do). To judge, therefore, God has to come down from the heavens, where he is only an abstraction; must assume human nature; by the same token, however, must also recognize that his judgment, while self-validating, is existentially determined. He, too, in other words, on taking on flesh becomes a beautiful soul; as such, in judging he must also confess, must ask for forgiveness while at the same time forgiving. The Christ on the cross is for Hegel the counterpart of the beautiful soul in religious imaging thought. The Christ dies but is resurrected on the third day, an event which is therefore both redemptive and salvific. The religious community of those whose reconciling language is one of confession and forgiveness is thus born: "The *universal* divine Man [is] the community."[119]

This reconciliation is nothing of the sort that Stoicism or Enlightenment reason pretended to provide. It is not a matter of recognizing, from a sufficiently universal standpoint, that the otherwise immediately perceived evils are in truth not so. The immediate presence of evil is incontestable. It is sin. In this regard Hegel is true to Christian consciousness. Confessing evil and forgiving it is not a return to a *status quo ex ante* which in Hegel's paradigm of experience would mean stepping outside the human situation and returning, *per impossibile*, to the innocence of nature. It means, rather, a commitment to a new start that leaves the past contained but not abolished. And the materially destructive consequences flowing from it are

---

[119] PS § 787 (p. 478); GW 9:421.4.

still in need of being checked and remedied, even when the passage of time might bring the relief of forgetting.[120]

For this reason Hegel is not proclaiming a "moral holiday," as has been said.[121] Justice still remains the cardinal moral virtue of a society, all the more seriously moral because there is no danger on Hegel's position that it be understood as an exercise in mental therapy. However, since a community's dispensation of justice is historically particularized, the degree of rational self-comprehension achieved by the community at any time will affect the tenor of its justice.[122] This is an existential, historically determined conditioning. And since in lived experience this comprehension is in the medium of imaging thought, it also follows that religion – not morality, as it would be for both Kant and Fichte – is the underlying matrix of any society.[123]

As we have seen, much of Hegel's reading of the sacred story is an attempt at showing not only that its plot corresponds to the internal articulation of the concept but that it spontaneously leads up to the concept itself until the latter finally comes on the scene *für sich*. We have also seen that, in the narrative of the Phenomenology, any leap in self-comprehension on the part of reason has direct consequences for the given structure of the society in which it occurs, on its religion in the first instance. A new sense of selfhood brought to an end the religion of the Ethical Order; the insight of the Enlightenment did the same for the faith of culture. This is because the new self-comprehension directly affects the imaging thought[124] in the medium of which religion, *every* religion, works its reconciliation. Hence the question that naturally arises: What happens to religion when the new self-comprehension is as conceptually articulated as Hegel thought was possible as of 1807; indeed, when the articulation is even prefigured in the current religion's sacred story and the religion itself is therefore in fact already aware of its rationality?

---

[120] Hegel's language, here and elsewhere, is unduly triumphalist, perhaps still a vestige of the Enlightenment. It does not follow, on Hegel's own terms, that there is no room for despair or, for that matter, that there are not evils that cannot be forgiven, for they are against Spirit itself. They might be materially healed (though not forgiven), only in the sense that time allows us to forget. Hegel's is not the last word on evil.

[121] William James, as cited by H. S. Harris (1997), pp. 521–522.

[122] In our society we do not burn witches. We do not even look for them.

[123] "It is in being thus related to religion that state, laws, and duties are in their actuality something determinate which passes over into a higher sphere and so into that on which it is grounded." *Philosophy of Right*. Hegel (1967), § 270, Addition, p. 166. But it is clear in the same Addition that Hegel is not speaking of Church/State relation. The issue is rationality, of which religion (as contrasted with Church) is a more fundamental realization than state and morality.

[124] Hegel quotes Diderot's *Nephew of Rameau*. Spirit, like an infection, penetrates all the vital organs of the body until "one fine morning it gives its comrade [i.e., the idol] a shove with the elbow, and bang! crash! the idol lies on the floor." PS § 545 (p. 332); GW 9:295.37–296.2.

Admittedly there is nothing definitive in Hegel on the issue, and there must be room for interpretation.[125] There can be no dispute, however, that the vocation of religion cannot be same as that of conceptual comprehension. To repeat a point already made, comprehending reconciliation is not the same as reconciling. Comprehension is objectifying; it aims at universalization. The work of religion is, rather, one of self-validation, an issue of identity which is both individual and communal; one which, as we have said, necessarily brings conflict and violence in train. Unlike comprehension, which is abstractive, religion is immersed in history; it is eminently historical. For this reason, while religion presupposes knowledge, this knowledge must be for it in the medium of imaging thought; it has to be historically particularized. Hegel says as much in a passage where immediately at issue is Spirit's movement of diffusion and self-recovery in all its aspects, as detailed in the Phenomenology, but the point is equally relevant in present context. As Hegel says, "Imaging thought constitutes the middle term between pure thought [i.e., such as is best expressed in the medium of the abstract concept] and self-consciousness as such [which is achieved in the historical validation of self-identity]."[126] Since Hegel's original intent in the Phenomenology is to demonstrate that knowledge which is truly such has been with us from the beginning, he is naturally driven by the logic of his narrative to move on to the pure concept after the speculative value of the sacred story has been demonstrated. But this does not mean that religion is thereupon made redundant, any more than, upon art ceasing to be religion, it ceases to be as art. The historical workweek of religion is at all times contemporary with the speculative Sunday of comprehension. The way to the latter is that of the cross.[127] Without the workweek, the speculative Sunday would be just an abstraction.

In other words, there will be myths with the advent of the explicit concept, and necessarily conflicting ones at that. There will equally be conflicting commitments as to what it means to be human. The presence in the age at large of the explicit concept will no doubt make a difference to the historical shape of the conflicting myths and the conflicting commitments. Nonetheless, myth will not be science, nor redemptive love intellectual.

Hegel apparently felt personally at home in his Lutheran confession. He did not anticipate, nor could he have anticipated, the long-term

---

[125] I suspect that, with the experience of secularism long behind us, we might be better positioned to appreciate the issue than Hegel himself could.

[126] PS § 767 (p. 464); GW 9:409.21–22. The translation is lightly modified; the glosses are mine.

[127] This is the underlying image in PS § 77; GW 9:55.32–39.

consequences of both the French and the Kantian revolutions.[128] For our part, the question still remains that has been pressing all along and must be confronted head-on in conclusion. Exactly what does Hegel mean by true knowledge, the kind that can only be expressed in the medium of the pure concept? For this we have to return to the beginning, to Spinoza and Kant.

6.5 Of Things Logical

6.5.1 *The Case of the Modal Categories*

Whenever in the Logic the modal categories are at issue, Hegel unfailingly uses them as a platform for criticizing Spinoza and Kant – in one breath, as it were – and both for the same reason: unlike him, they both deny that the categories have objectivity.[129] This is the defining difference of Hegel's relation to his two predecessors. And, since the modal categories are clearly the products of conceptual reflection, at stake is also Hegel's defining understanding of the nature of the concept and of the Logic which is the science of the concept.[130]

It is no easy task to lift Hegel's modal categories out of their immediate context within the Logic. They come at the concluding stages of the Objective Logic that roughly correspond to the transition in the Phenomenology from Consciousness to Self-Consciousness. We can nonetheless provide the right setting for discussing them by momentarily returning to the Fichte of 1804[2] lectures, specifically to his category of the *Soll*, with which, as we remember, he summed up the meaning of appearance.[131] A being that *should be* is one whose presence is effectively already at hand (it cannot be ignored), yet depends for its realization on conditions which, although still undetermined, when determined must be so from within the norm set by the being. In essence, the *Soll* is

---

[128] They belong to the history of modern secularism.

[129] These are the main texts. GW 21:10–44; 21:323–328; 11:369–409; 12:11–28; GW 20 §§ 142–149.

[130] Hegel's treatment of the modal categories in book II of the Objective Logic, published in 1812/1813 and never revised (GW 11), is not quite the same as their treatment in the 1830 revised edition of the Encyclopaedia (GW 20). In the former, the leading category is the absolute. In the latter, it is actuality; "absolute" does not occur at all as a category in its own right. Moreover, the treatment in the Encyclopaedia concludes with *Sache* (about which more momentarily), not with "absolute necessity," as in the Logic of 1812/13 (GW 11). Absolute necessity does not appear at all in 1830. These are substantial differences that would need closer consideration in the appropriate forum. We rely on the treatments of both 1812/1813 and 1830, but conclude more in line with the Encyclopaedia's (1830). In the following, the one volume English translation of the Logic is cited first, by page number alone.

[131] SK 155; GA II.8:318–319. Cf. Chapter 3. The modal categories occur as further determinations of appearance also in Hegel's Logic.

an expectation of rationality, exactly the expectation that an object would have to induce when presenting itself as object *absolutely*, that is, as self-validating being. The object *is*, not simply, but because of a *because* which it holds within. This "because" is the object's possibility – a possibility that Hegel also defines as a *Sollen*,[132] a reasoned demand for actuality. The modal categories parse out the sense of this demand. Hegel makes no metaphysical commitment in this parsing. He is engaged strictly in *Kategorienlehre*,[133] the reflective formulation of what must be said of an object in general in order that it be truly said of this object that it stands on its own.[134] The modal categories are the first articulation of what it means for an object to be *in-itself*; they define the object's objectivity, or again, they define its *in-itselfness* – as we must now explain, however briefly.

If for the right setting of the modal categories we turned to Fichte, for the outline of their articulation we must turn to Aristotle.[135] For Hegel, no less than for Aristotle, a being is whatever it is only by *becoming it*, that is, by way of an achievement. It is as if there were a space within the being, a distance between an inner and outer that marks the beginning and end of the being's becoming and also carries this becoming's genetic history within it; as if, moreover, the being validated its actual presence by virtue of this history. The being's self-validation as the being that it is – its in-itselfness, in other words – lies in the being's success in transforming determinations and conditions, which would otherwise affect the being only externally, into the being's own being. It reduces these, as independent realities, to mere accidentalities. In other words, the being's self-validation lies in the being's capacity to provide an exposition of its genetic history – exactly what Hegel blames Spinoza's Absolute for being unable to do.[136] As object, the being thus carries its own norm of truth.

---

[132] 479; GW 11:382.33.

[133] "Metaphysics falls entirely within logic. Here I can cite Kant as my precedent and authority. His critique reduces metaphysics as it has existed until now to a consideration of the understanding and reason." Letter to Niethammer, October 23, 1812. Hegel (1985), p. 277.

[134] "The thing of many properties, the concrete existing world," are examples of the kind of objects Hegel has in mind. Cf. 482; GW 11:385.30–31.

[135] Aristotle appears by name in the Addition to § 142 of the Encyclopaedia (1830) which is not in GW 20, since it is based on student notes of Hegel's lectures. It is, however, included in Wallace's translation of the work. "[Aristotle] establishes in opposition to Plato that the idea, which both recognize to be the only truth, is essentially to be viewed as an ἐνέργεια, in other words, as the inward which is quite to the fore, or as the unity of inner and outer, or as actuality, in the emphatic sense here given to the word." Hegel (1873), p. 259. Aristotle was not held in high reputation in Germany during the late Enlightenment, mostly because of Jakob Brucker, who presented him as an empiricist of the Locke-type in his *Historia critica philosophiae* (1742–1744). Hegel, the late Schelling, and Christian August Brandis were mostly responsible for his rehabilitation.

[136] For the key text, cf. 473–473; GW 11:376–378. In the preceding pages Hegel presents the correct way of relating attributes and modes to the Absolute, which he takes as standing for Spinoza's substance.

Hegel's modal categories detail the history of this exposition in the abstract, basically by distinguishing the various meanings of "possible" and the consequent meanings of "actual," "contingent," and "necessary."

"Possible" can be said in either a "formal" or a "real" sense. One is justified in presupposing a being as actual inasmuch as, in presupposing it, one also supposes that the being can explain its own actuality, that is, that the being's actuality has a ground which the being can account for from within. Accordingly, we say that the being is possible, although at first the presumed possibility is admittedly *only* a possibility. While excluding the impossibility of the presupposed being, the alleged possibility does not exclude the concomitant possibility that the being might as well not have been. We call this possibility "formal," or possibility in general. At the level of explanation that this possibility offers, we are justified in saying no more than that the presupposed being is actual because it is possible and possible because it is actual. This is the circumstance which, according to Hegel, constitutes the contingency, or the "might not have been," of the presupposed being. As Hegel puts it: "The *absolute restlessness* of the *becoming* of these two determinations [viz., possible and actual] is contingency."[137] This contingency is itself a kind of necessity, since the presence of the presupposed actual being is *ex hypothesi* undeniable. Contingency and *de facto* necessity are thus interchangeable. As Hegel says: "But for this reason [viz., the restless becoming of possible and actual], each determination immediately turns into the opposite, in this opposite each equally *rejoins itself*, and this *identity* of the two, of each in the other, is *necessity*."[138]

This is the circumstance that precipitates the move from formal to real possibility. Not that formal possibility is not a significant category. On the contrary, it sets the stage for the specific function of the modal categories *as modal*. As such, they define not the *what* of a presupposed being – not its being-determination, in other words – but the mode in which this determination is, or has been, achieved, that is, the existential status of the determination. This, incidentally, is what Spinoza failed to see, according to Hegel. Spinoza took the modes of substance as further determinations of the substance's attributes (thought and extension, which are being-determinations) instead of as referring such attributes back to substance as modes of its subsistence. For this reason, Spinoza's exposition of the Absolute failed to achieve closure, according to Hegel.[139] But to return to

---

[137] 481; GW 11:384.31–32. Also: "The contingent thus has no ground because it is contingent; but for that same reason it has a ground, because it is contingent." 481; GW 11:384.18–19.
[138] 481; GW 11:384.32–34. [139] Cf. the already cited text, 473–473; GW 11:376–378.

formal possibility, and still to play on the image of the distance within a being that marks the beginning and end of the being's becoming, formal possibility defines this distance in principle; it opens it, so to speak.[140] The point is to traverse this distance, and to this end one has to move from formal to real possibility.

We have real possibility when a content is added to the otherwise only formal possibility.[141] This is not, of course, a matter of adding extra-conceptual material, which, since it is extra-conceptual, would leave formal possibility unaffected and therefore still only formal. Rather, adding a content only means to suppose that the possibility of the presupposed actual being is based on being-determinations that already accrue to it as presupposed. They accrue to it by virtue of the relation that the presupposed actual being has to other beings, that is, by being presupposed as standing within an explanatory context of beings.[142] This also means that, by virtue of standing in such a context, other being-determinations can be added to the actual being until, so far as being-determination or content goes, the possible and the actual coincide in it.

However, the effectiveness of the presupposed being's possibility in grounding the being's actuality does not lie in this coincidence. For Hegel, the coincidence is the result of the grounding, not the grounding itself.[143] This is the all-important point. If the effectiveness lay in just this coincidence, the reality of the presupposed being would be dissolved into an indefinite number of determining relations directed at a universe of possible and actual beings, exactly the consequence that Jacobi refused to accept but attributed to Spinoza and rationalist metaphysics in general. In that scenario, the reality of the presupposed actual being (indeed, of any being) would be flattened, so to speak, spread out over a tapestry of in principle unlimited being-determinations.

For Hegel, the effective factor in the grounding of an actual being through its possibility is, instead, the very coming-to-be of the actual being. It is this being's ἐνέργεια, as Aristotle called it, or its internal

---

[140] Strictly speaking, this was already done with the distinction between essence and being. But the modal categories are the place where we can turn to the distinction at its most significant for our exposition purposes.

[141] 482; GW 11:485.21–29.

[142] All this according to the play of categories detailed in the Logic in the first book of the Objective Logic.

[143] I am basing this reading, which requires some glossing, on the Encyclopaedia Logic, §§ 146–149; GW 20:166–169. Actualization as the self-grounding of a well-founded fact (*die Betätigung der Sache*) is the point at issue. The long addition to § 147, available in Wallace's translation, is very helpful as a more intuitive expansion of Hegel's succinct statements. Hegel (1873), pp. 267–271.

entitling force (its "should-be"), by virtue of which being-determinations that are otherwise indifferent to it are transformed into conditions (*Bedingungen*) of the being's actually becoming itself *and no other* – whether these determinations are presupposed at any stage of this becoming or are further added to those that are presupposed because they are consistent with them. Moreover, since the range of available being-determinations is in principle indeterminate, and, in the course of the being's becoming, more than one set might be consistent with those already at hand, that one set is accepted rather than another is itself a function of the same force that drives the being's coming-to-be. In other words, it is the being's becoming that progressively generates the being's "might have been"; it generates it at different stages of the becoming, by positing possibilities but at the same time precluding some as effectively real. At the end, with the decisive realization (*Betätigung*) of the presupposed actual being, the contingency of the latter's immediate presence no longer denotes mere presence. Rather, it denotes the successful completion of the actual being's grounding. It is the witness to the completion. Contingency derives internally from the realized actual; immediacy is the actual's product.

Hegel calls this achieved actual being "*Sache*," an internally well-founded fact, a self-validating actual being.[144] In the Logic, Hegel is not concerned with the subjective activity of explaining. This is the task of the Phenomenology. At issue in the Logic is, rather, the constitution of an object that renders the object explainable, or the constitution of meaning itself. In documenting this constitution, particularly when the language of presupposing and supposing is involved, it is easy, even unavoidable, to lapse into the mode of subjective explaining. But it is the constitution of the *Sache* itself, since its actual presence is an achievement, that requires that the presence be presupposed. This presence can at first only be assumed provisionally, that is, barring further considerations that would disallow its presupposition. In any case, the presupposition cannot be based on immediate intuition. (Hegel is no Frau Bauer, as we remember from the Phenomenology.) It is made, rather, on the supposition that the

---

[144] *Sache* is a notoriously difficult term to translate in philosophical contexts. The most recent translation of the Logic (2010) has "fact," an adequate rendering provided one keeps in mind the Latin root of the word, *factum*, a "done deed." The *Sache* is the end-product of an actualization, a *Betätigung*. GW 20:167.11; 147. Wallace translates *Sache* in this context as "the actual fact or affairs in its all-rounded definiteness." Hegel (1873), p. 267. Wallace's translation of the Encyclopaedia Logic, although too free by contemporary standards of translation, is, in my opinion, eminently readable and accurate in meaning,

presupposed being internally justifies its being presupposed. This is the expectation. Presupposing an object is, at the same time, supposing that the object supposes its being presupposed.[145] Modally considered, an object is like a promissory note, a *Soll*, as we said.

Another way of making the same point is to say that real possibility, and the consequent real actuality and real necessity, can only be particular, relative. "Absolute necessity" is not determinable and therefore falls outside the scope of discourse.[146] One might think of it by taking one's start from the being-determinations of beings – their "what" and the "how much thereof" – and then supposing the totalizing of such determinations in an Absolute. However, this is a self-contradictory supposition, since determination means "being one thing rather than another and in opposition to such other," as if in one breath. To totalize determinations in fact amounts to suspending them as identifiable particulars. It amounts to denying their truth-value where it counts most, namely at the level of singularity where alone they are effectively determined. Here is where Kant's image of an "abyss of reason" has its proper place. To suppose an entity that would be all possible determinations of being at once (call it Substance, Absolute, God, or else) would be like precipitating all determinations into an abyss, which at the same time would be the abyss of reason, since reason is inherently discursive and, as such, depends for its explanatory power on the play of determinations. But to undermine reason necessitates that one rely on intellectual intuition, exactly what Spinoza and Kant had done – Spinoza, dogmatically; Kant, hypothetically. The net result was the same so far as the modal categories were concerned. They were denied objective validity. In essence, this was Hegel's criticism of his two predecessors.[147]

There might nonetheless be room to speak of an absolute necessity but only in the context just assumed, namely with reference to the self-validating becoming which is internal to a *Sache*. This becoming, as we said, renders the *Sache*'s immediate presence – by right and not just incidentally – its own presence and no other's. This is the logical

---

[145] At the opening of book II of volume 1 (Objective Logic), Hegel presents the play of supposing and presupposing (*setzen* and *voraussetzen*) as internal to the object itself. This play generates its own externality, which makes room for the language of external explaining.

[146] In the Logic, but, significantly, not in the 1830 revised edition of the Encyclopaedia Logic, Hegel concludes the treatment of the modal categories with "absolute necessity." It is not clear, however, what this necessity amounts to except as a reflection on what constitutes real or relative necessity, namely on the fact that necessity generates its own contingency. "It is necessity itself, therefore, that determines itself as *contingency*." 485; GW 11:390.25–26. In that case, absolute necessity simply marks the transition to substance.

[147] In the revised edition of the Logic (GW 21).

counterpart of the arrival in the Phenomenology of the individual who stakes her universality on her singularity; indeed, who, by virtue of this staking, makes the singularity (which would otherwise be just an incidental determination) significant *as singular*. But in this context, necessity truly devolves into freedom, an object for which the modal categories are inadequate. These are too abstract. To understand freedom, one must instead turn to the categories of the concept.[148]

6.5.2 The Concept

Hegel calls necessity "blind," "averse to light."[149] The image is an implicit reference to the kind of person, as portrayed in the Phenomenology (say, Antigone), whose still only implicit awareness of her own rationality leads her to believe that whatever happens to her does so according to a script inherent in things and that, therefore, she deserves the fate that befalls her, whatever this might be. It is this awareness that, if the person motivated by it could put it into words, would be canonized by the categories of real actuality. Within the context of the Logic, the image is, however, one way of saying that necessity, and the other modal categories associated with it, are not sufficiently self-reflective, that is, that although they in fact provide the internal exposition of what it means for an object to be in-itself, they do not *say* that they say it. In the language of the Phenomenology, the exposition is *in* the object but not *for* it; it is only *for* the "we" that reflects upon the object externally. (The "we," remember, is the one who already has a grasp of rationality. The counterpart in the Logic of this "we" is the logicality[150] that anonymously carries the whole categorial procession.) The task at hand, therefore, is to develop the categories of actuality so as to have them say explicitly, or reflectively, that they define – as they do indeed – the in-itselfness of an object. They define it, moreover, precisely as an achievement.

This is the task of the categories of substantial and causal relation that follow and which Hegel treats in the final segment of the Objective Logic under the overall title of "the absolute relation." These are the categories typical of classical metaphysics. On their basis one might indeed be

---

[148] Cf. "The concept of necessity is very difficult, for necessity is indeed already the concept, but with its moments still as actualities which, yet at the same time only forms, must be grasped as in themselves splintered (*gebrochene*) and transient." [My translation] GW 20:167.22–26; § 147. "This truth of *Necessity* is thus *Freedom*, and the truth of *substance* is the *concept*." [My translation] GW 20:174.15–16; § 158.

[149] 487, 488; GW 11:391.25, 392.1.   [150] This word is Hegel's, *das Logische*. 736; GW 12:237.2.

tempted to metaphysical commitments, as if in their medium one were not just explaining the determinations of an object in general but instead engaged in cosmology. But Hegel is definitely not a dogmatic metaphysician, let alone a Schelling. To repeat the point just made, such categories only say what the categories of actuality exhibit in fact. And (to telescope Hegel's detailed treatment into one sentence) the more explicitly they say it, the more they motivate the shift to a yet higher level of reflectivity – one that is unlike all the previous levels, because it marks the closure of the reflective exposition of an object in general (an exposition internal to it) that began with the Logic. The categories now introduced do not just *say* what the previous categories have expounded; *they say that they say it*. In effect this means that the object, which has been the subject matter of reflection from the start, has become fully transparent as object by assuming the form of a subject. As a result, it can do its own self-exposition, can give reasons for its in-itselfness, and, consequently, can demonstrate that its language, which only now comes into its own, has in fact supported all the previous forms of objectivity, including, notably, those of substance and causality, which are, significantly, typically Spinoza's.[151] The object, now a subject, generates its own norm of what it is to be an object.

In volume 2 of the Logic, "The Science of Subjective Logic,"[152] we thus enter the domain of the concept, which is also that of freedom. This is a step that, in the context of the Phenomenology, corresponds to the recognition that intelligibility is achieved *per se* and *a se* only in the works of the spirit, that is, in the medium of typically human existence. The concept is the form of this existence, in the sense that human existence is achieved as such only in conceptualization, or in such activities as are mediated by conceptualization. This is also the sense in which feeling is already reason in principle, as we said and have had occasions to repeat. These are claims that have ontological implications. They in fact make monism moot as a philosophical position. But, so far as Hegel's Logic is concerned, the significant presupposition (which is historical in nature) is

---

[151] I am diverging from Hegel's technical language which, precisely because it is technical, needs explaining. This is how Hegel himself makes the point: "In the *concept*, therefore, the kingdom of *freedom* is disclosed. The concept is free because the *identity that exists in and for itself* and constitutes the necessity of substance exists at the same time as sublated or as *positedness*, and this positedness, as self-referring, is the very identity. Vanished is the obscurity which the causally related substances have to each other, for the originariness of their self-subsistence that makes them causes (*Ursache*) has passed over into positedness and has thereby become self-transparently *clear*, the '*originary fact*' (*ursprüngliche Sache*) is "originary" because it is a "*self-causing fact*" (*Ursache ihrer selbst*), and this is the *substance that has been let go freely into the concept*." 513; GW 12:15.35–16.6.

[152] "Or The Doctrine of the Concept." 507; GW 12:5.

that the form of human existence (the concept) has been abstracted by itself – as have, therefore, the norms of the activity of conceptualization that gives rise to the universe of meaning which is the specific achievement of human existence. The Logic details such norms. And since it is in the course of discourse that that universe is generated, to detail the said norms is, in effect, to determine norms of discourse. The Logic is what one should expect a logic to be. It is a *Kategorienlehre*, a doctrine of categories, from beginning to end, and, in this final part – the Subjective Logic – officially such.

Accordingly, in the first section of this final part, Hegel introduces all the conceptual instruments normally associated with traditional formal logic but, in the present context, motivated by a completely different interest. They are, first, the concept itself, as universal, particular, and singular; second, judgment, in its several possible forms; finally, syllogism, also in its several possible forms. As treated by Hegel, these instruments are not presented independently but with the deliberate intent of demonstrating that each would not effectively discharge the function specific to it within discourse without presupposing, or without being mediated by, all the others. This is the case within each of the three distinguished levels of conceptual complexity (concept, judgment, syllogism), as well as, so far as conceptualization as such goes, within the procession from one level to the other. When the categories of actuality were at issue, Hegel demonstrated that an actual cannot effectively be such without an internal process of realization that entails distinct but interrelated moments. With the concept, Hegel is making a corresponding claim. To put it as intuitively as I can, a discourse (for it is of discourse that we are in fact talking) is successful only to the extent that, in making a point (which must be singular if it is to be recognized for what it is), this point must have been brought within a broader context of discourse and connected to the latter by means of relevant particular determinations. The net result is that, on the one hand, the singular point gains universal significance (it brings to a singular point a discourse that otherwise transcends it) and, on the other, the broader context is correspondingly validated precisely by the success of the discourse in rendering, by virtue of the broader context, the singular point significant. The richness in content of the discourse depends on the particular circumstances that the discourse brings in train. Discourse proceeds *pari passu* with an inner rhythm (*Lebenspuls*),[153] by virtue of

---

[153] Hegel repeatedly uses this term in connection with method. Cf.: PS §§ 56, 57, 58; GW 9:40.34, 41.8, 42.3. Logic 17, 35; GW 21:15.23 (*Lebenspuls*), 21:38.11.

which it maintains inner coherence as it constantly transcends itself only to return to one original point.[154] Like the process of actualization, this is a process of self-validation, except that discourse does it *for itself*, *sua sponte*.

"Objectivity," therefore, is the subject of the section that immediately follows. Hegel says that the transition from "concept" to "objectivity" is "essentially the same as the *proof* from the *concept*, that is to say, from the *concept of God* to his existence."[155] However, "the same as" in the quote is misleading, for it may give the impression that Hegel is revalidating the "proof from the concept."[156] And of course, in a way Hegel does – not, however, by lapsing into the metaphysics that Kant called dogmatic but, on the contrary, by deflating the traditional proof of its metaphysical content. The simple point that is made with the transition from concept to objectivity is that being becomes intelligible, and therefore knowable (an object), only to the extent that it is drawn into the space provided by the concept. We cannot make judgments of existence except within that space. Objectivity enters into the Logic at this particular juncture because the concept that makes it possible has been fully developed internally *as concept*. The more being, which is otherwise a flat landscape of immediate determinations, acquires in the course of the Logic internal depth, and incrementally gains the self-subsistence of substance that reflectively contains the being-determinations, the more it internally retreats to the concept, that is, reveals the latter as the source of its objectivity.

Accordingly, in the rest of the section Hegel examines three different levels of objectivity: mechanism, chemism, and teleology. In the Phenomenology, Hegel details the historical process by which the scientist arrives at the sciences, the objects of which fall under these three rubrics. What is at issue in the Logic, however, is exclusively the degrees of intelligibility of such objects themselves, that is, the extent to which, in

---

[154] For the point made in Hegel's technical idiom, cf. "The concept, as absolutely self-identical negativity, is self-determining; it was noted that the concept, as resolving itself into *judgement* in singularity, already posits itself as *something real, an existent*; this still abstract reality completes itself in *objectivity*." 626; GW 12:128.1–4.

[155] 625; GW 12:127.9–10.

[156] Dieter Henrich's early book on the ontological proof of God's existence (Henrich 1960) is very instructive on this subject. So far as I can see, Henrich's understanding of Hegel is not unlike the one I have just proposed. Hegel admits that Spinoza's concept of substance as *causa sui* is perfectly valid *as concept*, and even necessary for a complete conceptual determination of objectivity. Kant, too, admitted that much. However, this was not for Hegel – nor, for that matter, it was for Kant – the warrant for concluding to the existence of a substance which is *causa sui*. It was for Hegel, rather, the warrant for claiming that the truth about being *can*, and *only* can, be achieved through the concept. This is the work of Spirit. Here is where Hegel differed from Kant and took umbrage at the latter's claim that the categories are subjective. Kant had taken the subjectivity of the concept in a psychological sense. For Henrich's conclusion regarding Hegel, see especially pp. 216–219.

the context of the Phenomenology, each would support the scientist's discourse regarding it on its own, without the scientist in fact having to bring into play presuppositions external to the object's presumed specific form. In the context of the Logic, the issue is the degree to which an object carries its own exposition of its content – or fails to carry it, in which case it is led, by virtue of logicality in general, to give way to a more reflective form of objectivity – in effect, to another science.

Finally, in the last section of the Subjective Logic, which is also the conclusion of the Logic, this logicality itself (*das Logische*) is objectified as such, in the medium of "the idea" – a term which obviously recalls Kant's idealizing constructions that bring his Critique of Reason to systematic unity. For Hegel, too, the term carries systematic significance. For in teleology (the final stage in the elaboration of objectivity), the object closes its reflection upon itself. In this, it distances itself from itself and thus opens the space for itself as *object* and, by the same token, equally for itself as *subject* – the latter, however, as containing the object.[157] This closure, and the new space that the closure opens up, is what the idea expresses. As Hegel says: "Thus the concept is essentially this: to be distinguished, as an identity existing for itself, from its *implicitly existing* objectivity, and thereby to obtain externality, but in this external totality to be the totality's self-determining identity. So the concept is now *the idea*."[158] The self-exposition of the concept, which has in fact supported objectivity all along and has been explicitly reflected, progressively, in the detailed three stages of objectivity, is finally objectified.

In a way, this is a return to the self-exposition of the concept achieved at the beginning of the Subjective Logic. Real actuality and possibility were also a return, in their case to formal possibility and actuality. The parallel is instructive, for in both cases the return is not without an advance. In the latter case – that to formal possibility and actuality – the return was by way of demonstrating how, as reassembled within the logical space provided by these formal categories, previous being-determinations acquired new significance: they became factors in the determination of a well-founded fact (*die Sache*). In the case of the return to the formal structure of the life of the concept (what we have called discourse) by way of the objectivity that this structure has made possible, what is demonstrated (narrated, so to speak) is how, in the production of this objectivity, a new subjective universe is

---

[157] This should bring us back to Hegel's claim in the Phenomenology that the truth is subject rather than substance. See Section 6.4.1.

[158] 667; GW 12:172.14–17. Cf. Also, Encyclopaedia Logic, §§ 209–212.

generated, one of meaning, which, in the idea, is presented *per se*. The subject matter of this final section of the Logic, the Idea, is accordingly an exposition of the determinations of a life for which the concept is the form – in effect, an exposition of the idea of "the true" and "the good."

Fichte's *Wissenschaftslehre* – we remember – concluded with the idea of itself as science. So does the Logic, under the title of the "absolute idea."[159] This is where the idea, which (we must keep in mind) is the objectification of *das Logische* – the form of rational life – realizes itself, in the sense that all the categories introduced from the start of the Logic are retrieved but now explicitly exhibited as conditions for the Idea to come to its own. This takes place according to a process of distinguishing and opposing and, by the same token, reconciling, which constitutes the rhythm (*Lebenspuls*) of the life of the concept and which Hegel calls "method."[160] We see this process, of course, reflected in the flow of discourse in real time. In the case of the modal categories, the process constituted the limited realization (*Betätigung*) of formal possibility. It issued in the *Sache* – in effect, Spinoza's substance shorn of Spinoza's dogmatism. In the present case, the realization at issue is of rationality as such, and the upshot is none other than the idea of personality. As Hegel says:

> The richest [concept] is, therefore, the most concrete and the *most subjective*, and that which retreats to the simplest depth is the mightiest and the most all-encompassing. The highest and most intense point is the *pure personality*, which, solely by virtue of the absolute dialectic [i.e., the process just described] which is its nature, equally embraces and holds *everything within itself*, for it makes itself into the supremely free – the simplicity which is the first immediacy and universality.[161]

Hegel has made good on his claim that the Absolute, which in fact turns out to be the idea of knowledge as truly such, is to be conceived first and foremost as subject and not as substance.

In the Phenomenology, this conclusion corresponds to the coming on the scene of the beautiful soul, and of the human drama of evil and reconciliation which is further lived in the medium of religious feelings and religious myth. The logical counterpart is no doubt poor of content in comparison. It is the product of abstractive conceptual art, the hypostatization of the form of the rational life that makes evil possible, and of the

---

[159] "Absolute Idea" – not "Absolute" in the dogmatic sense of an absolute entity; nor, for that matter, the idea of an entity such as God (Kant). At issue is the idea of a knowledge that knows itself to be truly such (*Wissen*).

[160] 33: GW 21:38.24.   [161] 750 (slightly modified); GW 12:251.8–13.

history that goes with it. Hegel's Logic is only a shadow of real life. In Hegel's words: "The system of logic is the realm of shadows, the world of simple essentialities, freed of all sensuous concretion";[162] its "content is *the exposition of God as he is in his eternal essence before the creation of nature and of a finite spirit.*"[163] Or, in a comparison that I prefer, it is like the syntax of a language that readies one to speak before one engages in actual discourse. Nobody, of course, needs the Logic in order to live rationally (in Hegel's deep sense of "rational," which actually makes possible the presence of error and evil) – no more than one needs the knowledge of syntax to speak coherently. Nonetheless, the fact that a culture is in the position of generating a Logic is a reflection of the degree of critical self-awareness that the culture in question has achieved, just as for anyone to have a syntax betokens a special capacity of reflective control over one's actual discourse.

The Logic is a realm of shadows. But it is not without a content of its own, as Hegel insists. Hegel equally insists that its content is internally generated from within conceptual reflection.[164] This is the claim that might give rise to the belief that Hegel's system is a panlogism, as if the course of nature and history unfolded with the same necessity as the Logic unfolds and according to a schema as prescribed by it. But in fact, the claim precludes precisely this belief. It is because experience is internally rational – in effect, because history writes its own plot as it moves along – that its rationality can be abstracted on its own, in the medium of conceptual art, and in the form of a conceptual plot (so to speak) that documents, as I have tried to sketch, the constitution of an object in general. What all this amounts to in real life is a matter of historical reflection and historical discovery.

Only if one assumes that the truth of experiences lies outside it, in a principle that transcends it (call it God, the Absolute, Substance, or else), and to which one needs to refer experience in order to understand it, is one led to adopt strategies for looking at experience from the standpoint of this transcendent principle. The metaphysics that Kant dubbed dogmatic presumed that, by virtue of its logical categories, reason achieves an insight into – literally – God's essence before creation and also, therefore, comes into possession of the script according to which everything happens. On this assumption, one should be able to deduce all of experience from such a script – in principle, at least, though not in in practice. It would also

---

[162] 37; GW 21:42.30–32. [163] 29; 21:34.9–11.
[164] 24; GW 21:28.9–14. "[...] This objective thinking is thus the *content* of pure science." 29; GW 21:34.1.

follow that Hegel's Logic would have to be read as if it constituted the truth of experience *materially*. The distance between Logic and history, which, on the contrary, is essential to Hegel, is thus removed – hence the panlogism.

Hegel was a Kantian. He said that much himself, openly. He did not approve of Kant's language of the "I think," just as he also did not admit the language of consciousness within the precincts of logic, in both cases because of their psychologically subjective connotations. Hegel insisted on the language of concept and conceptualization. Nonetheless, as he said: "It is one of the profoundest and truest insights to be found in the Critique of Reason that the *unity* which constitutes the *essence of the concept* is recognized as the *original synthetic* unity *of apperception*, the unity of the '*I think*,' or of self-consciousness."[165] But this, according to Hegel, is just another way of saying that it is only by virtue of the concept and its conceptualization – that is, only in the intelligible space provided by the concept, and by virtue of the norms of intelligibility supplied by it – that an otherwise merely supposed manifold of intuitions and perceptions is recognized as belonging, or not belonging, to an object as the object's determinations. The objectivity of the object is thus validated internally to the object, and the concept, for its part, recognizes in this validation its own achievement. Subjectivity proceeds *pari passu* with the achievement of objectivity. In Hegel's estimate, Kant was already an idealist in his own sense of idealism. But, because of what Hegel calls Kant's "psychological reflex,"[166] Kant took the categories to be subjective in a psychological sense, as if their norms of intelligibility were to be applied to immediate experience externally, instead of taking the immediacy of the experience to be generated by the categories. Kant ended up accepting classical metaphysics as true by default – only hypothetically, of course, and behind the protection of the veil of critical ignorance. Nonetheless, the distance between the logical and the historical was in principle abolished.

Hegel was a Fichtean in perhaps an even deeper sense than he was a Kantian. Like Kant, Fichte started with the presupposition that experience would not be what it is if it did not bask in intelligibility from the start – in a Light, to use Fichte's image, that makes things visible while it itself remains invisible. But where Hegel saw this Light as the product of reason, Fichte instead saw reason's products as human constructs that in fact obfuscate the Light. Therefore, the constructs had to be, indeed not

---

[165] 515; GW 12:17.36–18.2; the whole of page 18 (English, 515–516) is relevant.
[166] 520; GW 12:22.34.

ignored (for that would be impossible), but disarmed when the immediate awareness of truth is concerned. And, since the *Wissenschaftslehre* was itself a product of reason, it, too, achieved its truth at the point at which it annulled itself as a product of conceptual art and transformed itself, instead, into a way of life – one for which, out of subjective conviction, Fichte presumed to preach the ideological norms.

This is what I meant when I said[167] that the difference between Hegel's idealism and that of his contemporaries ultimately devolves into the issue of whether, and why, a distinction can be maintained, as is maintained in Hegel, between philosophy and religion – where religion is experience at its most concrete. To be sure, "philosophy has the same content and the same purpose as art and religion,"[168] since they are all equally engaged in transforming nature into a typically human universe, all of them by virtue of the concept. And it can be added that philosophy is "the highest mode of apprehending the absolute idea [i.e., that human universe precisely as such], because its mode, that of the concept, is the highest."[169] But this is only to say that in the Logic philosophy abstracts the very form of rational life and objectifies it for itself, detailing it in its determinations precisely as such a form. But that is not the same as living that life (Fichte), let alone the same as living the life of a cosmic God (Schelling). Understanding reconciliation, which is at the existential heart of human experience according to Hegel, is not the same as reconciling.

Hegel says that the transition from the idea to the space and time of nature has to be grasped "in the sense that the idea *freely discharges* (*entläßt*) itself, absolutely certain of itself and internally at rest."[170] Schelling was right in pointing out that this self-discharge was only an image, a metaphor. But he was wrong in complaining that the use of imagery at this juncture was at odds with Hegel's declared intent of operating within the confines of conceptual reflection alone. Of course, once the Logic has fulfilled its vocation, the transition to the direct experience of nature, or, for that matter, to the particular sciences of nature and spirit, cannot itself be logical – no more than (say) the transition from syntax or grammar to actual discourse can itself be syntactical or grammatical. In determining the idea, the Logic determines the possibility of cognition as such, and hence the possibility of the sciences of nature and spirit. But this is not the same as providing particularized principles for them. The self-discharge of the idea is more like an existential move – the type of move that we make when, in

<hr>

[167] At the very end of Chapter 5.   [168] 735; GW 12:236.28–29.   [169] 735; GW 12:236.29–30.
[170] 753; GW 12:253.21–24.

actual life and according to the vicissitudes of the latter, we shift from one set of considerations, or one set of activities, to another. Of course, such moves all presuppose the logicality of experience, yet each constitutes by itself a new taking of a position with respect to experience and, accordingly, new possibilities of discovery. Regrettably, Hegel's *Encyclopaedia of the Philosophical Sciences in Outline* can give the impression (Hegel himself is responsible for this) that, in such a compendium, the sciences unfold from principles that are established by the Logic and that together they constitute one single logically knit vision of reality. But the truth that more closely accords with the Logic is, rather, that each science comes into its own by virtue of marking a new and creative starting point.

So far as Schelling goes, it is difficult to contrast him with Hegel. Schelling operated in the medium of poetic imagination, often overlaid by dubious scientific theory. Hegel's Logic simply sidelined this way of philosophizing. It might be possible, perhaps, to contrast the two on the issue of evil, which was important to both. For Schelling, evil was a cosmic event. For Hegel, it was instead a human creation, and all the more irreducibly real because of that. In this, Hegel remained closer to the biblical narrative than Schelling. In actual fact, Schelling had a much more profound historical influence in the nineteenth century than Hegel's Logic. But the point is that Schelling and Hegel simply never trod the same conceptual grounds as Hegel instead did in company with Kant and Fichte – or even in company with Jacobi, for that matter.

And Jacobi brings us back to the towering figure of Spinoza that has been behind all the ways and byways of thought we have tried to document. Jacobi loved Spinoza because of his conviction that truth is self-explanatory. As he said of him: "Few have enjoyed such a peace of the spirit, such a heaven in the understanding, as this pure and clear mind did."[171] It was because of this clarity of mind that Spinoza succeeded in distilling the essence of classical metaphysics, to the point, in Jacobi's eyes, of making its consequences clear so far as human existence was concerned. Classical metaphysics undermined the possibility of human personality. To save this possibility conceptually, with the same clarity of mind as Spinoza, was the challenge. Hegel met it.

---

[171] MPW 193.

Bibliography

Primary Sources

Eschenmayer, Carl August. *Die Philosophie in ihrem Übergang zur Nichtphilosophie*. Erlangen: Walther, 1803.

Der Eremit und der Fremdling, Gespräche über das Heilege und die Geschichte. Erlangen: Werther, 1806.

Die philosophie dans son passage à la non-philosophie, trans. Alexandra Roux. Paris: Vrin, 2005.

Fichte, Johann Gottlieb. *Gesamtausgabe der Bayerischen Akademie der Wissenschaften*, ed. Erich Fuchs, Hans Gliwitzky, Reinhard Lauth, and Peter K. Schneider. 42 vols. Stuttgart-Bad Cannstatt: Frommann, 1962–2012.

Fichte: Science of Knowledge (Wissenschaftslehre) with First and Second Introductions, ed. and trans. Peter Heath and John Lachs. New York: Appleton-Century-Crofts, 1970.

Characteristics of the Present Age, The Way towards the Blessed Life or The Doctrine of Religion, ed. Daniel N. Johnson, trans. William Smith. Washington: University Publications of America, 1977.

Early Philosophical Writings, ed. Daniel Breazeale. Ithaca, NY: Cornell University Press, 1988.

Fichte: Foundations of Transcendental Philosophy; Wissenschaftslehre nova methodo (1796/99), ed. and trans. Daniel Breazeale. Ithaca, NY: Cornell University Press, 1992.

Introductions to the Wissenschaftslehre and Other Writings (1797–1800), ed. and trans. Daniel Breazeale. Indianapolis: Hackett, 1994.

The Science of Knowing: J. G. Fichte's 1804 Lectures on the Wissenschaftslehre, trans. Walter R. Wright. Albany: State University of New York Press, 2005a.

The System of Ethics According to the Principles of the Wissenschaftslehre, trans. Daniel Breazeale and Günter Zöller. Cambridge: Cambridge University Press, 2005b.

Characteristic of the Present Age, trans. William Smith. Moscow: Dodo Press, 2008.

Attempt at a Critique of All Revelation, trans. Allen Wood. Cambridge: Cambridge University Press, 2009.

Fichte, Johann Gottlieb and Friedrich Wilhelm Joseph Schelling. *The Philosophical Rupture Between Fichte and Schelling: Selected Texts and Correspondence (1800–1802)*, ed. and trans. Michael G. Vater and David W. Wood. Albany: State University of New York Press, 2012.

Goethe, Johann Wolfgang. *Aus meinem Leben, Dichtung und Wahrheit*, ed. Karl Richter, Part 3, Vol. 16 of *Sämtliche Werke*, 19 vols. Munich: Hanser, 1985.

Götter, Helden und Wieland. Eine Farce. In *Poetische Werke*, Band 3, pp. 525–534, Leipzig: Auf Subscription, 1774.

Hegel, Georg Wilhelm Friedrich. *The Logic of Hegel: The Encyclopaedia of the Philosophical Sciences*, trans. William Wallace. Oxford: Oxford University Press, 1873.

Hegel's Philosophy of Right, trans. T. M. Knox. Oxford: Clarendon Press, 1967.

Hegel's Philosophy of Mind: Part Three of The Encyclopaedia of the Philosophical Sciences in Outline (1830) trans. William Wallace; *Additions* (1845), trans. A. V. Miller. Oxford: Clarendon, 1971.

Phenomenology of Spirit, trans. A. V. Miller. Oxford: Oxford University Press, 1977.

Hegel: The Letters, trans. Clark Butler and Christiane Seller. Bloomington: Indiana University Press, 1984.

Vorlesungen über die Philosophie der Religion, ed. Walter Jaeschke. In *Georg Wilhelm Friedrich Hegel, Vorlesungen: Ausgewählte Nachschriften und Manuskripte*. Vols. 4–5, 1985.

Foreword to Friedrich Wilhelm Hinrichs, Die Religion im inneren Verhältnisse zur Wissenschaft. In *Hegel, Hinrichs, and Schleiermacher. On Feeling and Reason in Religion. The Texts of Their 1821–22 Debate*, trans. Eric von der Luft. New York: Edwin Mellen Press, 1987.

"Solger's Posthumous Writings and Correspondence," trans. Diana Behler. In *Encyclopedia of the Philosophical Sciences in Outline and Critical Writings*, ed. Diana Behler, pp. 265–319. New York: Continuum, 1990.

Lectures on the Philosophy of Religion: One-Volume Edition. The Lectures of 1827, ed. Peter C. Hodgson. Oxford: Clarendon Press, 2006.

The Science of Logic, trans. George di Giovanni. Cambridge: Cambridge University Press, 2010.

Phenomenology of Spirit, ed. and trans. Terry Pinkard. Cambridge: Cambridge University Press, 2018.

Heine, Heinrich. *Religion and Philosophy in Germany: A Fragment (1835)*, trans. John Snodgrass. Albany: State University of New York Press, 1982.

Jacobi, Friedrich Heinrich. *The Main Philosophical Writings and the Novel Allwill*, ed. and trans. George di Giovanni. Montreal and Kingston: McGill-Queen's University Press, 1994.

Über die Lehre des Spinoza in Briefen an den Herrn Moses Mendelssohn. Breslau: Gottlieb Löwe, 1785.

Kant, Immanuel. *Kants gesammelte Schriften*, ed. Königliche Preußische Akademie der Wissenschaften. Berlin: Reimer/de Gruyter, 1900–.

Critique of Practical Reason, trans. Lewis White Beck. New York: The Liberal Arts Press, 1956.

"What Does It Mean to Orient Oneself in Thinking?," ed. and trans. Allen Wood. In *Religion and Rational Theology*, ed. Allen Wood and George di Giovanni, pp. 1–18. Cambridge: Cambridge University Press, 1996.

Religion within the Boundaries of Mere Reason: And Other Writings, ed. and trans. George di Giovanni. In *Religion and Rational Theology*, ed. Allen Wood and George di Giovanni, pp. 39–215. Cambridge: Cambridge University Press, 1998.

"Declaration Concerning Fichte's *Wissenschaftslehre*, August 7, 1799," in *Kant, Correspondence*, ed. and trans. Arnulf Zweig, pp. 559–562. Cambridge: Cambridge University Press, 1999.

Critique of the Power of Judgement, trans. Paul Guyer. Cambridge: Cambridge University Press, 2000.

Theoretical Philosophy after 1781, trans. Gary Hatfield, Michael Friedman, Henry Allison, and Peter Heath. Cambridge: Cambridge University Press, 2001.

Critique of Pure Reason, trans. Norman Kemp Smith. 2nd ed. New York: Palgrave Macmillan, 2007.

Kierkegaard, Søren. *The Concept of Anxiety: A Simple Psychological Orienting on the Dogmatic Issue of Hereditary Sin (1844)*, ed. and trans. Reidar Thomte and Albert B. Anderson. Princeton: Princeton University Press, 1980.

Lessing, Gotthold Ephraim. *Philosophical and Theological Writings*, ed. and trans. H. B. Nisbet. Cambridge: Cambridge University Press, 2005.

Paul, Jean [pseud. Jean Paul Richter]. *Sämtliche Werke. Abt. I. 3, Titan. Komischer Anhang zum Titan. Clavis Fichtiana seu Leibgeriana*, ed. Norbert Miller. Darmstadt: Wissenschaftliche Buchgesellschaft, 2000.

Rametta, Gaetano. *Le strutture speculative della dottrina della scienza: Il pensiero di J. G. Fichte negli anni 1801–1807*. Genoa: Patograf, 1995.

Rosenkranz, Johann Carl Friedrich. *Psychologie oder die Wissenschaft vom subjektiven Geist*. Königsberg: Bornträger, 1837.

Ueber Schelling und Hegel. Ein Sendschreiben an P. Leroux. Königsberg: Gebrüder Bornträger, 1843.

Georg Wilhelm Friedrich Hegels Leben (1844). Darmstadt: Wissenschaftliche Buchgesellschft, 1963.

Schelling, F.W.J. *Sämmtliche Werke*, 14 vols, ed. Karl Friedrich August Schelling. Stuttgart: Cotta, 1856–1861.

Friedrich Wilhelm Joseph von Schelling: Werke 13 = Nachlaßband, Die Weltalter. Fragmente. In den Urfassungen von 1811 und 1813, ed. Manfred Schröter. Munich: Beck, 1946.

System of Transcendental Idealism, trans. Peter Heath. Charlottesville: University Press of Virginia, 1978.

Ideas for a Philosophy of Nature: As Introduction to the Study of This Science, trans. E. E. Harris and P. Heath. Cambridge: Cambridge University Press, 1988.

On the History of Modern Philosophy, trans. Andre Bowie. Cambridge: Cambridge University Press, 1994.

Ages of the World, trans. Judith Norman, in Slavoj Zizek and F. W. J. von Schelling, *The Abyss of Freedom/Ages of the World*, pp. 105–182. Ann Arbor: University of Michigan Press, 1997.

Philosophical Investigations into the Essence of Human Freedom, trans. Jeff Love and Johannes Schmidt. Albany: State University of New York Press, 2006.

Historical-Critical Introduction to the Philosophy of Mythology, trans. Mason Richey and Markus Zisselsberger. Albany: State University of New York Press, 2007a.

The Grounding of the Positive Philosophy: The Berlin Lectures, trans. Bruce Matthews. Albany: State University of New York Press, 2007b.

Historisch-Kritische Ausgabe. Reihe I, Werke 10, Schriften 1801: 'Darstellung meines Systems der Philosophie' und andere Texte, ed. Manfred Durner. Stuttgart: Frommann-Holzboog, 2009.

Philosophy and Religion, trans. Klaus Ottmann. Putnam, CT: Spring Publications, 2010.

Historisch-Kritische Ausgabe. Reihe I, Werke 12:1, Schriften 1802–1803, ed. Vicki Müller-Lüneschloß and Paul Ziche. Stuttgart: Frommann-Holzboog, 2019.

Secondary Sources

Altmann, Alexander. *Moses Mendelssohn: A Biographical Study*. Alabama University Press, 1973.

Barth, Roderich. *Absolute Wahrheit und endliches Wahrheitsbewußtsein*. Tübingen: Mohr Siebeck, 2004.

Beach, Edward A. *The Potencies of God(s): Schelling's Philosophy of Mythology*. Albany: State University of New York Press, 1994.

Beiser, Frederick. *Hegel*. London: Routledge, 2005.

Bowie, Andrew. *Schelling and Modern European Philosophy: An Introduction*. London: Routledge, 1993.

Brown, Robert F. *The Later Philosophy of Schelling: The Influence of Boehme on the Works of 1809–1815*. Lewisburg, PA: Bucknell University Press, 1941.

Brucker, Jakob. *Historia critica philosophiae*, 5 vols. Leipzig: Breitkopf, 1742–1744.

Bruno, G. Anthony. "The Appearance and Disappearance of Intellectual Intuition in Schelling's Philosophy," *Analecta Hermeneutica* (5) (2013) 1–14.

"Genealogy and Jurisprudence in Fichte's Genetic Deduction of the Categories," *History of Philosophy Quarterly* 35(1) (2018) 77–96.

Caird, Edward. "Review of Otto Pfeidler's *The Development of Theology in Germany since Kant and Its Progress in Great Britain since 1825* (1890)," *Mind* 16(63) (1891) 405–408.

Collins, Ardis B. *Hegel's Phenomenology: The Dialectical Justification of Philosophy's First Principles*. Kingston: McGill-Queen's University Press, 2013.

Dickey, Laurence. *Hegel: Religion, Economics, And the Politics of Spirit, 1770–1807*. Cambridge: Cambridge University Press, 1987.

di Giovanni, George. "Faith without Religion, and Religion without Faith: Kant and Hegel on Religion," *Journal of the History of Philosophy* 41(3) (2003), 365–83.

Freedom and Religion in Kant and His Immediate Successors: The Vocation of Humankind, 1774–1800. Cambridge: Cambridge University Press, 2005.

"Reinhold's Criticism of Fichte and Schelling: The Commonality at a Distance between Reinhold's Late Thought and Hegel's Logic," *Archivio di filosofia* (73) (2006) 271–284.

"Sacramentalizing the World: On Fichte's Wissenschaftslehre of 1810," in *Grund- und Methodenfragen in Fichtes Spätwerk, Fichte-Studien 31*, ed. Günter Zöller and Hans Georg von Mainz, pp. 219–233. Amsterdam and New York: Rodopi, 2007.

ed. *Karl Leonhard Reinhold and the Enlightenment*. Studies in German Idealism. Dordrecht: Springer, 2009.

"How Intimate an 'Intimate of Lessing' Truly Was Hegel?" in J. Stolzenberg, K. Ameriks, and F. Rush, eds., *International Yearbook of German Philosophy*, pp. 178–197. Berlin and New York: de Gruyter, 2010.

"Review: On Robert R. Williams, Hegel on the Proofs and the Personhood of God (2017)" *SGIR Review*, 1(1) (2018) 8–19.

di Giovanni, George and Harris, Henry S., eds., *Between Kant and Hegel: Texts in the Development of Post-Kantian German Idealism*. Indianapolis and Cambridge: Hackett, 2000.

Dorrien, Gary. *Kantian Reason and Hegelian Spirit: The Idealistic Logic of Modern Theology*. Hoboken, NJ: Wiley-Blackwell, 2012.

Dufour, Dany-Robert. *Lacan et le miroir sophianique de Boehme*. Paris: EPEL, 1998.

Estes, Yolanda and Curtis Bowman. *J.G. Fichte and the Atheism Dispute (1798–1800)*. Farnham: Ashgate, 2010.

Frank, Manfred. "Schelling's Critique of Hegel and the Beginnings of Marxian Dialectics," *Idealistic Studies* 19(3) (1989) 251–268.

Franks, Paul W. *All or Nothing: Systematicity, Transcendental Arguments, and Skepticism in German Idealism*. Cambridge, MA: Harvard University Press, 2005.

Gardner, Sebastian. "Sartre, Intersubjectivity, and German Idealism." *Journal of the History of Philosophy* 43(3) (2005) 325–351.

Gueroult, Martial. "L'Initiation à la Vie Bienheureuse," in *Etudes sur Fichte*. Hildesheim: Olms, 1974, 96–144.

Harris, Henry Silton. "Review of Stephen Houlgate, *Truth and History: An Introduction to Hegel's Philosophy* (1991)," *Philosophy of the Social Sciences*, 24(4) (1991) 517–519.

"Fichtes Verdienst," *Revue Internationale de Philosophie* 191(1) (1995) 79–91.

Hegel's Ladder. Vols. 1–2. Indianapolis and Cambridge: Hackett, 1997.

Haym, Rudolf. *Hegel und seine Zeit*. Berlin: Gaertner, 1857.

Heidegger, Martin. *Schelling's Treatise on the Essence of Human Freedom* [1936], trans. Joan Stambaugh. Athens, OH: Ohio University Press, 1985.

Henrich, Dieter. *Der Ontologische Gottesbeweis*. Tübingen: J. C. B. Mohr, 1960.

Between Kant and Hegel: Lectures on German Idealism, ed. David S. Pacini. Cambridge, MA: Harvard University Press, 2003.

Hodgson, Peter C. *Hegel and Christian Theology: A Reading of the Lectures on the Philosophy of Religion*. Oxford: Oxford University Press, 2005.

Horstmann, Rolf-Peter. "Hegels Phänomenologie des Geistes als Argument für eine monistische Ontologie," in Klaus Vieweg and Wolfgang Welsch, eds., *Hegels Phänomenologie des Geistes*, pp. 58–78. Frankfurt: Suhrkamp, 2008.

Houlgate, Stephen. *Hegel's Phenomenology of Spirit: A Reader's Guide*. London: Bloomsbury, 2013.

Hyppolite, Jean. *Genesis and Structure of Hegel's Phenomenology of Spirit*. Evanston, IL: Northwestern University Press, 1979.

Ivaldo, Marco. "The Doctrine of Manifestation in Fichte's *Principien*," *Laval théologique et philosophique* 72(1) (2006) 35–64.

Janke, Wolfgang. *Sein und Reflexion – Grundlagen der kritischen Vernunft*. Berlin: De Gruyter, 1970.

Die dreifache Vollendung des Deutschen Idealismus: Schelling, Hegel, und Fichtes ungeschriebene Lehre. Amsterdam: Rodopi, 2009.

Kojève, Alexandre. *Introduction à la lecture de Hegel*. Paris: Gallimard, 1947.

Kroner, Richard. "Mure and Other English Hegelians," *The Review of Metaphysics* 7(2) (1953) 64–73.

Kuehn, Manfred. *Kant: A Biography*. Cambridge: Cambridge University Press, 2001.

Lauth, Reinhard. "Spinoza vu par Fichte," *Archives de philosophie* 41(1) (1978) 27–48.

"Über Fichtes Lehrtätigkeit in Berlin von Mitte 1799 bis Anfang 1805 und seine Zuhörerschaft," *Hegel-Studien* 15 (1980) 9–50.

Lewis, Thomas H. *Religion, Modernity, and Politics in Hegel*. Oxford: Oxford University Press, 2011.

Mann, Wolfgang-Rainer. "The Origins of the Modern Historiography of Ancient Philosophy," *History and Theory* 35(2) (1996) 165–195. http://links.jstor.org/si ci?sici=0018656%28199605%2935%3A2%3C165%3ATOOTMH%3E2.0.CO %3B2-K

Mayer, Paola. *Jena Romanticism and Its Appropriation of Jakob Boehme: Theosophy, Hagiography, Literature*. Montreal: McGill-Queen's University Press, 1999.

McCumber, John. *The Company of Words: Hegel, Language, and Systematic Philosophy*. Evanston, IL: Northwestern University Press, 1993.

McGrath, Sean J. *The Dark Ground of Spirit: Schelling and the Unconscious*. London and New York: Routledge, 2012.

"*The Late Schelling and the End of Christianity*," *Schelling Studien* (2) (2014) 63–77.

"The Ecstatic Realism of the Late Schelling," in *Continental Realism and Its Discontents*, ed. Marie Eve Morin, pp. 38–58. Edinburgh: Edinburgh University Press, 2017.

McTaggart, J. McT. E. *Studies in the Hegelian Dialectic*, 2nd ed. New York: Russell & Russell, 1910.

Studies in Hegelian Cosmology. Cambridge: Cambridge University Press, 1918.

A Commentary on Hegel's Logic. Cambridge: Cambridge University Press, 1931.

Mollowitz, Gerhard. "Kants Platoauffassung," *Kant-Studien*, 40 (1935) 13–67.

Nitzan, Lior. *Jakob Sigismond Beck's Standpunktslehre and the Kantian Thing-in-Itself: The Relation between a Representation and Its Object*. Dordrecht: Springer, 2014.

O'Reagan, Cyril. *The Heterodox Hegel*. Albany: State University of New York Press, 1994.

Pinkard, Terry. *Hegel: A Biography*. Cambridge: Cambridge University Press, 2000.

Pippin, Robert. 2012, "Back to Hegel?" *Mediations*, 26(2) (2012). www.mediationsjournal.org/articles/back-to-hegel

Schmid, Dirk. *Religion und Christentum in Fichtes Spätphilosopie, 1810–1813*. Berlin: de Gruyter, 1995.

Snow, Dale E. *Schelling and the End of Idealism*. Albany: State University of New York Press, 1996.

Taylor, Charles. *Hegel*. Cambridge: Cambridge University Press, 1975.

Tilliette, Xavier. *Schelling: Une philosophie en devenir*, 2 vols. Vrin: Paris, 1970.

Williams, Robert R. *Hegel on the Proofs and the Personhood of God*. Oxford: Oxford University Press, 2017.

Žižek, Slavoj. *The Abyss of Freedom*, in *The Abyss of Freedom/Ages of the World*. Ann Arbor: University of Michigan Press, 1997.

Index

244

For EU product safety concerns, contact us at Calle de José Abascal, 56–1°,
28003 Madrid, Spain or eugpsr@cambridge.org.

www.ingramcontent.com/pod-product-compliance
Ingram Content Group UK Ltd.
Pitfield, Milton Keynes, MK11 3LW, UK
UKHW020354140625

459647UK00020B/2469